City of Nature

Expulsion from the Garden of Eden by Thomas Cole.

City of Nature

Journeys to Nature
in the Age of American Romanticism

Bernard Rosenthal

Newark
University of Delaware Press
London and Toronto: Associated University Presses

Associated University Presses, Inc.
Cranbury, New Jersey 08512

Associated University Presses
Magdalen House
136-148 Tooley Street
London SE1 2TT, England

Associated University Presses
Toronto M5E 1A7, Canada

Library of Congress Cataloging in Publication Data

Rosenthal, Bernard, 1934-
    City of nature.

    Bibliography: p.
    Includes index.
       1. American literature--19th century--History and
criticism. 2. Romanticism--United States. 3. Nature in
literature. I. Title.
PS217.R6R64   810'.9'14   78-68879
ISBN 0-87413-147-2

Also by Bernard Rosenthal
Race and the American Romantics (coeditor with Vincent Freimarck)

Printed in the United States of America

For Evelyn

Contents

Acknowledgments

Since scholarly publications in part propose new ideas or refute old ones, they are necessarily indebted to studies that have preceded them. In acknowledging that debt, one can specifically engage all the individuals who have spoken to similar subjects, or one can assume an audience learned enough to recognize the rejection of one theory or the acceptance of another. As much as possible, I have chosen the second route. The general reader who may profit from my study will have little interest in scholarly controversies, while the specialist will readily recognize points of contention without having them gratuitously emphasized. If I do not name every study that I have considered, I am no less grateful to those who have written about problems directly or indirectly raised in this book. Since my study depends heavily on minor works of the early nineteenth century, many of which I cite, I am particularly grateful for the studies that have helped me locate a canon of literature difficult to retrieve. I also owe much to the librarians who have been so generous in helping me at this task.

I wish to express my appreciation to the library staff of the State University of New York at Binghamton and particularly to John Briggs, Janet Brown, Michael Jasenas, and Rachelle Moore. I am also grateful to Eva Benton for library services at the University of Illinois. With the assistance of these individuals I have been able to locate information from various other libraries. I wish especially to thank the New York State Public Library, the library of the College of William and Mary, and the Boston Public Library. I am also grateful to Joan Winterkorn and other rare book librarians at Cornell University, as well as to the microfilm librarians there. For various clerical services, I am indebted to Marge Allen, and for secretarial help I owe much to Mary Peters.

In preparing this study I have been fortunate in receiving financial assistance from the University of Illinois in the early stages of my work, and from the National Endowment for the Humanities at a later date. In addition to the two full years of support I received as a result of grants from the University of Illinois and the National Foundation for the Humanities, I received a summer award from the Research Foundation of the State University of New York.

One of the great pleasures in writing this book has been the opportunity to share my perceptions about literature and society with students and colleagues. Although I cannot name all who have assisted me in various ways, I do wish to thank those who have read and commented on all or part of my study. Norman Burns, Charles A. Carpenter, and Sheldon Grebstein have offered valuable stylistic suggestions, while Vincent Freimarck and Roger Stein have made very helpful remarks regarding theoretical aspects of the book. In addition to reading the manuscript and offering suggestions, William Bysshe Stein has spent many hours with me in provocative discussions of literature. I am also deeply indebted to Jane Lewis for her wise suggestions and for her many hours of patient work in helping me prepare the manuscript for publication. It is not possible to express how much I have appreciated her help.

For granting me permission to include the chapter entitled "The Urban Garden," I express my appreciation to *Texas Studies in Literature and Language,* where the essay appeared in slightly different form in the Spring 1978 issue.

I also want to acknowledge a debt of long standing to Edward H. Davidson. For over a decade he has followed my research and the conclusions I have drawn from it. He has been my constant friend and teacher.

Finally, I thank my wife and children. They have shared and understood.

B.R.

Textual Note

The current editorial projects on American texts leave scholars in a quandary. Since major collections are in various stages of reediting, consistent principles of citation are difficult to attain. Generally, I have cited the newest, most authoritative texts. However, in some cases, the more practical approach has been to use older texts. For example, Emerson's *Journal* has been only partially reedited, and rather than send the reader from one edition to another, I have stayed with the older standard text while remaining alert to changes in the new volumes that have appeared. Novels, on the other hand, present less difficulty. When appropriate editions are in print, I use the latest authoritative texts. Otherwise I rely on the standard, older editions. Minor writers present an entirely different problem. Much of this study treats works so obscure that one is almost grateful for any edition. With these, I have employed the best available texts. Many of the works only appear in one edition.

City of Nature

O my brave soul!
O farther, farther sail!
O daring joy, but safe! Are they not all the seas of God?
O farther, farther, farther sail!
                    —Walt Whitman, ''Passage to India,'' 1871

Through yonder strait, for thee, perdition lies. And from the deep
beyond, no voyager e'er puts back.
                    —Herman Melville, *Mardi,* 1849

Columbus has sailed westward of these isles by the mariner's compass, but neither he nor his successors have found them. We are no
nearer than Plato was. The earnest seeker and hopeful discoverer of
this New World always haunts the outskirts of his time, and walks
through the densest crowd uninterrupted, and, as it were, in a
straight line.
—Henry David Thoreau, *A Week on the Concord and Merrimack
                                        Rivers,* 1849

Nothing will stand the eye of a man—neither lion, nor person, nor
planet, nor time, nor condition. Each bullies us for a season; but
gaze, and it opens that most solid seeming wall, yields its secrets,
receives us into its depth and advances our front so much farther on
into the recesses of being, to some new frontier as yet unvisited by
the elder voyagers. And yet alas for this infirm faith, this will, not
strenuous, this vast ebb of a vast flow! I am God in nature, I am a
weed by the wall.
                    —Ralph Waldo Emerson, *Journal,* 1840

1

Introduction: Journeys to Nature

The common denominator of American Romanticism, probably of all Romanticism, may be found in the attempt to create a private world free from the constraints of time and history. Romantic writers want to reject predestination, mechanism, or any theory of history that denies individual preeminence in the shaping of events. Accordingly, in articulating a theory of history, Emerson found an understandable appeal in a rhetorical question Napoleon asked: "What is history. . .but a fable agreed upon?" In the same essay, "History" (1841), Emerson further concludes that "All history becomes subjective; in other words there is properly no history, only biography."[1] If history as an absolute process could be turned to private biography, malleable in the mind of the poet, the individual would be free to enter a world of infinite possibility—the location of Romanticism.

But the Romantic writer is also compelled to acknowledge the constraints imposed by linear history, as Emerson indeed does in "History":

> But along with the civil and metaphysical history of man, another history goes daily forward—that of the external world—in which he is not less strictly implicated. He is the compend of time; he is also the correlative of nature. His power consists in the multitude of his affinities, in the fact that his life is intertwined with the whole chain of organic and inorganic being. (Pp. 35-36)

Out of the vast quantity of critical study on American Romanticism, agreement has emerged on at least one point: American
Romantics experienced a conflict between themselves and the
culture within which they lived, between the myth they sought to
create and the historical world in which they were "implicated."
Whether, as A N Kaul argues, they sought to resolve this
through creating an ideal of community, or whether, as Richard
Poirier affirms, they looked for "a world elsewhere,"[2] modern
scholarship has correctly acknowledged the fundamental tension
between the Romantics and their "external world." But the relationship between the two has been only partially understood,
since comprehensive attempts at examining such American concepts as "nature," the "garden," or the "city" have generally
presupposed that these terms had meanings common to the
Romantics and to the other people who inhabited the country in
which they shaped their art. If such a supposition is false, then the
definitions need to be clarified, and the premises underlying the
"tension" between the artist and society require reexamination.

American Romantics, being "implicated" in linear history,
took their language, their metaphors, their tropes, from the "external world." Primarily, they shaped into private meanings
American categories of thought centering on images of nature.
Stated another way, Americans of the day generally held a set of
myths about nature, and from these public myths the Romantics
reconstructed a vocabulary to express radically different private
myths. Regardless of how odd their definitions of nature may appear upon close examination, the people who inhabited
Emerson's "external world" had reasonably common
understandings of nature's meanings. These understandings differed profoundly from romantic perceptions of nature, even
though romantic writers appropriated national images of nature
to their own ends.

The Americans of Emerson's "external world" perceived
nature primarily as participating in a teleological process shaped
in part by man and culminating in civilization. Nature in its most

important and pervasive metaphorical use connoted the values of civilization and often implied civilization itself. In its purest form, nature took the shape of urban America, and the journey to nature became the journey to the city. In a world that held to this sensibility, Emerson and his contemporaries came of age. Because of their implication in an "external world," the American Romantics defined their interior journeys in a language that also brought them from nature to the city. If Leo Marx has drawn different conclusions from observing this pattern of their journeys, he has nevertheless accurately noted that "our American fables" lead heroes through "a raw wilderness. . .back toward the city."[3]

But toward what city, and through what nature do our fables lead us? The answer to this depends on whether the journey occurs in historic America or in private myth, a distinction Thoreau suggests in his essay "Walking":

> I walk out into *a* [my italics] nature such as the old prophets and poets, Menu, Moses, Homer, Chaucer walked in. You may name it America, but it is not America; neither Americus Vespucius, nor Columbus, nor the rest were the discoverers of it. There is a truer account of it in mythology than in any history of America, so called, that I have seen.[4]

The truest history of nature, Thoreau tells us, cannot be found in any history of America. Nor is nature one phenomenon, as his indefinite article indicates. Thoreau walks to "a" nature, discovered earlier by poets, explorers of man's interior world. In the region of romantic myth, Thoreau can walk the same ground they did. But it is a different ground from that upon which the people of his day walk. Put another way, Thoreau has not simply posed history against myth; he has confronted his myth with his culture's myth.[5] Americans had constructed a story about nature, which Thoreau rejected, though he would use the frame of that story in describing his own interior journey. This story of nature in early nineteenth-century America, whether told in novels, travel narratives, or political orations, recounted the transformation of nature into its purest form, civilization. It was not the only story of the time, but it was the most pervasive, and it found its greatest teller in James Fenimore Cooper, to whom I shall return at length.

The counterpart to the myth Cooper essentially endorsed exists in the myth of nature as spiritual place, the region comparable to where Thoreau walks in the paths of Menu, Moses, Homer, and Chaucer. One does not need trees or lakes here, although one may certainly use them, as one uses whales. Similarly, one may use America, as Whitman does in "Passage to India," as he passes through America's historical triumph over the West to embark on a "Passage to more than India," to a mythic sphere that leaves the linear history of America behind. It is an interior journey to a private place, one that ultimately takes the poet as far from an American location as Thoreau takes the reader in "Walking," where he finds the "truer account" of "nature" in "mythology" rather than in America. All our classic writers of the Romantic period, except for Cooper, explored mythic regions analogous to those found by Whitman and Thoreau.

Although the journey motif has a history older than America, writers understandably fashioned their literary enterprises after the models of their day. Consequently, while our classic writers differed radically in their intentions from their compatriots in the "external world" of America, they found their metaphors in the ordinary myths of society. When juxtaposed, private myth against national myth, interior myth against exterior myth, the language of each illuminates the other. Concepts of nature and the city emerge from seemingly indiscriminate language and form definable patterns of thought that would defy coherent analysis without the recovery of lost definitions. The reacquisition of these meanings, bearing crucially on America's exterior political journey and the interior literary ones, requires an examination of forgotten fiction, travel narratives, newspapers, and magazines, as well as belles-lettres. As in the present, popular images are discovered, by definition, quantitatively rather than qualitatively.

For common attitudes of the nineteenth century, we look to Timothy Flint before examining Thoreau. But we can understand neither without studying both.

All writers, of course, do not fit neatly into one category or the other, nor is the canon of any given author ever wholly devoted to a single view. Yet, broadly speaking, a distinction may be made between those primarily concerned with the ''external world'' and those who sought to find a different order of understanding in a new religious myth generally called Romanticism.

It is no understatement to say that Romanticism has many connotations, but without entering into the debate Arthur O. Lovejoy precipitated by his moderate insistence that the term requires definition,[6] I want to cite Northrop Frye's *A Study of English Romanticism* to establish my own use of the term. According to Professor Frye, the

> Middle Ages itself, like all ages, had its own anti-mimetic tendencies, which it expressed in such forms as the romance, where the knight turns away from society and rides off into a forest or other ''threshold symbol'' of a dream world. In Romanticism this romance form revives, so significantly as to give its name to the whole movement, but in Romanticism the poet himself is the hero of the quest, and his turning away from society is to be connected with. . .the demoting of the conception of man as primarily a social being living in cities. He turns away to seek a nature who reveals herself only to the individual.

Additionally, ''the great Romantic theme is the attaining of an apocalyptic vision by a fallen but potentially regenerate mind.''[7]

Literary historians reasonably enough associate this regeneration with an ''Adamic myth,'' but there must be no misunderstanding about the state of Adam in this myth as it took shape in America. Adam was fallen and not innocent.[8] The successful romantic quests, such as those found in *Nature, Walden,* or ''Song of Myself,'' all posit the fallen figure seeking to *restore* a diminished or lost spirituality. Conversely, the quests of

Melville, Hawthorne, and Poe generally reveal probings at regeneration accompanied by a failure to achieve it, at least if one reads these writers as governed by Melville's "blackness." But whether finding success or failure in the quest for regeneration, all of them—Emerson, Thoreau, Whitman, Melville, Hawthorne, Poe—explore "the great Romantic theme."

Cooper, however, does not, although he misleads the reader who has not taken into account typologies of nature basic to Cooper and his contemporaries. Cooper writes primarily in Emerson's "external world." His heroes and heroines, Natty Bumppo included, perceive nature as existing in America rather than in mythology, to use Thoreau's dichotomy.

The "mythology" in which Thoreau found his true account of nature may certainly have been a timeless one, as he suggests, but it was probably most accessible to him and other Romantics as part of what Northrop Frye calls "an encyclopedic myth."

> In Western Europe [this] myth, derived mainly from the Bible, dominated both the literary and the philosophical tradition for centuries. I see Romanticism as the beginning of the first major change in this pattern of mythology, and as fully comprehensible only when seen as such. (P. 5)

This new mythology does not reject the past. On the contrary, it seeks to recapture something that has slipped away. While romantic concepts of *apocalypse, fall,* and *regeneration* lost much of their traditional meaning as speculations about them moved from historical Christianity, the continuing vitality of the ideas, particularly those of *fall* and *regeneration,* strongly indicate an adherence to Christian categories if not to Christian history. As M. H. Abrams cogently observes, the basic thrust of Romanticism is conservative: "Despite their displacement from a supernatural to a natural frame of reference, . . .the ancient problems, terminology, and ways of thinking about human nature and history survived. . . ."[9] The observation is as appropriate to American Romantics as to English ones.

This "displacement" had little to do with Cooper or with most of the people living in the geographical location of America because for them the concepts of *fall* and *regeneration* required no radical redefinitions. While many Americans had modified the theological rigor of their forebears, they basically held to the old beliefs. Emerson's myth of man as a ruined divinity, his Adamic myth, carried a theology antithetical to the beliefs of most Americans, including James Fenimore Cooper, the great articulator of a secular American myth of nature. Cooper tells adventure stories, and sometimes very good ones. He comments extensively on the society in which he lives. He is attracted to the magic of the wilderness, and if this is Romanticism then Cooper is a Romantic. But by no stretch of the imagination does Cooper or his most venturesome soul, Natty, seek to reconstruct Christian categories into a new theological myth. None of his "good" people are ruined divinities, and his "bad" people are simply ruined. Cooper, alone, among the major American writers of his day, created relatively innocent individuals in the wilderness, a tangible region comprehensible in terms of America's idea of nature as process tending toward civilization and incorporating its values. The obligation of individualists inhabiting Cooper's nature is to disappear. Which Natty does. He lives in linear history, lives out its joys and sadnesses, and then moves on before an advancing civilization. The inhabitants of Cooper's world do not whittle sticks, as Thoreau's artist of Kouroo does, while eons pass. Unlike Emerson, Cooper does not seek to build a new world. God had built him a fine one already. He would justify it in his writings.

Although America was obviously not of one mind in the early nineteenth century, readers charmed by the novelty and freshness of Cooper's writings generally shared the underlying premises of his Leatherstocking stories. Written as historical fiction—for the events Cooper chronicles had long since passed—the Leatherstocking stories combine two visions of America, both very familiar to his audience. One treats the West and nature as a

region that inevitably must and should be transformed into
civilization. The other constructs the fantasy wilderness of noble
savages, a location imaged first in Europe. But American readers
knew which was fantasy and which was not, and Americans in
general, Romantics included, had few illusions about geographical
America as an Edenic region. Although various Europeans fixed
their view on the Edenic mirage they had long seen in the
American wilderness, few Americans succumbed to images of
primitive utopianism. Many, however, did see in America the old
European image of endless possibility for new beginnings. Seen
this way, America was a vast region into which one could journey
either to escape the past or to create a new future, or both. The
geographical space offered room for establishing or reestablishing
social, economic, political, or religious order suitable to individual desire. But central to this image, no matter how ecstatic,
was the idea of America as a geographic place, the outcome of
history's most recent revelation.

The Romantics found such a view of the new world constrained
and insufficient. For them, the newness was spiritual rather than
geographical, apart from America rather than of it. In Melville's
words, "You must have plenty of sea-room to tell the Truth in;
especially when it *seems* [my italics] to have an aspect of newness,
as America did in 1492, though it was then just as old, and
perhaps older than Asia, only those sagacious philosophers, the
common sailors, had never seen it before, swearing it was all
water and moonshine there."[10] Only in the context of this
perception can we comprehend his often-quoted statement that
the "world is as young today as when it was created; and this
Vermont morning dew is as wet to my feet as Eden's dew to
Adam's."[11] *His* Vermont belongs to Thoreau's "mythology."
The "Idea of Man," as Roy Harvey Pearce calls it in his *Continuity of American Poetry,* takes precedence over the idea of
America, even in the basic Adamic formulation. Readers having
noted England's Adamic motif, if only in Mary Shelley's
Frankenstein, understand how remote from nationality and

America's newness the myth of "Adam's" regenerative quest was in the nineteenth century. The great "experience" of American Romantics was private rather than national; it was visited upon individuals caught in that moment of history when, even prior to Nietzsche's crystallization of the idea, the possibility of God's death haunted the poetic imagaination. In response, a new religious pattern began to emerge, even among writers like Longfellow and Whittier, who waivered between newer and older myths, just as the major Romantics did.

At some point in the nineteenth century, and historians may debate exactly when, the American journey into nature ended. The political frontiers had been conquered, and Western man, as Whitman affirms in "Passage to India," had circumnavigated the globe. If the American West was not a totally idyllic place, it nevertheless essentially redeemed the pledge of material prosperity nature had held. Political and economic problems remained, but the American journey to nature had been relatively successful. The romantic journey was also largely over in the sense that new methods of literary exploration engaged the attention of leading writers such as Adams, Crane, James, and Twain, although inquiries into the meaning of being remained fundamental to their writing. What had generally changed was the pattern of metaphor. Whether coincidental or not, the *romantic* trope of a journey to nature in search of salvation ended at about the time that American fully possessed the promised land.

Except for Melville's *Clarel* and *Billy Budd,* the last richly poetic nineteenth-century exploration of what had already become an old dream appeared in Whitman's "Passage to India." The poem, dated 1871, explores again the romantic myth that by then bordered on nostalgia. Since Melville's later writings offer only bleak possibilities, "Passage to India" remains as the final great nineteenth-century example of the romantic dream that in the "Passage to more than India," as Whitman phrased it in his poem, a truly new metaphysical and redemptive frontier could emerge. Melville, as early as 1849, had insisted in *Mardi* that such quests led to places other than those Whitman imagined in his poem. Yet both writers probed the "mythology" of Thoreau's "Walking." In the polarities of human possibility outside of geographical America, one thrusting toward hope and the other toward a hopeless endurance, "Passage to India" and *Mardi* exemplify the similar meanings to be found in so many journeys to nature taken by romantic writers.

Both narratives recognize that, in Whitman's words, "the shores of America," or of this world, are too confining, that "this separate Nature," as Whitman calls the tangible world, is "so unnatural." One must shed the temporal, as the poet does in seizing command of his soul and launching "out on trackless seas" in search of "unknown shores." Whitman is "bound where mariner has not yet dared to go," and is ready to "risk the ship, ourselves and all." Whitman's "trackless seas" may be equated with Melville's "endless sea" and "chartless" voyage across "untracked" waters.[12] Whitman, who will "steer for the deep waters only," is like Melville's hero Taji, who grasps possession of his own soul, seizes the helm of his ship with "eternity. . .in his eye" (p. 654), and daringly plunges forth. Before the final moment of these two journeys, where the heroes leave all temporal things behind and move toward the mystical "unknown shores," each author has first taken the reader through a linear history. Both writers have invoked Europe and America; each has found them "so unnatural"; each has sought to redefine the self in a region beyond the world of physical things, regardless of different expectations. In "Passage to India" an old Walt Whitman still follows the promise that

Nature and Man shall be disjoin'd and diffused no more,
The true Son of God [the poet] shall absolutely fuse them.

We recognize in the vision its kinship to Emerson's prophecy of 1836 that the "problem of restoring to the world original and eternal beauty is solved by the redemption of the soul." This world defined by Emerson as one that "lacks unity, and lies broken and in heaps"[13] will be put together again. Melville, in sending his hero across the "endless sea," makes no such promise. But the quests are similar in their intentions, and they have little to do with Cooper's American journeys.

In 1855 when Whitman announced himself to the world in *Leaves of Grass* he did so with the implicit promise that the words of Emerson would be validated. In "Passage to India" he was still uttering the promise, as if by a kind of Shelleyan incantation he could make it happen. Emerson was saying little at this time about putting the world back together again. By 1871, for a generation of writers, the restless, longing dream that art might in some way make coherent the incoherent world was for the most part over.

Their dream had generally implied that if science rendered chaotic the old divine order, perhaps the world might yet be held together by something called *nature*. Not the nature that Whitman thought of as "unnatural," but something else: the peculiar amalgam of all tangible things seen through the religious eye that transformed them into an idea whereby nature would transcend its physical qualities. To this region of nature beyond India, heroes of a literary era embarked on their inner journeys to Walden, or to Ishmael's sea, or to the "place" in *Nature* where Emerson's "poet" found a way of knowing that would transform old beliefs into a new myth. Such explorations are neither peculiar to America nor to the nineteenth century. But the American writers who created such journeys drew heavily from an image fundamental to those living in their "external world." The discovery of nature became the discovery of civilization, or the self, as the Romantics modified the pattern.

The American journey was successful; it was a rewarding passage whereby a nation transformed the wilderness into something approximating the urban dream it held for nature. The romantic journey had a different outcome. Cast often in the lyric language of success, as in *Walden, Nature,* or "Passage to India," the inner quest for what these works of art prophesied was generally unfulfilled, and nature rarely kept the promise it had seemed to make. Indeed, nature often evoked a threatening myth, often suggested that all the seas might not be those of God. On the other side of Walden Pond one might find "A Winter Walk," where Thoreau thinly covers with snow the death and decay he implicitly defines as something other than nature:

> The wonderful purity of nature at this season is a most pleasing fact. Every decayed stump and moss-grown stone and rail, and the dead leaves of autumn, are concealed by a clean napkin of snow.[14]

This world of death and decay lurked just underneath the "clean napkin" of nature. When the "napkin" was probed, however, when the world was explored, it often appeared in its ambiguity of whiteness. "Think what a mean and wretched place this world is," writes the creator of *Walden* in another book, "that half the time we have to light a lamp that we may see to live in it. This is half our life. Who would undertake the enterprise if it were all? And, pray, what more has day to offer? A lamp that burns more clear, a purer oil, say winter-strained, that so we may pursue our idleness with less obstruction. Bribed with a little sunlight and a few prismatic tints, we bless our Maker, and stave off his wrath with hymns."[15]

"Who would undertake the enterprise if it were all?" That was the crucial question, and the Romantics hoped that it would not be "all." Somewhere there might be something else; not in the realm of America's nature, but in the private vision of the questing individual. This is by no means to say that all the Romantics spent their entire lives monomaniacally searching for God or some equivalent. Obviously, they found other satisfactions. But when nature served as the metaphor for the regenerative quest, when artists sought their location in the universe, the passage took them to a region away from geographical America, away from any geographical place, to a mythic nature where they could escape from an "unnatural" plight. And they dared the search, even though the "seas of God" proclaimed by Whitman in 1871 had too often proved to be, in Melville's words, the "realm of shades."[16] They searched in the region of Thoreau's "mythology" rather than in the America from which they took much of the imagery that described their separate journey.

Two ideas of nature, then, need to be explored, each with its attendant ambiguities and complexities, each illuminating the other. One belongs to the history of nineteenth-century America, to a journey into the wilderness from which would emerge nature and the city. The other belongs to the search for a new religious myth, a journey that would lead to nature and the city of the self. In each case the image of nature begins in fragmentation and seeks order. In its extremest form, the typology of each journey presents the wilderness as the trope for fragmentation and the city as the image of order. Two journeys toward this city took place, both "implicated" in the linear history of America.

2

Nature in the Land of Milk and Honey

The earliest imaginative European conceptualizations of America all posited an untouched world of nature to be shaped into whatever one's deepest yearning might create. As the object of personal fantasy, America variously promised the acquisition of gold, conversion of savages, escape to a new order of life (whether primitive or civilized), and the countless private dreams forever out of recorded history's reach. By the time America had become a country, the rhetoric associated with these early visions continued to suggest the miracle of nature revealing a magnificent new world to Europe. In the nineteenth century travelers were still coming to examine this world, although the enduring dream was focused more specifically. The questions that urgently emerged more and more centered on the values of an evolving democracy within an existing culture. What the future held was still in doubt, but dreams were now also taking place in a framework largely created by the relatively new society that still fascinated Europe. This is not to say that the dreams could not remain large now that their boundaries were clearer. Much might yet be expected of America and the wonderland of nature, but the East was already settled, and however attractive America might be—at least to those who were not ridiculing it—the more extravagant dreams reached farther west and centered upon

28

whatever region remained untouched. So it has always been with fantasy.

But the association of America with nature remained a powerful idea, and the most contradictory notions often found expression in identical metaphors growing from that association. In the extravagant praise of nature, which in the nineteenth century was already a heritage of America's past, one finds astonishingly mundane concerns garbed in a rhetoric so bombastic as to suggest, misleadingly, a mystical commitment to nature shared both by the creator of *Walden* and multitudes of pioneers. Language about the grandeur and glory of nature is readily available to anyone seeking evidence for some past American spiritual commitment to it. Thus, Perry Miller draws on such rhetoric to argue that nature provided the whole rationale for America, that it became "the American TEMPLE"; and a passage he cites from an article in *The Knickerbocker Magazine,* appearing in 1835, surely seems to support his claim:

> God speaks this promise [of American greatness] in the sublimity of Nature. It resounds all along the crags of the Alleghanies. It is uttered in the thunder of Niagara. It is heard in the roar of two oceans, from the great Pacific to the rocky ramparts of the Bay of Fundy. His finger has written it in the broad expanse of our inland seas, and traced it out by the mighty Father of Waters. The august TEMPLE in which we dwell was built for lofty purposes. Oh! that we may consecrate it to LIBERTY and CONCORD, and be found fit worshippers within its holy walls.

Furthermore, Miller indicates that he could cite "millions" of similar statements.[1] The hyperbole of this claim notwithstanding, similar rhetoric was widespread. Yet in *Godey's Lady's Book,* also in 1835, there appeared the calm complaint that "the loveliest scenes of nature so soon lose their power to charm."[2] In which of the two journals, neither radical, is an American truth to be found? Certainly, even cursory examinations of nineteenth-century scenic descriptions frequently reveal perceptions of nature antithetical to the exuberant view expressed in *The Knickerbocker Magazine.*

The problem is one of language, and Perry Miller, when not momentarily captured by the kind of rhetoric he quotes, is perfectly aware that behind the facade of spiritual commitment America's most important sense of nature had less to do with temples than with the price of cattle. We see this in his perceptive explanation of the difficulty one individual, Daniel Drake, had in spreading the gospel of nature as a spiritual force:

> Frequently Dr. Drake had to answer the objection that arose from the society of early Cincinnati—where men were infinitely more concerned with real estate, slaughtering pigs, improving steamboats, canals and railroads, than with solitary feasts of the soul amid October forests—whether in Ohio there were not multitudes ''who spend their whole lives in new countries, and yet die uninstructed in mind, unelevated in feeling, by the scenery around them?''[3]

Those slaughterers of pigs may not have seen nature in Dr. Drake's terms, but as workers in the temple their own fondness for nature provided food for the priesthood.

Even those who praised nature most lavishly had reservations about American scenery. Thus, George Ripley, who earned his ''transcendentalist'' credentials on the staff of *The Dial* and as a manager of Brook Farm, assured readers in *The Harbinger* that rural scenery in America was ugly.[4] And James Fenimore Cooper, while lamenting in *The Pioneers* (1823) the passing of America's pristine nature, decorated his nostalgic town with poplar trees imported from Europe. Nor was he a curiosity in this planting of foreign seeds (literal and symbolic), since even the first American horticulturist had a good enough sense of his market to be in the business of importing and selling English seeds.[5] Cooper saw nothing inconsistent in having British seeds in America's virgin wilderness. Unlike Hawthorne in ''The Maypole of Merry Mount,'' he missed the symbolic possibilities of this particular cross-fertilization, although he faithfully depicted American indifference to an indigenous landscape appreciated more as literary convention than as natural object.

The incongruity of having English trees in the magic region of the western settlements exists only to the degree that we take literally the abundant glorifications of America's nature. Nineteenth-century Americans knew better than to do this, although they rarely concerned themselves with precise definitions of nature. The word was fluid, its meaning rarely consistent.[6] Unlike extraordinary people such as Emerson or Thoreau, most individuals found no need to see nature as part of a theoretical concern. Although rhetorical expressions about nature often suggest what surely seems to approach a national religion, the exegesis of these utterances generally leads us to relatively mundane concerns. Under the verbal legerdemain of shifting rhetorical uses of the word *nature,* one finds concepts quite remote from any association with a national "temple." We see this, for example, in the fascinatingly eclectic connotations of nature found in the writings of Timothy Flint, an American reporter of nature far better known and appreciated in his day than Emerson or Thoreau. This remarkable missionary, land speculator, and travel writer was so widely recognized that Harriet Beecher Stowe in *Uncle Tom's Cabin* mentioned his works in the same sentence as she did the Bible, *Pilgrim's Progress,* and *Paradise Lost.*[7] In spite of Flint's personal frustrations with farming and of his own retreat from an agricultural life in the West, he defined himself to the American public as "an earnest lover of nature."[8] And he probably believed it even as he wrote about the cypress, which "grows. . .in deep and sickly swamps, the haunts of fever, musquitos, [sic] moccasin snakes, alligators, and all loathsome and ferocious animals, that. . .*seem to make common cause with nature against* [man]" (my italics).[9] There is no reason to suppose that an American public impressed with Flint's accounts of the West was in any way disturbed by this separation of nature from a swamp. On the contrary, Americans were quite used to it, and even our best writers were unperturbed by the verbal divisions that, for example, allowed Thoreau to create a poetry of nature while in *Civil Disobedience* pejoratively comparing men to dogs.

Clearly, nature meant more than the sum of natural things. When one writer describes a river that flees nature,[10] while another sees the death of a tree as a pause in nature's work,[11] readers must conclude that out of context *nature* defies definition in nineteenth-century America. Yet some generalizations are possible, and one applies with particular force: more than anything, nature serves as a trope to affirm one's private view of truth. This definition does not have universal application, but it recurs often enough to require special acknowledgment. More particularly, in regard to the notion of private truth, the concept of nature fundamentally perpetuates the American value of civilization. Therefore, the nineteenth-century reader found nothing startling, not the slighest incongruity, in reading about nature as a cosmic urban planner dispensing its blessings to Alton, Illinois, [12] even as it withheld the same blessings from Michigan City in spite of the citizenry's best attempts to build a great commercial center there.[13] For in the myriad associations of nature with truth, the verity most forcefully proclaimed was the value of civilization. Nature was the builder of cities, the codifier of laws, the guiding spirit of commerce. But since nature did not build its cities in a day, since it remained unfulfilled until the wilderness became civilization, nature as wilderness carried a pejorative connotation. The common phrase, "in a state of nature," denoted something untouched by civilization. Something "in a state of nature" was incomplete, uncivilized. But as nature came to imply civilization, its value increased accordingly.

Such a process is nicely illustrated in the experience of a Philadelphia ornithologist, John K. Townsend, with three frontier girls described as "perfect children of nature." These girls lived alone with their father, their mother having died. Because of their isolation from civilization the girls had "no opportunity of aping the manners of the world." At first it seems as if Townsend is applauding some pure value antithetical to the artifices of civilization. After all, the girls did not have "the manners of the world." But Townsend also encountered some Indian women picking "vermin" from each other's hair and eating them—an activity he squeamishly observed to be "so universal amongst Indians." Since here Townsend did not even associate Indians with nature, they obviously were not "children of nature" like their white counterparts. The superiority of the white girls, their identification with nature, was only partly due to their decorous avoidance of vermin-picking. These "children of nature" had a highly civilized proficiency in needlework and had been educated by their father in "a good, plain" way.[14] So nature's meaning becomes clearly revealed as a metaphor for Townsend's particular values. Yet the larger point has to do with more than an insight into one ornithologist's values. His insistent identification of nature with valued civilized accomplishments exemplies a process encountered over and over again. And with this in mind, the "millions" of phrases comparable to the grand rhetoric in *The Knickerbocker Magazine* may be understood to reveal the pervasive belief that civilization and nature are part of a common enterprise having little or nothing to do with the monotonous scenery mentioned in *Godey's Lady's Book.* One concept referred to civilization and commerce, the other to ordinary landscape. This was a distinction in nature clearly understood by Americans. Writers of European travel narratives, often busily ridiculing America, rarely comprehended this, but it was so evident to American travel writers that they had no need to spell it out.

One of those countless writers of travel narratives describing the American West was C. W. Dana, whose *Garden of the World, or the Great West* (1856) offers a fairly typical example of the American travel narrative genre. Where ancient poets direct their opening remarks to the muses, Dana begins with an invocation to an almost magically presented region: *"The Land of Promise,"* writes Dana, "and the *Canaan* of our time, is the region which, commencing on the slope of the Alleghanies, broadens grandly over the vast prairies and mighty rivers, over queenly lakes and

lofty mountains, until the ebb and flow of the Pacific tide kisses
the golden shores of the El Dorado.'' America presents ''to the
nations a land where the wildest dreamer on the future of our race
may one day see actualized a destiny far outreaching in splendor
his most generous visions.'' As a representative American
writer, however extravagant the statements may seem, he is sure
to give cities a central place in this vision. Every child knows, he
tells us, ''how Cincinnati, Chicago, and St. Louis, the spots on
which they stand, but a few years since unbroken forests, have
sprung into existence and grown with such rapidity and power that
they now outrival in wealth and population the older cities of the
East.'' He does not mean that for all its perfection the region could
be left to its own devices. Rather, it should be directed by ''New
England minds,'' whose thoughts would help generate a haven
for the oppressed of the Old World in a land where resources exist
''such as Nature has vouchsafed to no other clime.''[15] Having
presented his soaring invocation, Dana turned to the specifics of
his subject, the poetry of America.

What follows in Dana's book will suggest to the modern reader
contemporary high school geography books, which may even owe
their form to this old American travel genre. With few exceptions, Dana scrupulously avoids matters of scenic beauty and
treats instead boundaries, navigable rivers, climate, agriculture,
internal improvements, government structure of the territories,
education, religion, population, and, of course, development of
cities. Although these subjects are all potentially fascinating to
the modern reader, Dana's plodding discourse, in sharp contrast
to his breathless introduction, is more likely to be soporific than
exciting. But for the reader of his day, the book was not at all un-
faithful to its opening promise, since the ''El Dorado'' of the
West, the land of ''milk and honey,'' had its poetry in the growing urban and commercial interests of America. The news of
America's progress needed no embellishment to make it exciting;
it only needed reporting. For Dana, as for so many others, the
American West had little to do with a spiritualized biblical land of
''milk and honey.'' Dana's poetry of America was so closely tied

to a commercial vision that he found Madison, Wisconsin almost alarming, since its scenic attractions had "diverted attention, to some extent, from its advantages as a business and manufacturing town,"[16] albeit the region's commercial growth would later prove his fears unfounded. As for the kind of sentimental regret about the fading wilderness that some modern readers are tempted to take seriously (although nineteenth-century Americans rarely did), Dana has nothing to say. On the contrary, in a typical response, memories of the virgin forest are recalled with horror rather than nostalgia.[17] Even political acts are seen basically through the prism of commercial vision; for example, the Missouri Compromise is hailed primarily because it will allow the territories of Kansas and Nebraska to be filled with "populous cities."[18] Although America's journey into the wilderness might not have been quite as crassly conceived as, for example, Mrs. Frances Trollope suggested in observing the struggling frontier settlers as "a race that are selling their lives for gold,"[19] she understood, just as Dana did, the commerical meaning of nature in America. Unlike Dana, however, she could not comprehend that in an American context the equation of nature and commerce implied no hypocrisy.

Nor was there much in Dana's vision of nature as commodity to suggest the potential dilemma—noted often today, although less disturbing to people of his time—that if the wilderness is becoming the "milk and honey" of St. Louis or Cincinnati, does not the very creation of the city destroy the benevolent nature that yields it? This question is more appropriate to the present time than to Dana's, only in part because America then seemed inexhaustible. More germane is the fact that nature in its best sense did not exist until man created it. Once completed, the city would stand by itself, and the wilderness could *become* nature. The task would be completed. This idea is exemplified in the popular *American Scenery* (1840), where N. P. Willis, in writing the text for W. H. Bartlett's illustrations, refers to America as "an Eden."[20] Such a region of nature, one would think, ought to be sufficient, but Willis approvingly tells us that the "first thought'' of the American for his Eden ''is of the villages that will soon sparkle on the hill-sides, the axes that will ring from the woodlands, and the mills, bridges, canals, and railroads, that will span and border the stream that now runs through sedge and wild-flowers.''[21] This is a picture of that ''middle landscape'' so accurately described by Leo Marx in his *Machine in the Garden,* although Willis's vision goes beyond a compromise between nature and art. From Willis's perspective, as from that of so many other writers, *the American is turning the wilderness into "nature."* Conceivably, one may fail to see this nature because the ''imperfect state of settlements,'' the forests that cast ''gloom,'' and the ugly felled trees reveal the landscape as incomplete. But Willis is confident of his nation's capacity to look past these appearances. The imaginative power of Americans allows them to project their vision beyond the wilderness, to ''see the form of nature, which is now in dishabille, *restored* [my italics] to her neat drapery.'' But the previous ''drapery'' was the thing so alien to ''nature,'' the ''prostrate wilderness.''[22] Thus, what is ''restored'' is a ''nature'' true to man, the ''Eden'' of human art. From this perspective there is no dilemma for an advancing civilization, since nature is finally art, and when the wilderness is gone, America will have been completed. However unreal or incongruous this sense of nature may seem now, it was broadly assumed in nineteenth-century America.

Such an equation between art and nature was certainly not new. As M. H. Abrams has noted, Coleridge took issue with Wordsworth's belief in the superiority of nature by citing *The Winter's Tale,* where Polixenes refuted ''Montaigne's preference for nature, as opposed to art, by pointing out that art (the intervention of man's planning and skill) 'itself is nature.' ''[23] But the matter took a special turn in an American context, as seen from Poe's exploration of the problem in his story ''The Landscape Garden,'' published by *Ladies' Companion* in 1842 and republished three years later by *Broadway Journal.*

Poe's narrator is struck by the superiority of an artificial garden to a natural one. He is puzzled because in ''all other matters we are justly instructed to regard Nature as supreme,''[24] but he manages to reconcile this poetic view of nature with a broader, cultural perception of art either as equal to nature or as superior to it when nature is associated with the wilderness. His rationale begins with what we recognize as the Emersonian idea that apparent imperfections in nature exist only because of man's imperfect vision, although Poe's solution is anything but Emersonian. His story describes the scheme of a fabulously wealthy man's attempt to create through art the kind of beauty that angels can perceive in nature. By attempting to work out the metaphysics of nature's relation to art that Willis only suggests, Poe grapples with a problem far more difficult than the question of whether art or nature is superior—an intellectual game already old in the first century when the Roman agrarian Columella regretted the passing of rural virtues. On the one hand, Poe shared the European rationalism of a perfectly ordered universe, of the innate superiority of the cosmic clock—itself a metaphor from art—over the crude artifices of man. On the other hand, his perceptive fear of urban blight notwithstanding (as revealed, for example, in his ''Colloquy of Monos and Una''), Poe also shared the national belief that nature as physical phenomenon must become civilization. To reject such a view would leave the wilderness intact—an idea not even pursued in Concord.

Poe's solution in ''The Landscape Garden,'' whimsical though it may have been, was to intensify, to exaggerate the basic American sense of art's relationship to nature—the merging of one into the other. Through his wealth, Poe's character creates nature of a spectacular kind, well beyond the raptures of Dana and others. Although this offers no solution to the metaphysical puzzle of art's relation to nature, the story does reveal how closely the question, in an American context, was tied to the subject of commodity and commerce. By creating a character of fabulous wealth, Poe establishes his framework for exploring the question and concludes, to put it crudely, that with sufficient wealth one could demonstrate the superiority of nature by buying, as it were, one's own visions.

The metaphysical issue, which intrigued Poe, was not, however, a serious concern to those further removed from the world of belles-lettres. Indeed, many individuals confronted the whole myth of nature as a force special and beneficent to America by ridiculing rhetorical extravagances about nature. Such individuals were willing to dispense with the whole verbal apparatus of nature as "golden," or as "the land of milk and honey," or as the "El Dorado" region. Uninterested in seeing nature as anything other than starkly realistic, they nevertheless subscribed to Dana's underlying assumptions, even while eschewing the linguistic adornments found in *The Garden of the World,* or in numerous works similarly conceived. George Ogden in his *Letters from the West* (1823) exemplifies the writer who condemns the seductive rhetoric of nature's promise, even while subscribing wholly to the great American image of nature being transformed into civilization.

A New England Quaker merchant, Ogden shared with most writers of the West a concern for the economics of the region, particularly its potential for growth. However, he saw the region in harsh terms reminiscent of the early Puritans. The fulfillment of the West would come when the area is populated, when "wild beasts" are destroyed, and "when the silence of nature is succeeded by the buzz of employment." The emphasis here is not so much on nature being transformed as on it being defeated. Nor would anything less than the total subjugation of nature do for Ogden, who seemed to have little doubt that it was inevitable and would be a sign "of the benevolent intentions of Providence!"[25] The triumph over this inimical force that stood in the way of civilization and God's will was the means by which America would fulfill the great destiny Ogden visualized with certainty; but to eulogize nature, to describe it as "flowing with milk and honey," was for Ogden the fabrication of "scribblers and land speculators."[26] Yet, even in this attack on misleading claims for the West, Ogden keeps faith with the view that nature will become civilization. Neither Ogden nor Dana, nor any travel writer I have read, doubted that the destiny of the West was to be realized in the emergence of great cities and prosperous farms. Only the price to be paid or the langauge to describe the outcome seemed at issue.

One version of the cost, and of course the most famous one today, is the frontier myth Cooper launched in 1823 with the creation of Natty Bumppo. It will come as no surprise to scholars of Cooper that in spite of widespread pride in him as living proof that America really could produce good writers, many people had serious reservations about his version of America's encounter with nature. The basic complaint is exemplified in a bit of praise Cooper received from an admirer, Francis J. Grund, who, having lived many years in America, wrote an important account of the nation, in part to offset the stinging British criticisms by Frances Trollope and Basil Hall.[27] Here is a portion of what Grund observes about Cooper:

> Whatever may be said of his imitation of Walter Scott, he is original in his scenes and conceptions, and will forever remain a rival competitor of the great master. His works have been translated into all European languages, and, despite of the illiberal criticism of his own countrymen, will be read and admired as long as there shall be a heart capable of enthusiasm for liberty. Whatever the Americans may now think of Cooper, he is, and will, probably, for a long time remain, the most manly and national representative of their literature.[28]

Although Grund admired Cooper's originality, others called it distortion. But such a charge against Cooper was really unfair, since it measured his conception of the West and nature against the kind of unsentimentalized view appearing in Ogden's book, published the same year as *The Pioneers*. Moreover, Cooper's critics sometimes missed the fact that he was writing historical fiction, telling stories of the past and not of contemporary America. Thus, he was faulted for not comprehending the actual frontier, and ironically he was even criticized by Daniel Drake, perhaps one of the very few people in America actually holding the kind of spiritual commitment to nature Cooper attempted to create in his art. Drake's criticism of Cooper—and of J. K. Paulding as well—is indeed harsh, and fair only if Cooper is to be measured as a reporter of his contemporary West, which he certainly was not. According to Drake,

> The failure of Mr. Cooper in his Prairie [1827], and Mr. Paulding in his Westward Ho [1832], is conclusive evidence, that in delineating the West, no power of genius, can supply the want of opportunities for personal observation on our natural and social aspects. No western man can read those works with interest; because of their want of conformity to the circumstances and character of the country, in which the scenes are laid.[29].

Although Paulding was a witty writer, and his Dangerfield family in *Westward Ho!* can still provide an evening's entertainment, no historian would look to him for an illuminating delineation of the West. Nor, in most cases, to Cooper, one would hope, although in the "conception" of his frontier story there was one crucial element, grounded in the same assumptions made by Dana and Ogden, that indeed told the truth about America's West. This was Cooper's portrayal of the West as a wilderness upon which civilization must be imposed. His admirers and detractors could agree to that. On this key point, Cooper spoke for America. Whether the forces standing in the way of civilization were removed brutally or with loving tenderness, nobody doubted that America's destiny was to remove them. And very few people, if any, really regretted that fact. Only in the literature of imagination did such perceptions appear.

Although writers of the American West who had actually traveled there would, on occasion, note the presence of individuals reminding them of Natty, the most important character Cooper created who existed more in reality than in fantasy was Ishmael Bush, who appeared in *The Prairie* in 1827. Bush is a character whose type emerges frequently in observations about the West. He very well might be a figure out of any number of travel narratives, whether sympathetic or not in their approach to

America. He was the pioneer who, in Ogden's work, was degraded by intimate contact with nature. It was axiomatic for Ogden
that one could not live so far from civilization without acquiring
the habits of savages.[30] This was a widespread view, one reflected
in the depictions of Bush and Natty, although in the latter case
the "savage" is idealized. But the premise is the same: one
transforms nature into civilization, or one is transformed.

Although nobody doubted that America's nature would be
transformed into civilization, many were concerned that intimate
contact with the natural world would adversely affect American
character in the West. Thus, Bush was the embodiment of an
American fear. Cooper handled it fictionally by sending him to
the socially redeeming settlements, or by killing him in his later
incarnation as Tom Hutter. Yet the person degraded by nature
endured in American thought. Ogden had described "Bush" in
1823, Cooper had invented him in 1827, and Dana was still affirming in 1856 that he could be controlled from the East. To the
memory of that dream, whereby the West would be populated by
ruggedly skilled men with minds trained by Harvard Divinity
School, Dana offered the invocation in his introduction. At about
the same time, in 1855, Walt Whitman wrote his song to the
democratic man who would be skilled and moral, who would
work the land and build the nation with his superior mind and
body. But the Ishmael Bushes were not reading *Leaves of Grass*.
And certainly by the 1850s the misleading claims for the West,
about which Ogden had warned, were widely—if not univer-
sally—kept in perspective. Those who went West had no reason
to believe that the region offered more than an opportunity for
radical economic transformation at great personal risk. Even
leaders of utopian communities understood this for the most part.
The journey west was speculative, and no literate person could
be expected to believe that life on the frontier was mediated by the
decorum of Dana's "New England minds."

As Cooper accurately reported, the settlements absorbed
Bush's descendants and made them respectable. These descendants may even have become some of the people about whom

Sinclair Lewis was one day to write, for in freeing themselves from Bush's "savage" state his descendants assimilated the values of an emerging society, widely boasting of its increasing population, proud of its special virtue and particularly of its commercial success. The boosterism and attachment to material things that Lewis would attack mercilessly represented the degeneration of a dream for some, but primarily it was the logical extension of America's larger dream envisioning a great western, commercial empire. For although much was written in the early nineteenth century about national destiny being fulfilled in the context of religious or democratic ideals, the dominant American idea of the West and nature is recorded in the text of Dana's *Garden of the World.* Whatever ancillary benefits developed from the conversion of "milk and honey" into factories and other enterprises, the controlling vision of America as a great nation remained largely commercial. Once America was populated and wealthy there would be time enough for varying visions. First, nature had to become "El Dorado."

Some, of course, dissented from this particular vision, as Whitman did in his famous warning issued in the preface to his 1855 edition of *Leaves of Grass.* Here he insists that a nation so heavily endowed by nature would be monstrous—as nature itself would be monstrous—without a corresponding greatness of spirit. Although Whitman offers a solution by converting through the alembic of art this potentially dreadful outcome into a joyous prophecy for the future, the horrible possibility inherent in his warning disturbed those unable to be reassured by the euphoria of transcendental poetry. Actually, the warning had been published long before Whitman offered his version of it. Two decades earlier, in 1832, a perceptive Presbyterian clergyman from Pennsylvania, Robert Baird, had warned that "the Christian [cannot] be inattentive to the inceptive character and forming manners of a part of our country [the West] whose influence will soon be felt to be favourable, or disastrous, to an extent corresponding with its mighty energies, to the cause of religion."[31] According to Baird, who had journeyed west to establish a network of Sunday schools, nature alone would be ''impotent'' to shape properly America's national character. But with marvelous prescience, he saw in nature the extraordinary capacity ''to supply striking and appropriate similes, metaphors, and create the language of wonder,''[32] as Emerson would indeed do a few years later in *Nature*—although one doubts if this could have pleased Baird—when he reshaped Christianity's formulation into a personal mythology.

But the metaphors of Emerson generally did not celebrate a national impulse toward the ''land of milk and honey,'' and America was scarcely moved by his gentle admonishments or by the vigorous beratings of foreigners such as Harriet Martineau, who saw her grand hopes for the fresh, redemptive new world of ''nature'' crushed by ''selfish adventurers, who drive out the red man, and drive in the black man, and, amidst the forests and the floods, think only of cotton and of gold.''[33] The ordinary citizen, whom Richard Hofstadter perceptively has described as an ''expectant capitalist. . .for whom enterprise was a kind of religion,''[34] had personal interests more compelling than an old European dream for a spiritually regenerative America. In search of philosophers and poets, Harriet Martineau found instead these expectant capitalists. ''The chance,'' she protested in 1837, ''which opens to the meditative the almost untouched regions of nature, is a rare one; and they should not be left to the vanishing savage, the busy and the sordid.''[35]

Harriet Martineau's criticisms were this severe because, in part, her expectations had proved too high and wholly unrealistic. Her thoughts ran toward a poetic idea about America that had been born in Europe, while those who had chosen to settle the land usually had more mundane intentions. The new man of the New World had become in large measure a participant in democracy's sacred group, the majority; he enthusiastically endorsed Jacksonian contempt for Indian rights and regarded abolition as a dirty word because it struck at property rights. And if ever there were a time in history when an old European dream for America was out of place, this era may very well have been a singular

example—not merely for the new nation, but for Western civili-
tion. Doctrines rooted in the denigration of materialism were in
direct conflict with the views of a civilization infatuated by the
theory of enlightened self-interest, codified in 1776 by Adam
Smith. This concept, called by Max Lerner "a cardinal principle
of the faith of the age,"[36] held that society will reach its highest
potential as each individual seeks his own selfish ends. That such a
premise retained vitality in the nineteenth century can be seen by
the eagerness with which the doctrine of social Darwinism would
be embraced. Smith's *Wealth of Nations* may not have been a fix-
ture in the settlements or in the average home libraries of the
East, but the rationale of laissez-faire capitalism was an integral
part of the social theory on which America was built. And even
the intense individualism in Concord—the quest for private solutions—had something to do with this idea. Nor is there really
much reason to believe that the West would have been very different if Dana's "New England minds" had directed the process
of nature becoming civilization. One only has to look to Timothy
Dwight to see exemplified what Dana had in mind, for as a Congrega-
tional minister and president of Yale, a solid representative of
Christian orthodoxy and the "New England mind," Dwight
wrote an eastern "truth," as well as a western one, in assuring
his audience that only through instilling in the Indian "the *love
of property*" could he be civilized.[37] This was the spirit that
prevailed when eastern minds did indeed shape the developing
West, as Washington Irving's *Astoria* (1836) affirms in
celebrating the commercial triumphs of John Jacob Astor, "the
master-spirit of the enterprise who," as Irving writes, "regulated
the springs of Astoria, at his residence in New York."[38]

Nature in America was defined in many ways, from a
mysterious, threatening force to something loved, or to almost
anything one could imagine. But within the great variety of
meanings two irreconcilable connotations emerged as the most
important definitions of the word *nature*. In the ideas of Dana,
Ogden, Dwight, and Astor, nature represented commodity being
transformed into civilization. In the ideas of some of Harriet Mar-

tineau's "poets," nature became the metaphor for a new spiritual mythology. In visionary art—and then only rarely—the two images of nature might merge. But generally they remained apart—separate images carried by the common metaphor of *nature,* a word that had its broadest cultural meaning in the concept of commodity rather than spirit. Although Americans were surely not the greedy barbarians so often portrayed by European writers—and these were mostly of an economically privileged class—the myth of new civilizations in the West had an immediate meaning to a society holding little interest in the myth of a new theology. For most Americans, Christianity remained healthy enough to address concerns of the spirit.

3

The Garden of America

In the apparently tangled rhetoric of early nineteenth-century America, religious phrases such as ''milk and honey'' were often used to convey an aesthetic enthusiasm for aspects of nature that in retrospect seem secular and unrelated to aesthetics. Yet when the language reveals its meanings, the apparent paradox of a nation that praised the beauties of nature while generally ignoring the aesthetics of the natural world becomes clarified. There is no denying that the praise does exist in an abundance that would *seem* to define early-nineteenth-century America as a culture fascinated by the beauties of nature, in the East and in the West. The glut of adulation at times seems to approach ubiquity, appearing as it does in magazines, in newspapers, and in the voguish gift or ''flower'' books—anthologies of poems and pictures celebrating flowers while explaining their symbolic meanings. Painters, such as those of ''the Hudson River School,'' depict beautiful landscapes, while travelers repeatedly marvel at the attractions of the Natural Bridge in Virginia or of Trenton Falls in New York State, or of Niagara Falls, or of numerous other places. And our modern anthologies have carefully preserved the paeans to nature by the ''grey-bearded'' poets. That a litany of praise existed is certain, although to accept it at face value is to recover a nation that never quite existed.

European travel writers visited a different nation, and, in their almost ritualistic comments on America's indifference to the

46

beauties of nature, they fairly accurately portrayed America's aesthetics of nature. Certainly these writers do have to be examined skeptically, for they so often deserve the kind of satire Melville aims at them in *Mardi*, where he stingingly entitles a book, " 'Three Hours in Vivenza [America], containing a Full and Impartial Account of that Whole Country: by a subject of King Bello [King of England].' "[1] We are perhaps correctly suspicious of Fanny Kemble (Frances Anne Butler), the British actress, who, adored by the American public—even praised in Catherine Sedgwick's best-selling *Linwoods*[2]—ungratefully replied by publishing in 1835 her scarcely disguised disdain for an American insensitivity toward nature's beauties. She found this attitude "nothing short of amazing," especially since anyone with "half a soul" would respond "with feelings almost of adoration."[3] Or one may be skeptical of Tocqueville's companion, Gustave De Beaumont, whose outraged feelings against slavery, as revealed in his semifictional polemic book *Marie* (1835), may have clouded his judgment about Americans to the point where he could write that "the European who admires beautiful forests is much surprised to find that the American has a deep hatred for trees."[4] But when the much more sympathetic Frenchman, Michael Chevalier, genuinely fascinated by American commercial enterprise, observed that he was "mistaken" in claiming that Americans speculate in everything, since "the American, essentially practical in his views, will never speculate in tulips, even at New York although the inhabitants of that city have Dutch blood in their veins,"[5] we begin to wonder what prompts such views about a nation committed to nature. Certainly the sense that these European observations might be valid quickly increases as similar perspectives are found in the words of a young Fanny Wright, still in love with America, of Harriet Martineau, and, to give one American example, of Charles Fenno Hoffman, the well-known writer of his day, who, like many of his countrymen, conceded that nature was not aesthetically appreciated in his native land.[6] Moreover, when the greatest nineteenth-century social critic of America, Alexis de Tocqueville, concludes that

Americans are indifferent to the beauties of nature, we know that
the proposition must be taken seriously.

"In Europe," Tocqueville writes, "people talk a great deal of
the wilds of America, but the Americans themselves never think
about them: they are insensible to the wonders of inanimate
nature."[7] Tocqueville could hardly have been blind to all the
celebrations of nature's beauty, yet the word "insensible" confronts us. One clue to the apparent contradiction is found in an
observation by the German naturalist and soldier, Alexander
Philip Maximilian, that Americans—with the exceptions of
Cooper and Irving—avoided "clear and vivid description of the
natural scenery of North America" because they were so familiar
with it.[8] Although Maximilian was wrong in thinking that
Americans avoided scenic description, the words "clear and
vivid" offer a key insight, for it is generally safe to say that praise
of nature was overwhelmingly in the form of obligatory phrases
rather than in precise, lucid descriptions. At least this is the case
in accounts by American travel writers. A passage written in
1834 by Theodore Dwight is instructive and typical.

Traveling through New York State, Dwight came upon a scene
that caught his attention. *"The Great Falls,"* he writes, "is a
romantic cascade, of 150 feet, about 9 miles from Hudson, near
the old post route." For him this exhausted the scenic dimension.
Dwight then turned his attention to practical matters: "Various
plans have been proposed, for the improvement of the navigation
of Hudson river, and some have been attempted. Nearly
$150,000 have been expended since the year 1797, about
$30,000 of which was by the state."[9] Or consider the similar
paean by Timothy Flint: "Pittsburg is a considerable town,
generally built of brick, and has been so often described as to
render uninteresting any new attempt of the kind. The site is
romantic and delightful. It is well known as a manufacturing
place, and once almost supplied the lower country with a variety
of the most necessary and important manufactures. But the
wealth, business, and glory of this place are fast passing away,
transferred to Cincinnati, to Louisville, and other places on the

Ohio.''[10] Like Dwight, Flint had tucked his praise unobtrusively and perfunctorily in with the commercial facts that captured his imagination.

These descriptions by Dwight and Flint are so characteristic that they might be called the modus operandi of numerous American writers. Their method consisted of giving the reader a vapid word or phrase in tribute to scenic appeal, followed or preceded by a discussion of serious questions relating to commercial potential. So frequent was this process that words such as ''romantic'' existed as substitutes for the ''clear and vivid'' scenic descriptions Maximilian mentioned. Thus, Dwight revealed the Delaware Water Gap as ''romantic and beautiful,''[11] and another writer described Saratoga as ''pleasant, with Hudson below, divided by two romantic islands.''[12] Catherine Sedgwick, ranked in her own time with Cooper and Irving, used ''romantic'' to perform a similar task in fiction, as, for example, in the enormously popular *Hope Leslie* (1827), where some Indians, after destroying a settlement, return to ''the forest with as little apparent uncertainty as to their path, as is now felt by travellers who pass through the same still romantic country.''[13]

Such empty rhetoric forces upon us the question of why writers bothered to praise at all. Certainly in the relatively new world of America, as in the old one of Europe, many of nature's component parts offered little to celebrate. Complaints about bugs, disease, intolerable climate, or miasma were far more numerous than paeans to nature. Yet there is no avoiding the fact that praising nature was stylish. Some of this praise was genuinely related to an aesthetic feeling about the texture of one's world. A painter, for example, did not need a national ideology to find the landscape an attractive subject. Moreover, the most venal persons were perfectly capable of aesthetic appreciation. But however much a given painter or land speculator may have enjoyed the scenery, the ubiquity of praise requires an explanation not contingent on random admiration. Part of the larger solution is found in the aping of British fashions, one of which was the broad use of nature in poetry. Although the preeminent nature poet, Wordsworth, did not begin his real American vogue until 1849, [14] the British had been exporting the topic in poetry for some time.

The broader explanation relates to the lingering power of Europe's old idea of America as a place of special imagination. America's peculiar burden has always been to carry the rhetorical encumbrances of fantasies spawned before its birth. In the nineteenth century, however odd the notions of the Rousseaus and the Chateaubriands may have struck most Americans, the whole concept of America as the land of magic—of Shakepeare's *Tempest*—carried the lingering rhetorical vestige of an idea that had now, to a large extent, been reduced to the place Dwight and Flint gave it. Historians may reasonably argue as to when the idea of America turned from a renaissance poetry of imagination to a later poetry of commerce, but by the nineteenth century the suggestion that America was Edenic, at least in European poetic terms, or that noble savages inhabited the wilderness, offered an almost certain reply of ridicule and contempt in America. Europeans met such reactions even though their fantasies of the American Indian as Adam before the Fall, or of the wilderness as an earthly paradise, found their way into derivative American writing. And although Americans scattered their paeans in commercial discourses, European visitors uncomprehendingly responded with astonishment at how ''insensitive'' Americans were to the beauty of nature.

Although European travelers were not so naïve as to expect an American Eden, they were often unprepared for a society more concerned with the practical business of existence than with shaping America to Europe's rigorous poetic standards long ago imposed upon the New World. This disparity between two ideas about America helps explain how a writer such as Charles Dickens, who knew poverty and squalor well, could fail to see any beauty in an American landscape covered with rotted trunks and burned trees,[15] American symbols of nature in the process of becoming civilization in a land of opportunity. Moreover, neither Dickens nor countless other Europeans ever comprehended how this same ''ugly'' landscape could be regarded by Americans as one of the beautiful manifestations of nature. Europeans had little experience in looking past the immediate landscape—as Willis had done—and visualizing the completed artifact of civilization that adhered within the raw stuff hiding it from penetrating eyes. Americans grew up looking at nature that way. Indeed, America's sense of beauty in this respect can be understood by analogy with the transcendental theory of sight, the notion whereby one ''sees'' the mystical or romantic truth in nature before one even looks at objects such as trees or other natural phenomena. The crassest, most materialistic land speculator could easily agree with Emerson's idea that nature looked ugly only to those who did not know how to see it properly. They only differed in what the eye should ''see.'' So an Emerson might discover transcendent beauty in the landscape, or a Willis—not a crass land speculator—might see the glowing beauty of civilization, and a Dickens could find rotted tree stumps. But neither Emerson nor Dickens really participated in the dominant American vision of what the journey into nature meant.

The rotted stumps that bothered Dickens were, as Flint writes, ''To the eye of a Kentuckian. . .pleasant circumstances,'' although on the particular occasion that he wrote this, Flint was himself not very pleased with the sight.[16] Yet he was reporting America, and there is every reason to believe his accuracy in this. Americans understood, for example, what C. W. Dana meant when he wrote that ''this structure,'' referring to landscape not yet dominated by cultural artifacts, ''is yet in process of erection: the materials of construction, workmen ascending and descending, mar its present appearance; but when the work is finished the scaffolding will fall, and the noble edifice will start in its wondrous beauty before an astonished world!''[17] Somewhat less exuberantly, Timothy Dwight offered an impressively succinct equation: *''beautiful country,''* he writes emphatically, ''means appropriately, and almost only, lands suited to the purposes of husbandry: and has scarcely a remote reference to beauty of landscape.''[18] Or as Flint observed: ''East Pennsylvania is a beautiful country in every point of view. I have no where seen an agriculture apparently so rich as here.''[19]

This kind of association held little room for any idealization of a primitive, untouched world, except as it might offer the opportunity for cultivation or for escapist literature. Only two years after Cooper began his wonderful myth of Natty Bumppo and Chingachgook, America's famous ethnologist and explorer, Henry Schoolcraft, articulated a basic value of his society by claiming that ''the poet and the painter may look with fond admiration upon the attractions of a warrior age [of Indians], which knew nothing but ferocious passion, and lawless freedom, or the faithless and sudden transitions of wild and unchastened indulgence. But to the mild reign of letters and civilization, belong that subjection of passion and direction of reason which impart form, and system, and permanency, to all the essential blessings of life. . . .''[20] Civilization: this was the prophecy implicit in nature, and this was the context in which Americans read Cooper, whose own attachment to civilized values was sufficiently clear to his audience. But Europeans such as Rousseau or Chateaubriand were remote from these values, and Americans therefore thought such Europeans mad or stupid. It would be hard to find two names appearing more often in American writing as examples of European obtuseness, however accurately or inaccurately these two Frenchmen were understood. Their absurdity, as seen by Americans, offered an irresistible target for people eager to return Europe's insults.

Europeans, Flint writes of many people who came to examine America, arrive here ''deluded. . .by the pastoral dreams of Rousseau or Chateaubriand. . . .''[21] Certainly all Europeans were not so ''deluded,'' but neither was Flint creating straw men. Indeed, a decade after Flint's statement, one could find Beaumont writing the following:

Atala, René, the Natchez, were born in America, children of the wilderness. The New World inspired them, old Europe alone has understood them.

When the Americans read Chateaubriand, as when they see the marvel of Niagara, they say, "And what does that prove?"[22]

Surely Beaumont was not "deluded," but he carried a dream alien to most Americans, and he accurately defined a poetic relationship between the New World and Europe. Beaumont offers much truth in what he says about Americans and Niagara Falls, although one could nevertheless almost drown in the myriad American panegyrics to those waters. Not at issue, however, is the fact that Beaumont, in his view of Americans as aesthetic barbarians, represented a common European view. Likewise, Flint reflected a basic American attitude in belittling Europe's poetic idea of America. Idealizations of primitivism, concepts of a beauty or value in nature independent of civilization, belonged to the fool or to the writer of fantasy. America's normative idea of the Indian, for example, was far less likely to be found in the writings of Rousseau and Chateaubriand, or even in Cooper's myth of the Indians, than in the chilling words of Robert Baird:

> An uncivilized state of mankind is one of constant tendency to annihilation, all the world over. Nor need we marvel at it. From the very nature of the human mind, and the condition in which men are placed in this world, it cannot be otherwise. A state of barbarism, is a very miserable one. Its uncertainty, often, of the means of sustenance; its great destitution of social or individual happiness; its gloom and dreariness; its want of happiness here, and its ignorance of life and immortality beyond the grave—are unfavourable to a rapid propagation of the species, or indeed to propagation at all.

Taking direct issue with Rousseau and Chateaubriand, Baird denied that Indians were, or could be, happy.[23]

Whether it was Baird or Rousseau who made the more egregious anthropological judgment is beside the point. Baird, along with Flint and so many others, voiced an American perception, uttered a national belief even about the fascinating subject of

Indian fecundity—or lack of it—which in a nation almost
obsessively concerned with population growth was indeed a telling point against Indian values. But this contempt for the Indian
was in itself only symptomatic of America's larger conception of
what beauty and the wilderness meant in the land of nature. For
the wilderness of the present—as opposed to the beauty one might
"see" in the wilderness of the future—remained as hideous, if
not as frightening, as it had appeared to the Puritans. Baird's
equation between the "uncivilized state" and "annihilation"
contained more than prophetic judgment; it revealed how inimical an untouched wilderness was perceived to be in America.

Such cultural assumptions are central to Cooper's wilderness
myth. Not all the nobility of Cooper's idealized Indians could im-
munize them from the fate pronounced by Baird. Cooper lovingly
tells of the Indian's movement toward Baird's promised "annihilation." Indeed, take this premise from Cooper's story of the
American Indian, and he has no story to tell. The wilderness
promises "annihilation," and Cooper confirms this even in the fate
of the white man who chooses to live in such a world. Only in
Cooper's sentimentalization of the receding wilderness and its
vanishing inhabitants, in his atypical richness of scenic description, does he depart from the basic premises his society held about
the wilderness. Americans knew Indians as neither the grandly
evil Magua, nor the deeply noble Chingachgook, nor even the
comically stupid characters emerging from Mark Twain's
reading of Cooper. None of these types is likely to be found in
travel narratives describing Indians, who were generally reported
to be opportunistic, shiftless, generally unhappy, and, most unlike
either Magua or Chingachgook, easily intimidated. In short,
Baird's miserable barbarian. Although few modern readers
believe that nineteenth-century Indians resembled Cooper's
literary creations, we may be assured that most of Cooper's contemporaries made an even sharper distinction between "real" Indians and his version of them. But although Cooper's more
perceptive readers always understood that in his depiction of Indians he was inventing rather than reporting, much searing

criticism was directed at his presumed inability to comprehend Indians. Such criticism came from quite disparate sources.

One such critic was Achille Murat, an émigré in America for about nine years, profoundly sympathetic toward his host country, and a defender of almost all its institutions—including to a large extent democracy's great embarrassment, slavery. And he lauded Cooper's fiction.[24] But as for his Indians, Murat drew the line. "You must not form any opinion of them from the descriptions of Cooper," he warns his readers, particularly European ones, since Cooper "has always wished to make *gentlemen* of them, and. . .has even endowed them with delicate sentiments towards the fair sex, which, however, is by no means natural to them. . . .As to the Indian himself, he is physically brave, morally a coward, patient from necessity, while some among them possess much natural sagacity."[25] Of Cooper, and indeed the Indians themselves, this was fairly sympathetic criticism, as was Washington Irving's broader statement not specifically applied to Cooper, though obviously suggesting him: "As far as I can judge, the Indian of poetical fiction is like the shepherd of pastoral romance, a mere personification of imaginary attributes."[26]

The unsympathetic criticism was another matter. J. Watson Webb, editing *Altowan* (1846) by the Englishman William Stewart, observes the following in a footnote to his prefatory remarks:

Among the deluded mass, our countryman Cooper stands conspicuous. In common with all of us, he listened in infancy to the nursery tales which had been handed down from generation to generation, with such additions as the love of the marvelous among nursery maids, very naturally prompted; and as Mr. Cooper is not accustomed to doubt the accuracy of his knowledge on any subject, it should not be matter [sic] of surprise with those who know him, that he assumes perfectly to understand the Indian character. In consequence of this assumption of knowledge—based solely upon the sources to which I have referred [i.e., the nursery tales]—he has written a series of exceedingly clever books, the chief tendency of which is to perpetuate his own crude conceptions of Indian character, by embodying all the nursery gossip of two centuries, and handing it down to posterity as a picture drawn from life, instead of what it really is—the tradition of the ignorant, embellished by the lovers of the marvelous, to frighten into silence, if not sleep, the restless inmates of the nursery.

Whereupon Webb proceeded to insist that "I do not make these remarks in any spirit of unkindness to Mr. Cooper, but in the way of protest against his delineation of Indian character."[27] Whether or not Webb offered this disclaimer ironically or sincerely, his protest against Cooper's characterizations missed the point. Cooper had no serious interest in "Indian character." He had a story to tell about the transformation of the wilderness into civilization, and in taking aesthetic liberties he had a right to assume that literate readers could distinguish fact from fancy.

Webb's criticism nevertheless accurately suggests the distance between the perceived reality of Cooper's day and the wilderness of his imagination (albeit *Altowan* scarcely closes the gap). Whatever Cooper may mean to us today, people who appreciated him in his own time—except those believing in nursery tales—did so with the full capacity to distinguish between a poetic fantasy and a life true to American perceptions. Moreover, if Cooper distorted the West for literary purposes, he erred on the side of restraint rather than of excess. That is, Cooper's wilderness was a safer place than the wilderness of America. His fiction conjured perils that were easily and predictably contained. By contrast, Americans associated the wilderness with terrors Cooper declined to portray in his celebration of the process whereby nature took the shape of civilization. So alien was the wilderness to America's dream of the West, so remote was the idea of a contemporary wilderness as beautiful (when not properly "seen"), that with few exceptions a clear cultural equation emerges between proximity to civilization and beauty in nature. Natural beauty in America was appreciated most where it was thoroughly domesticated, where nature had already taken the shape of civilization. As the frontier extended westward, the equation held. There were a good many more encomiums to the *aesthetic* beauties of Trenton Falls, near Utica, New York, than to the whole Mississippi Valley.

The ultimate symbol of America's aesthetic sense of nature as process toward civilization may be found in the fascinating emergence of cemeteries in which the dead were interred in a "natural" setting of carefully pruned foliage amid paths named after domesticated flora. Greenwood in New York and Mt. Auburn in Massachusetts, for example, drew effusive praise from writers such as Catherine Sedgwick,[28] even while the then-little-known writer named Thoreau responded to these cemeteries with contempt—specifically, in his essay "Autumnal Tints." The voguish cemeteries—progenitors of Forest Lawn and other contemporary "resting places," with their elaborate ornaments and sentimental poetry inscribed in rock—appropriately represented America's most extravagant monuments to the aesthetics of nature, for the cities of the dead excluded any hint of the wilderness. The intense identification of these cemeteries with conspicuous artifacts of civilization reflected a society's commitment, even in death, to triumph over the disorders of an uncultivated world, to avoid the kind of horror evoked in Hawthorne's "Roger Malvin's Burial."

Although Hawthorne's story endows the wilderness with a complex set of meanings, its suggestion of the land ultimately possessing man draws heavily on a nightmare image of nature. But the appearance of nature truer to an ideal American dream takes shape in the design of Greenwood Cemetery. Whether in images of life or death, the perception of nature as beautiful faded as civilization—or its promise—receded. Had Charles Dickens explored the barren lands at the approaches to Oregon, he might have found American aesthetic perceptions more consistent with his own, since few Americans believed that these lands would become civilized. Therefore, they were as devoid of beauty as the Mississippi Valley was to the bewildered English writer, who—like many of his countrymen—failed to grasp the American equation of beauty in nature with the potential for civilization.

The force of this association had such power in America that when Poe sought in his abortive *Julius Rodman* (1840) to describe as beautiful a region thought hopeless for the emergence of civilization, he was almost by definition writing a tale of fantasy. Describing the barren region along the way to Oregon, Poe offered a tale that could have been based on any number of travel narratives describing the familiar route his hero followed. As in the earlier sea story, *Pym,* Poe sought to exploit public interest in a remote, exotic area. Although Poe's final intentions for *Julius Rodman* must remain speculative, the story seeks to invert America's equation between beauty and civilization. No other attempt of its kind exists, and perhaps Poe never finished the story because the task proved too difficult. Whether Poe failed to complete the piece for this or other reasons, Rodman's journey ends finally with the totally implausible image of the barren West as a floral wonderland. This was a fantastic proposition for a society that equated such beauty with civilization, whether in the cities of the West or the cemeteries of the East.

The stated destination of Poe's hero is a region west of the Rocky Mountains and north of the sixtieth parallel. Never mind that, cartographically, Julius Rodman seems headed for a campsite somewhere in the Bering Sea. Poe's heroes manage these things, and whatever experience was envisaged for him Julius Rodman apparently survives. The narrative, however, does not take us across the Rockies, nor does it offer any poetic view of the barren lands; it stops somewhere near the juncture of the Yellowstone and Missouri rivers. Before reaching this point—at which the manuscript ends—the explorers in Rodman's party had traveled north on the Missouri River on a route frequently taken by American explorers, widely written about, and well-known to the American reading public. Poe alluded to familiar sites, lending an air of plausibility to the imaginative journey that described the same scenery found in *Astoria* and other travel narratives. What makes Poe's work extraordinary in the context of his society is his aesthetic transformation of the West. Although this happens only once in the story, at Council Bluffs—which Irving and others found strikingly beautiful—Poe outdoes these writers as he creates a uniquely exotic setting. Rodman, he writes,

> was enchanted with the voluptuous beauty of the country. The prairies exceeded in beauty anything told in the tales of the Arabian Nights. On the edges of the creeks there was a wild mass of flowers which looked more like Art than Nature, so profusely and fantastically were their vivid colors blended together. Their rich odor was almost oppressive. Every now and then we came to a kind of green island of trees, placed amid an ocean of purple, blue, orange, and crimson blossoms, all waving to and fro in the wind. These islands consisted of the most majestic forest oaks, and, beneath them, the grass resembled a robe of the softest green velvet, while up their huge stems there clambered, generally, a profusion of grape vines, laden with delicious ripe fruit. The Missouri, in the distance, presented the most majestic appearance; and many of the real islands with which it was studded were entirely covered with plum bushes, or other shrubbery, except where crossed in various directions by narrow, mazy paths, like the alleys in an English flower-garden; and in these alleys we could always see either elks or antelopes, who had no doubt made them. We returned, at sunset, to the encampment, delighted with our excursion. The night was warm, and we were excessively annoyed by mosquitoes.[29]

Although there is little else in America's literature of the West that offers quite such rapturous tribute to this region, the passage nevertheless adheres to some fundamental American assumptions about the aesthetics of nature. The measure by which Poe pays his highest tribute is that of an English flower garden; the richest compliment he can gave is that ''flowers. . .looked more like Art than Nature.'' This basic response to the West dates back at least to the account of the Lewis and Clark expedition, specifically conceived as an attempt by Jefferson to assess the potential for civilization in the uncharted wilderness. In the account of the *History of the Expedition Under the Command of Lewis and Clark,* ''shelving rock'' in the Missouri River is described as so regular in its features that it seemed ''formed by art.'' The sight was ''singularly beautiful, since, without any of the wild, irregular sublimity of the lower falls, it combined all the regular elegances which the fancy of a painter would select to form a beautiful waterfall.''[30] Or in the words of one Dr. Willard, ''Art has a neatness and finish, which we look for in vain in the great scale of nature's rough operations.''[31] In a society where such ''rough operations'' culminated in civilization or art, nature as aesthetic phenomenon could hardly be expected to emerge as something extraordinarily valued, let alone as a cultural deity. Poe, in his poetic extension of that society's values, shaped his ideal West into an English flower garden. By transforming the region into this garden, he remained true to an American dream of civilization in the West, even as he falsified it by equating the region's beauty with flowers instead of with railroads, canals, and cultivated farmland. Only the pesky mosquitoes whose presence ended the idyllic vision were wholly true to other accounts of the area.

But Poe's attempt to shape nature into art nevertheless reflected the essence of early nineteenth-century American aesthetic sensibility, and the impulse to subsume nature within art reflected itself in the very fads of civilized America, where flowers had a more recognized place than in Julius Rodman's fantasy land. The popularity of ''flower books'' is to be understood in the context of this American aesthetic sensibility. Typical of these books is Henrietta Dumont's *Language of Flowers: The Floral Offering* (1851), or, better known to students of Melville as the source for much of his floral symbolism in *Mardi,* Frances S. Osgood's *The Poetry of Flowers and Flowers of Poetry* (1846). Such books, and their numbers seem limitless, generally share predictable characteristics, as they bind ''nature'' between their covers. In celebrating countless varieties of flowers —though not ragweed—they use British poetry or verses deriving from it. Indeed, Mrs. Osgood's book was actually an adaptation of an English book called *The Sentiment of Flowers.* These works often contain lovely pictures of flowers to accompany the sentimental poems, and each volume includes a dictionary of floral meanings, such as "true love," "falsehood," "maternal love," or other ideas conforming to a highly civilized, sometimes decadent sensibility. Emerson gave the delicious sobriquet, "the fop of fields"[32] to the adherent of this sensibility, but he, not the fops, represented the minority.

In their reliance upon British poetry, the flower books suggest not only America's attempt to fit nature into civilization, but the conscious effort to use Europe as an aesthetic model. This aping of European literature, of which flower books represent only one example, did not go unnoticed by American literati. The great search for a "national literature" is familiar enough, and in retrospect one can be as confident as were these literati that America's nature poetry was Europe's. One can see, too, the striking irony of Americans in the promised land imitating European manners—to the dismay of how many Beaumonts we will never know—by adopting its civilized nature cult, the roots of which lay largely in Europe's poetic search for an escape from the oppressiveness of civilization, a quest that often led imaginatively to America. Each contained the dream of the other. And however little the consolation may have been for those uncountable Beaumonts, America expressed many of its dreams in a European vocabulary.

Although the flower books furnish one pervasive example of this, nowhere was it more manifested than in the visionary rhetoric about the West. One recalls here Dana's *Garden of the World,* a title evoking the almost religious European idea that had been associated with the New World in the earliest days of its discovery, or, as Edmundo O'Gorman has suggestively argued, its "invention."[33] And one recalls at the same time the drably secular, coldly commercial vision of Dana's "garden" in contrast to the marvelous European poetic conception of a new Adam in a new world. But the "garden" in America was remote from the European vision. Its meaning differed radically. "The sturdy plant of the wilderness," Thomas Farnham writes in regard to civilization's triumph over the Indian, "droops under the enervating culture of the garden."[34] If that does not explain what the "garden" had come to mean, perhaps a comment by Charles Fenno Hoffman that made perfect sense to nineteenth-century Americans will clarify it. "Railroads and canals will make one broad garden of Michigan,"[35] and in this image is found the meaning of America's "garden." We show more restraint today in speaking of an "industrial park," which grows from the American "garden," and which no more needs grass than did the nineteenth-century garden need an agrarian ideal. Although there were those who worried about the "garden" of pastoral imagination becoming mechanized, as Leo Marx has shown, they were few. For most, the machine *was* the garden, just as the industrial park *is* the factory complex.

This garden of Hoffman, Farnham, and Dana, this garden of America so intimately associated with railroads, canals, and the whole network of transportation and communication that with astonishing speed was transforming America into a commercial giant, was the pride of the nation. In the task of building this garden Americans spared no effort. The very design of western cities conformed to a thoroughly tested European commercial model. Michael Chevalier, who, unlike his countryman Beaumont, was enormously impressed with the way America was cultivating its garden, observed that the towns springing up in America were organized for the great commercial task: "Everything is here arranged to facilitate industry; the towns are built on the English plan; men of business, instead of being scattered over the town, occupy a particular quarter devoted exclusively to them. . . ."[36] Americans knew better than Beaumont how to cultivate their garden.

The nineteenth-century word *garden* had moved from older religious and aesthetic referents toward a commercial metaphor. The ancient trope of the garden as man's lost place to which he might, in an archetypal sense, "return," admirably suited America's ambition of crossing the land to reach a better place, even an ideal one at times. Nor did any genuine incongruity exist in giving the word *garden* to a place of cities, railroads, and canals, as well as farms. After all, the Christian source for this metaphor of harmony and bliss, the biblical garden, had as little to do with farming or agrarianism, as with railroads and canals. Thus, in a land whose very birth implied the idea of a journey toward something better, it was entirely logical that in the passage to the West, the ultimate goal—however remote from nature—could be the garden. This garden, which in imagination—if not always in practice—might be the wonderful cities rising in the West, became in America the verbal configuration for the journey's end, just as the "garden" or the "city" has traditionally been the goal in the Christian model from which America in large measure drew its paradigm.

As in the sacred journey, however, the American secular journey had inimical forces to overcome before reaching its garden. The most alien of these forces, and the most hideous, was the wilderness. Indeed, it was not *natural,* or so Americans tended to think, for nature, in its unfulfilled state, to occupy the space properly belonging to what would one day be the garden. A sense of this fascinating paradox emerges from Edmund Flagg's response to the appalling discovery of finding himself in an Illinois forest, surrounded by wild vegetation, isolated from civilization: "As I wandered through this region, where vegetation towering in all its rank and monstrous forms, gave evidence of a soil too unnaturally fertile for culture by man, whose bread must be bought the 'the sweat of his brow,' I thought I could perceive a deadly nausea stealing over my frame, and that every respiration was a draught of the floating pestilence." "Nature" too unnatural! Yet America would restore nature to Illinois by turning it into the garden that Hoffman envisaged for Michigan. "Cultivation and settlement," writes Flagg, "will, *of course,* [my italics], as in the older states, remedy this evil to some extent in time."[37] In his secular solution to a secular problem, Flagg had in mind an "unnatural nature" quite different from the one Whitman wrote of in "Passage to India," since the poet's "seas of God" were far removed from Flagg's wilderness in Illinois.

Flagg may have been engaging in rhetorical hyperbole in depicting "monstrous forms," but as a writer he certainly played on

assumed cultural beliefs by associating pestilence with uncultivated vegetation. Flagg was surely not inventing a myth, for
the horror he perceived in the wilderness was already a cliché when
years earlier Charles Brockden Brown had a terrified Edgar
Huntly ask whether "some mysterious power snatched me from
the earth, and cast me, in a moment, into the heart of the
wilderness."[38] No matter what verbal embellishment Flagg gave,
he was uttering commonplaces. As another writer observes,
"[L]ike most travellers from the populous seaboard of our states I
began to expect, in proportion as I receded from the vale of the
Mohawk, to meet with less cultivation—to traverse a hideous
wilderness. . . ."[39] Between the East and the garden was the
wilderness—no insurmountable obstacle, but a force that had to
be transmogrified from its "unnatural" and "hideous" aspects
to the beautiful, commercial garden of nature. That this would
eventually happen was assumed in nineteenth-century America.
However, a vague uneasiness appeared that the wilderness might
triumph occasionally after all, though rarely outside the context
of imaginative writing or iconographic representation.

For example, Thomas Cole's well-known graphic sequence,
"Course of Empire" (1836), ends with vegetation threatening to
engulf a destroyed civilization. The terrible specter of wilderness
overrunning the land led to the morbid account in one travel narrative after another of the famous landslide that engulfed the
Willey family in August 1826, the event that would serve as the
frame for Hawthorne's "Ambitious Guest."[40] Writers less frequently associated with high art than Cole and Hawthorne also
employed this image of the wilderness threatening to engulf man,
although with quite different implications. Timothy Dwight, for
example, writes of the beach near Province Town as "a barrier
against the ambition and fretfulness of the ocean, restlessly and
always employed in assailing its strength, and wearing away its
mass. To my own fancy it appeared as the eternal boundary of a
region, wild, dreary, and inhospitable, where no human being
could dwell, and into which every human foot was forbidden to

enter.''[41] But if Dwight used the same metaphor as Cole and Hawthorne, his was antiseptically safe. The ocean threatened the shores, wore away at the mass, but the beach was finally revealed as an ''eternal boundary'' against it. Countless examples exist of what Dwight imaginatively constructed; fewer will be found of what Cole and Hawthorne created. The narratives about the Willey family's destruction in a landslide—an event fascinating partly because of the irony in the family's flight from the very place that was spared— treated this historically singular occurrence of the wilderness overrunning man as a marvel that had to be told over and over again. Hawthorne's variation of the story described an event that awaits us all. He had in mind something other than America's relation with the wilderness. His ''garden'' was closer to that of an ancient mythic one than to railroads and canals.

Hawthorne, of course, was atypical, not only in his genius, but to some extent in his very use of the wilderness in fiction. The more popular stories of his contemporaries—those with whom he could not compete successfuly—tended toward the decadent sensibility of the flower books, although popular writers were more likely to use drawing rooms than forests for their settings. Moreover, in spite of the countless nature poems and paintings, artistic depictions of America's garden of the West were relatively rare and not likely to present industry and nature with arcadian evocations, as did George Inness in his painting, ''The Lackawanna Valley'' (1855).[42]

A comment revealing just how remote any arcadian idea was for most Americans occurs in J. K. Paulding's *Westward Ho!* Although his famous novel is hardly a useful source for life on the American frontier, Paulding had a taste for pastoralism, and he created his own version of it in *Westward Ho!* But he knew enough about his countrymen's assumptions to apologize for what he did. Describing a scenic wonderland encountered by Virginia Dangerfield, Paulding writes, ''it was such a little paradise as whilom the shepherds haunted in the pastorals once so

admired, but now eschewed as fantastic pictures of a state of society which never had an existence." He went on to complain, "So
much the worse, so much the worse," but he knew his
audience."[43]

Although one can scarcely doubt that pastoral ideals had some
place in America, as even Paulding knew, they often existed in
radically different terms from the Inness picture of a vast natural
setting comfortably containing a technology that blends so nicely
into the landscape. The frontispiece to the well-known *Home
Book of the Picturesque* (1852) transforms what appears to be
Virginia's celebrated Natural Bridge into a finely formed structure for supporting the train that is crossing it. Although the tiny
train indeed blends into the dominating pastoral landscape, the
much-admired Natural Bridge is now an artifact of man. Perhaps
more noteworthy is a lithograph by Currier called "Railroad
Suspension Bridge Near Niagara Falls" (1856). Although a
rather pretty picture, it could almost have been commissioned by
Beaumont to prove his point about Americans and Niagara
Falls,[44] for in the background those falls appear quite
diminutive—anything but sublime. In the foreground,
dominating the landscape, is a magnificent bridge with a train,
horses, and people. The bridge—and not the Falls—dominates
this picture. It is a picture of nature as seen in nineteenth-century
America.

I would not want to guess which kind of representation occurs
more frequently—that typified by Inness or by Currier—since in
either case their conceptions, as discussed here, are rare. The
whole notion of whether or not factories or railroads and canals
were to fit organically into the landscape was not a very important
question in relation to America's vision of its garden. The
ultimate aesthetic shape that America's garden finally took—the
modern city—testifies to the relative unrepresentativeness of
those few people who saw the garden of the future in a special
poetic mode. Economic expansion was aesthetic enough for most,
and Americans in the early nineteenth century did not even produce public parks for their cities, let alone conceive Arcadian

landscapes for the wilderness. Indeed, no American city *had* a public park of any substantial size until New York's Central Park was built, and that project, not begun until 1853, succeeded only after the initial conception had been modified in the face of strong political opposition. Americans were not as interested in adorning their environment for the living as they were for the dead at Greenwood and Mt. Auburn. Arcadian ideals, whether those of Jefferson before he accepted the idea that they would be unrealized in America, or of poetic visionaries, belonged to an imaginative realm far from the utilitarian thrust of American culture. It must even be conceded that for all their appalling misconceptions of America, European travelers were reasonably accurate in writing so disparagingly about America's aesthetic response to nature. But they were writing about the nature of flowers and of landscape—the nature of adornment.

In spite of the incredible contradictions found in their observations, the Europeans' general conception of American aesthetic indifference to this nature of adornment found confirmation in the writings of Americans themselves, who were quite as savage in attacking a national aesthetic philistinism. None other than Lydia Sigourney, whose poetry graced America's most popular magazines, as well as its most elegant cemeteries, laments that "in many other countries, we see the love of flowers, a far more pervading and decided sentiment than in our own." Conceding that everybody cannot have a garden (that is, a literal one and not a railroad and a canal), Mrs. Sigourney actually pleaded for at least a few window boxes.[45] No doubt the situation was less desperate than this, but American writers, famous and obscure, readily conceded the larger point. A writer in *The Western Farmer,* responding to the criticism that the regions of the West usually lacked decorative gardens, observes that this "picture of ourselves we take in all honesty and candor to be a pretty true one. . . ."[46] In "The New England Village," another writer observes that in such a town the "love of nature" is "practical" rather than "sentimental."[47] And it was in vain that Emerson appealed for public gardens in America similar to the lovely ones he had seen in Europe.[48] The capitol of America, where one might expect the new nation to parade its beauty, earned the following reaction from N. P. Willis: "The waste lands which lie at the foot of Capitol Hill might be marshes in the centre of a wilderness for any trace of cultivation about them. . . ." A projected "botanical garden" in the area languished because of Congress' refusal to appropriate the funds.[49] Such an unwillingness to spend money for urban beautification appears to have been a cultural pattern, and it was an American—not a foreigner—who, noting the lack of public squares in Pittsburgh, observed that the citizens there were "more bent upon increasing their 'fathers' store' than on beautifying the favoured spot in which they dwell. . . "[50]

But more was involved than American aesthetic barbarianism, and a comment by Charles Fenno Hoffman—the greater significance of which he himself missed—reveals much to us. Hoffman observes—and other writers confirm his general observation—that soon after planting his food garden the western settler would go "out into the forest, and selecting two of the straightest maple saplings he can find, they are at once disinterred, their heads chopped off, and a pair of poles, thrust into the ground within two feet of his door, are whitewashed and called trees."[51] Hoffman did not quite know how to explain the fact, but Beaumont, his indignation notwithstanding, had a shrewd insight into this American phenomenon. "The Americans," he writes, "regard the forest as a symbol of the wilderness, and consequently of backwardness; so it is against the trees that they direct their onslaughts."[52] Beaumont attributed to the Americans a kind of monomania against trees that can only be equated with Ahab's feeling about the whale. But for all its indignant exaggeration, Beaumont's discernment is telling. Like the almost ubiquitous wooden fences that surrounded American homes, the transformed trees symbolized the impulse to turn the wilderness into an artifact of civilization. The whitewashed trees become the whitewashed fences, giving to the new home its emblem of triumph. Though fences also obviously existed for staking out one's claim, the two ideas associated with the transformed "trees" were not at all incompatible, as is nicely revealed in a casual statement by John Pendleton Kennedy in his *Swallow Barn* (1832): "Until this time [1790], ever since the miscarriage of the unfortunate enterprise of the mill, this part of the domain had been grievously neglected. It was a perfect wilderness. No fences had ever been erected, on either side, to guard the contiguous territories from encroachment." On one level of understanding this threat of "encroachment" came from other people, but in a deeper sense it emanated from that "perfect wilderness."[53] Of course, once a fence existed, the region would no longer be quite so "grievously neglected." Hoffman's frontier people understood this, as Beaumont did. All that the Frenchman failed to appreciate was that the "onslaughts" against the forests represented part of an American aesthetic perception, the object of which was to impose the beauty of civilization upon the wilderness and transform it into fulfilled nature. In the future, when Dana's "scaffold" would fall, there would then be flowers along the canals, gardens by the railroads, and parks in the cities. Meanwhile, the most scenically unattractive region held a beauty comprehended by many Americans, however incapable most Europeans were of seeing it.

A marvelous sense of this perceptual discrepancy emerges from contrasting two observations about America's garden in the Mississippi Valley—one by Charles Dickens and the other by Robert Baird. Arriving at Cairo, Illinois, where the Ohio and Mississippi rivers meet, Dickens came upon

> the junction of the two rivers, on ground so flat and low and marshy, that at certain seasons of the year it is inundated to the house-tops, lies a breeding-place of fever, ague, and death; vaunted in Europe as a mine of Golden Hope, and speculated in, on the faith of monstrous representations, to many people's ruin. A dismal swamp, on which the half-built houses rot away: cleared here and there for the space of a few yards; and teeming, then, with rank unwholesome vegetation, in whose baleful shade the wretched wanderers who are tempted hither,

droop, and die, and lay their bones; the hateful Mississippi circling and eddying before it, and turning off upon its southern course a slimy monster hideous to behold; a hotbed of disease, an ugly sepulchre, a grave uncheered by any gleam of promise: a place without one single quality, in earth or air or water, to commend it: such is this dismal Cairo.[54]

Now compare Baird on the Missisippi Valley: "In beauty and fertility it is the most perfect garden of nature; and by means of its thousand streams, wonderful facilities are extended to every part of it for commercial intercourse."[55] Baird readily and without the least sense of incongruity commented on the "unhealthy" aspect of the very region Dickens was observing. Disease, Baird affirms, is "the general scourge of the Valley."[56] Yet Dickens saw a "sepulchre," and Baird saw a "garden."

Both men were reasonably accurate, although Dickens could not understand that the region really did contain its "promise," its "Golden Hope." He did not know how to look past the "scaffold," as Baird did. As for the adornments of the present—the scenic view divorced from the garden—Baird quite agreed with the jaded comment of the writer in *Godey's Lady's Book*. Indeed, Baird outdid that writer, since it hardly mattered for him that "there is not probably on the earth an equal extent of territory, which is of so level and monotonous a character."[57] Nor is it likely that he would have quite comprehended anyone who suggested that this comment was inconsistent with his vision of the region as a garden.

Baird's nature was America's nature, the image predominantly held by those who inhabited Emerson's "external world." But for the romantic writer, such gardens tended to elicit the contempt exemplified in Thoreau's famous description of his ascent of Mt. Ktaadn. As was common with this genius of wordplay, Thoreau's language engaged multiple issues with a single rhetorical thrust. "Here was no man's garden," he writes of the mountain top. It was a marvelous appropriation of America's metaphor, as it related his own contempt for that place of railroads, canals, and other economic miracles; at the same time it implied his more serious affirmation of a private inability at this moment to transform the universe into the magic of transcendent vision. And, although it did not have to be said, Thoreau's description spoke also to the lost garden of Christianity. In his complete isolation Thoreau "felt a presence of a force not bound to be kind to man. It was a place for heathenism and superstitious rites—to be inhabited by men nearer of kin to the rocks and to wild animals than we."[58]

Here was a nature that did not promise to emerge as civilization, one that might after all engulf man, as Willey's slide engulfed an "ambitious guest" passing through this world. There was no promise of the garden at the end of such a journey, no assurance that outside such wonderful artistic achievements as *Walden* man would awake to something other than a universe after all "not bound to be kind to man." Thoreau's nature—the romantic nature in general—never guaranteed the prophecies in *Walden* or *Nature;* it offered only the possibility. The "presence" it embodied was often in stark contrast to the "presence" that in "Tintern Abbey" filled Wordsworth, whom Thoreau may have had in mind, "with the joy/Of elevated thoughts. . . ." Thoreau clearly understood the existence of those "mixed instrumentalities" that Emerson found in nature.[59] In seeking to comprehend the mysteries of those "instrumentalities," American romantic writers found in nature their prime metaphor, although in their lexicon it might be as far removed from trees and grass as was the American garden. In America, the abstraction called *nature* came to be defined as the civilization that emerged from the wilderness; for the Romantics, who found their vocabulary in the country they inhabited, *nature* came to be equated with the civilization of the self, the world of inner vision.

4

Mammon's Cave

Although writers of "realism" would one day find fertile material in America's "garden," romantic writers found very little to explore in such a region. Even James Fenimore Cooper, whose literary efforts assumed a sure understanding of the world's meaning, had almost no fictional concern with a contemporary West of railroads and canals. Although many Americans envisioned the West in other terms, the commercial image so dominated American thought about the contemporary West that not a single important literary figure, including Cooper, extensively exploited this region for artistic purposes. Its appeal lay in matters other than fiction. As a location for Dana's poetry it was ideal, though it would never do for Cooper's stories; and this explains, at least as much as his "indebtedness" to Scott, why Cooper set his Leatherstocking saga in America's past.

That Cooper did not even address his contemporary West in the Leatherstocking series may seem surprising, especially when one considers all that has been written on the West, both by and about Cooper. But no matter what theory one wishes to construct for Cooper and the meaning of his contemporary West, the fact is that Natty Bumppo answered his final roll call around 1804, roughly a quarter of a century prior to publication of *The Prairie* (1827). Natty was anywhere between eighty and eighty-seven (depending on which part of the novel a reader may wish to believe), an old man in any case, and one who even then was living beyond the time when the future of the West had been clearly determined. All this implies more than an idle exercise in numerology, since *The Prairie,* in the internal time of the Leatherstocking saga, concludes Cooper's examination of the conflict between man in the wilderness and man in society. Natty's way loses, and the civilized Middleton's wins, but the point is that by the time Cooper wrote *The Prairie* the conflict had ended. The ''annihilation'' of the ''savage,'' whether white or red, that Baird had discussed emerges in Cooper's story as an event from the past. Cooper, in other words, was writing a historical novel, or a series of historical novels, none of which was significantly germane to the conditions of his own time. Although they do treat the West as commodity in the sense that much of the series examines the question of who has a right to the land, the saga is always told in the context of assumptions shared by the author and his audience that the outcome of the contest is either settled or had never been in doubt. To retain any degree of plausibility, Cooper had to turn to history, since the idea of the West as a contested area between two human societies was simply not a serious proposition in his day. While in retrospect we see the conquest of the West as a battle against Indians, Cooper's contemporaries—although surely believing them an irritant—hardly considered Indians serious obstacles to the emergence of nature as America understood it. Something of this early-nineteenth-century view of American history is conveyed in an observation by Francis J. Grund, who saw not a trace of incongruity in genuinely admiring Cooper's art while denying even a modicum of glory to the white man's triumph and the Indian's defeat: ''There was no renown attached to their [Indians'] subjugation; it was the victory of intelligence over the barbarism of savages. No poetry, therefore, attaches to the conquest of the American soil, and the history of it is only remarkable from its conjunction with that of Europe.''[1]

Well then, what did he see in Cooper? The answer is that he thought him ''original in his scenes and conceptions.''[2] That is, Grund, like others, admired Cooper for his capacity to invent an ''original'' version of history. Only those who believed in "nursery tales" considered Cooper's ideas of the West as accurate. If stories set in the past were vulnerable to such doubts about their authenticity, one can scarcely imagine what an object of ridicule Cooper would have been had he tried to pass off his idea of the West as a version of contemporary America. This does not mean that Grund's analysis is fair to Cooper's intentions. Cooper did want his entire version of America's past to be taken seriously. He was certainly attracted by the exciting world of his invention, and to the extent that his saga dealt with the emergence of civilization it was intended to reveal historical truth. The noble savages, however, were inventions—embellishments so remote from reality that only in the obscurity of the past could they find a place even in fiction. Quite a few Europeans, and an occasional American, missed this point, but Cooper understood it. He wrote no novels about the West of his day. Its poetry was in commerce and not in the ferocities of noble savages or the pieties of young "females" or of wise old men.

Cooper, as all are aware, was a secular mythmaker. But Grund's compliments and Webb's insults notwithstanding, Cooper himself did not seek to falsify the meaning of America's past. On the contrary, he earnestly revealed a version of history that Americans could believe in its outlines even while enjoying the fabrications of its details. In certain aspects he was firmly wedded to historical realism. Surely the incredible pedantry that led him to footnote so many "facts" about America was not inspired by artistic attempts to heighten suspense. Cooper always remembered his English audience, toward whom he directed much of his history. After all, England was the arbiter of taste, and Cooper certainly enjoyed his reputation as one of the few exceptions to American literary mediocrity. Along with most American writers, Cooper very much wanted to please his English audience. His footnotes often jar us to this recognition. "The Americans," he explains in annotating *The Prairie,* "call the autumn the 'fall,' from the fall of the leaf."[3] We may laugh at such pedantry, or even apologize for it, but Cooper knew what he was doing. Regardless of how "unreal" his fiction may seem to us and to many Americans who experienced the West, he was not striving to be a mythmaker. And it was his wonderful good fortune, either through exquisite luck or through a shrewd sense of his audience, that the embellishments to his version of history fit so nicely into some of the richest dreams that Europe had imposed upon America. If ever an American novelist played out Europe's fantasies, Cooper did. From across the ocean he loomed as our very best writer, as the individual who understood what the new world might and might not be. But his American audience generally accepted as fantasy what gullible Europeans took for truth.

The inability to distinguish between Cooper's myth and Cooper's history formed the basis of Mark Twain's famous attack on him—one brilliantly stated, but scarcely original, since J. Watson Webb had preceded Twain in misrepresenting Cooper by identifying him as an accurate reporter of the West and its particular details. Unerringly, Twain found the statement of Brander Matthews that claimed authenticity for Cooper. ''The craft of the woodsman, the tricks of the trapper, all the delicate art of the forest, were familiar to Cooper from his youth up.''[4] He also cited Wilkie Collins, who credited Cooper for his skill in writing ''romantic fiction,'' but here Twain was on shakier ground. Certainly, Cooper did write *romance* as the term is conventionally used. That was his particular skill. He had the capacity to tell in one story a version of history and a version of romance that coalesced, and he did not have to distort *his* version of history to do this. Although his characters belong to romance, they act out America's larger historical truth: Europe's noble savage yields to America's civilization. For Americans who enjoyed fantasy—they never did believe in noble savages—and for Europeans who could not recognize it, Cooper had wonderful stories to tell. He also had the good sense not to place his tales in a contemporary setting. The West of his day was too intimately identified with commerce. Like almost all of America's other writers, Cooper found little material for fiction in the contemporary garden of America.

In spite of the many nineteenth-century claims about America's lack of history, such a problem was more imagined than real. This was true at least for our major writers of fiction, who regularly found sufficient historical material for their art. Hawthorne, like Cooper, found the wilderness of America's past a far more useful place than that of America's present.[5] *The Scarlet Letter* (1850), where Hawthorne offers his most serious consideration of the wilderness, is some two hundred years removed from his own time—farther away from his day than he is from ours. When writing about the present, as he does to a large extent in *The House of the Seven Gables* (1851), his contemporary wilderness forms no part of the book, although the wilderness of the past—the contested land—contains the roots of the particular civilization he examines. His one other major work set in America, *The Blithedale Romance* (1852), can scarcely be called a tale of the wilderness or of the West, although the story does conform to America's common idea of leaving civilization for the sake of gain. But Hawthorne redefines the journey by turning the quest into a search for spiritual rather than commercial gain. The failure of the journey represents Hawthorne's way of mocking the notion that man can find such a value in nature, whether at Brook Farm or elsewhere. Yet Hawthorne does more than ridicule transcendental rebirth in nature. He addresses the stubbornly enduring European postulate—as old as the idea of America itself—that all things are possible in a world that may begin again. Hawthorne's decision to examine at the same time a concept as relatively old as the European idea of refashioning the self and the newer transcendental idea of rebirth in nature is not at all extraordinary, since transcendentalism was, in part, a child of that older vision. But Hawthorne, of course, would not be comfortable with theories of regeneration.

Nor did he endorse the American journey to nature for gain, even though he structured *The Blithedale Romance* around this paradigm. But Hawthorne's feelings about the materialistic rather than the spiritual aspect of the American journey into nature is better understood from "The Hall of Fantasy," a tale that gives a rare example of Hawthorne's fictional use of America's commercial westward impulse. The story of the narrator's discovery of himself in a room containing human fantasies is tantalizingly ambiguous. It vacillates between ridiculing dreamers and thanking God that a world of fantasy exists where man may escape from the gloom of life. It is at the same time a place where Bunyan truly finds heaven and where some fool builds a machine for turning a woman's smile into sunshine. Moreover, while insisting upon ''the gloom and chillness of actual life,''[6] the tale passionately expresses the desire for mother earth to endure, so that her sunshine and joy may continue. The contradictions are never resolved, and the story ends with a Franklinesque injunction that fantasy in moderation is desirable. But we are too familiar with the way Hawthorne so often undercuts his own statements, as does Franklin, to be comfortable with that kind of resolution. Therefore, one is at first inclined to wonder just where Hawthorne stands when the narrator comments on a group of men dreaming about the commercial possibilities of America. The narrator's ''friend'' points

to a number of persons, who, manifest as the fact was, would have deemed it an insult to be told that they stood in the Hall of Fantasy. Their visages were traced into wrinkles and furrows, each of which seemed the record of some actual experience in life. Their eyes had the shrewd, calculating glance, which detects so quickly and so surely all that it concerns a man of business to know, about the characters and purposes of his fellow-men. Judging them as they stood, they might be honored and trusted members of the Chamber of Commerce, who had found the genuine secret of wealth, and whose sagacity gave them the command of fortune. There was a character of detail and matter-of-fact in their talk, which concealed the extravagance of its purport, insomuch that the wildest schemes had the aspect of every-day realities. Thus the listener was not startled at the idea of cities to be built, as if by magic, in the heart of pathless forests; and of streets to be laid out, where now the sea was tossing; and of mighty rivers to be staid in their courses, in order to turn the machinery of a cotton-mill. It was only by an effort—and scarcely then—that the mind

convinced itself that such speculations were as much matter of
fantasy as the old dream of Eldorado, or as Mammon's Cave,
or any other vision of gold, ever conjured up by the imagination of needy poet or romantic adventurer. (Pp. 176-77)

While Hawthorne obviously ridicules these men and their
dreams, he refrains from rejecting their premise. Although he did
not expect "streets. . .where now the sea was tossing,"
Hawthorne was nevertheless serenely confident that America
would indeed produce the kind of wealth envisioned by the
dreamers. The "magic" of cities being "built. . . in the heart of
pathless forests" was taken for granted as part of a national
destiny by almost everyone, from European travel writers to
American poets. Hawthorne knew this, and he believed the
premise. In *The House of the Seven Gables* he affirms an American
cliché in writing that when "the pathless forest" gives "place—as
it inevitably must, though perhaps not till ages hence—to the
golden fertility of human culture, it would be the source of in-
calculable wealth to the Pyncheon blood.'"[7] However, the ironist
in Hawthorne will not let it go at that. The "Pyncheon blood"
gets its mixture of Maule in the presumed offspring of Phoebe and
Holgrave, and the wealth is dispersed; still the fundamental image
of nature becoming civilization continues, as does the concurrent
image of the land yielding *temporal* riches. Hawthorne was not
oblivious to America, and he understood that civilization and
wealth tended to be indistinguishable in American imagination.
The narrator of "The Hall of Fantasy," in responding to this image of cities and wealth forming in the wilderness, has to persuade
himself that he really is in contact with fantasy. But he is wrong.
Like many of Hawthorne's other narrators, he fails to perceive
the situation, for Hawthorne is not doubting the materialistic
destiny of the West. It is not the fantasy of potential wealth that
Hawthorne ridicules. What he does address in "The Hall of Fantasy" is the unworthiness of this commercial dream, as well as
the likelihood that in search of gold many a dreamer would lose
his way. Hawthorne understood the American dream of wealth in

the West; he expected it to come true for many individuals and for the country as a whole, but he could only belittle those who spent their dreams on such a vision. As for a thorough fictional treatment of this tangible American quest, rather than the limited one he gave in "The Hall of Fantasy," Hawthorne simply was not interested. The human heart attracted his literary imagination more than the human pocketbook. That is why his wilderness of the past is not so much a geographical region as an imaginative place in which his particular concerns are explored. Given the assumptions of his society about the West as a place for commercial dreams, Hawthorne's decision to use a historical wilderness rather than a contemporary one was almost inevitable.

Even less concerned with America's geographical West than Hawthorne was Poe, who directly mentions the wilderness only infrequently. In "Metzengerstein" he writes of a demonic horse emerging from the forest, and in "Silence" he creates a hideous realm of nature, where the devil torments man. But Poe had little to say about America's West, except in the abortive *Julius Rodman,* predictably set in the past. Historical setting, however, could not make America's West a sufficiently remote realm for the imaginative adventures Poe sought to formulate. Certainly, a story about America's West that yielded the kinds of events which occur in, for example, Poe's antarctic narrative, *Arthur Gordon Pym* (1838), would have been imaginatively incongruent with America's sense of the West. No matter how much we may wonder at it, there really were people taken in by *Pym,*[8] but not even those in the nursery would believe such a story if it had been set in the West. Thus, there may indeed be some validity to the claim that *Pym* had aspects of a disguised western story. One would have to disguise such an idea about the American West if he were to sell a story.

The uninviting aspect of this region as a literary possibility, nevertheless, did not prevent Poe from utilizing the wilderness. As might be expected, the gloominess and dreariness of the forest, its primeval evocation of terror, appealed to him, a fact demonstrated in "Metzengerstein," even though the story is often considered a parody. Yet with the whole wilderness of America so close at hand, Poe set his tale in the *Hungarian* woods. A marketplace would not do, nor would anything in the American West, unless one accepts the much-discussed thesis that *Pym* is a disguised version of Washington Irving's *Astoria,* or at least heavily influenced by it—depending on which theory one reads. Whatever the soundness of the argument—and there surely are parallels to be found in the two books—*Astoria* treats the West of America's past and not its present, while Pym's journey takes him to the Antarctic. Which leaves Poe, for the most part, without a contemporary West in his fiction and which leaves us with the one novel that does address the subject, fortunately by a literary genius who knew how to tell his own story while giving America a version of the West it recognized. The book is Melville's *Confidence-Man* (1857).

Like the Drummond light revolving in *The Confidence-Man,* Melville's novel illuminates myriad perspectives. Among the book's numerous subjects are the obvious ones of faith, hope, and charity, allegorically examined in a region richly "American." Here is a novel that, among other things, places in the American West those dreamers of wealth described by Hawthorne in "The Hall of Fantasy" and that subjects to dark satire the speculators who invest in this world, as well as those who have—or have not—faith in the next. For the setting, Melville probably took his description of the Mississippi Valley from none other than Timothy Flint.[9] As so many others had done, such as Baird and Dickens, Flint gave special attention to Cairo, Illinois—a city believed to hold special importance for the region's economic future. It is no insult to the intelligence of Flint, Baird, or Dickens to observe that neither the Englishman nor the Americans fully comprehended each other's ideas about the region. An author wishing to reconcile the conflicting assumptions about America's West would have a formidable task, especially if he sought to comprehend the archetypal rather than simply the geographical West. Melville, alone among American writers, had the interest and the capacity to use America's promised land for an exploration of meaning.

As the *Fidèle*—the ship of faith—approaches Cairo, the Confidence Man, "glancing shoreward, towards a grotesquely-shaped bluff," remarks, " 'there's the Devil's Joke.' "[10] The Devil's "bluff" and the Devil's "Joke" in part mock the commitment to extract material wealth from nature—a wealth Melville never denied was there. The people of "The Hall of Fantasy," oblivious to the spiritual emptiness of their quest, are lured by the promise of America's wealth to prey upon one another in a world that finally yields only the guarantee of death. In playing out this parable, which is at least as old as Chaucer's "Pardoner's Tale," Melville's dupes of America have come "West, whose type is the Mississippi itself," (p. 8) in search of wealth; but as *The Confidence-Man* makes clear, these people represent all mankind. They move toward a place from which neither the geographical East nor West offers escape; they journey to the dark archetypal "West" that Melville evokes. "At Cairo, the old established firm of Fever & Ague is still settling up its unfinished business; that Creole grave-digger, Yellow Jack—his hand at the mattock and spade has not lost its cunning; while Don Saturninus Typhus taking his constitutional with Death, Calvin Edson and three undertakers, in the morass, snuffs up the mephitic breeze with zest" (p. 147). Melville is after more than a sociological critique of thieves along the Mississippi River, just as he seeks more than a repetition of Dickens's moral outrage. The river and its towns represent not merely graveyards for Dickens's greedy men. The river traces the journey all of us take—sometimes with faith, and sometimes without it. In Melville's version of our universal journey, we must contend with a divinity, however anthropomorphic he may appear in his guise as the Confidence Man, who is finally as inscrutable as the one Ahab sought in anger. In *The Confidence-Man,* Melville created some "original" incarnation of the devil or of God or of both in one, who walked among us, not as God in the Garden of Eden, but as a con man in America's very own "garden" of material pursuits. Given some basic cultural premises about the devil and the West, Melville had good reason for placing his strange incarnation in the Mississippi Valley. The devil had a history of haunting America's West, although by 1857 American attitudes on this subject had undergone some radical changes.

Henry Nash Smith in *Virgin Land* (1950) very accurately observes that by the beginning of the eighteenth century, "The unsettled forest no longer seemed, as it had to Michael Wigglesworth in 1662, a 'Devils den.' "[11] What the West did have, however, was a lingering rhetorical association with the devil, born in the same diversity of imagination that had once defined the region as Edenic. These polar identifications were verbal commonplaces in nineteenth-century America, regardless of how much the idea behind them may have diminished. Thus, there is nothing unusual in the observation of James Hall that "Some laud it [the West] as a paradise, others denounce it as a hell."[12] Part of this "hell" reflected the genuine difficulties settlers encountered, but part of it also sprang from a rhetorical bravado, a note of pride in labeling the region demonic. "The divinity, most frequently invoked by boatmen" along the Mississippi River, Timothy Flint writes, "seems to have imparted his name oftener than any other to the dangerous places along the river. The 'Devil's' race paths, tea table, oven, &c. are places of difficult or hazardous navigation, that frequently occur."[13] Such demonic place names rarely evoked images of terror; indeed, the Jesuit missionary P. J. De Smet casually describes "a beautiful defile, commonly called, by the mountaineers or Canadian hunters, the Devil's Gate."[14] Even Indians, as we certainly know from Cooper's novels, carried the old rhetorical associations with the devil that the Puritans had given them. Yet no matter how real the threat from Indians may at times have appeared to Americans in the West, the rhetorical associations of Indians with the devil hardly offer metaphors of genuine terror. Their "demonism" is more likely to be as harmless as the places along the Mississippi mentioned by Flint. One sees this, for example, in James O. Pattie's description of a Pawnee victory celebration: "When they began their triumphal yelling, shouting, singing and cutting antic capers, it seemed to us, that a recruit of fiends from the infernal regions could hardly have transcended them in a genuine diabolical display.''[15] Pattie's hyperbole is transparent enough, for the devil—like the Indian—remained some sort of a joke. Though not the "Joke" that Melville turned it into as he used this American identification of the West with the devil, just as he used America's identification of the West with the promised land. And he had more than an "antic caper" in mind.

For the journey he shaped in *The Confidence-Man,* Melville created some form of a real devil and joined him with the mocked, harmless devil of the American West. He held before his reader the recognizable image of the West as a commercial region, while having his "original" character embody the innocuousness of America's present devil; he evoked the full demonic power of the devil once sensed in America's idea of the West; and he fused it all into one astonishing parable of cosmic ambiguity.

From the outset, *The Confidence-Man* directs the reader to its theological subject. The mysterious avatar, whose shape-shifting presence defines the novel and the universe—or, examined more closely, reveals the impossibility of such definition as one assumption after another reduces itself to nothingness—makes his appearance in the first sentence of the book. That this harlequin avatar has something to do with a world divinity is suggested at the outset by his association with "Manco Capac at the Lake Titicaca," an allusion to an incarnation of the sun in Incan mythology. He is in quick order further defined by "his advent," by his "fleecy" appearance, and by his arrival from "the East." The title of this opening chapter is "A Mute Goes Aboard a Boat on the Mississippi," and in his portrayal of this first embodiment in the novel of an otherwordly visitor, Melville insists upon the voicelessness of the mysterious avatar. Silence was a divine characteristic Melville had explored in *Pierre* (1852), the novel immediately preceding *The Confidence-Man,* and the muteness of this April Fools' divinity recalls Melville's discourse in *Pierre* on the notion of God's silence. In *Pierre* he had written about a fool of virtue who comes to grief. In *The Confidence-Man* he writes about unvirtuous fools who are also victimized in a world of ambiguities. Although one may choose the kind of fool one wishes to be, Melville tells us that in each case God is silent; yet in His shape-shifting presence in *The Confidence-Man,* He takes on guises wherein He speaks to man by uttering Pauline theology as the devil might use it. Indeed, God and the devil become inseparable manifestations of one unified principle containing all the irony—or horror if one insists—of the world as cosmic joke, while promising none of the blessings traditionally associated with Christianity. To identify the Confidence Man as simply God or the devil is not quite accurate. Nor will it do to call Melville a Manichaean, reducing the complexity of his thought to a rubric. Melville was creating a new myth, deliberately, insistently, calling his character ''original,'' as he perversely played on the quest of American literati for ''original'' literature in America. But the genuine originality went unnoticed, as this swindler of souls coming like the biblical thief in the night, as well as in broad daylight, stalked the world that Melville was redefining. Certainly there are Manichaean overtones to Melville's vision, just as there are gnostic suggestions, of which the Manichaean theology was only one form. There are also Christian, Incan, and Hindu aspects, as well as others. But the point is that in the American West Melville creates an individual perception of meaning, a remarkable new theology. He had, as it were, followed the Emersonian injunction and had built his own world. It was a different one, but, like Emerson, Melville dared the enterprise and accepted the consequences. They were not very pleasant in 1857, when *The Confidence-Man* was published.

Although Melville gives the general reader a recognizable picture of the American West—including its commercial lure, its innocuous demonic place names, and its diversity of inhabitants—the book scarcely could be popular on those grounds; readers could get similar material in much more coherent form from Flint and others. But Melville had long since lost his chance for popularity, and not even his use of the familiar Mississippi could save him from the response of a public generally bewildered by what he was attempting. Still, some aspects of the book were praised. As seen by one critic, ''the controversalists pause ever and anon while a vivid, natural Mississippi landscape is rapidly painted before the mind; the narrative is almost rhythmic, the talk is cordial, bright American touches are scattered over the perspective.''[16] A shrewder critic writes: ''We are not quite sure whether we have cracked it ourselves—whether there is not another meaning hidden in the depths of the subject other than that which lies near the surface. There is a dry vein of sarcastic humour running throughout which makes us half suspect this.''[17] Others were clearer in their recognition of Melville as metaphysician, although for the most part it did not please them entirely. But perhaps the comment most revealing of what Melville could expect from a contemporary audience came from the well-known writer Fitz-James O'Brien: ''We desire him to give up metaphysics and take to nature and the study of mankind. We rejoice, therefore, to know that he is, at this moment, traveling in the Old World [Melville was on the trip that would take him to Jerusalem and one day lead to *Clarel*], where, we hope, he will enjoy himself heartily, look about him wisely, and come home ready to give us pictures of life and reality.''[18]

O'Brien's idea that the ''Old World'' might cure Melville was only in part related to the benefits of rediscovering his religious roots in Jerusalem. After all, what had ''metaphysics'' to do with ''nature'' and ''mankind?'' The first term was theological, otherworldly; the others were temporal, of America and its West. ''[N]ature and the study of mankind'' were one, akin to the study ''of life and reality.'' Americans of O'Brien's day understood very well that their panegyrics to nature had little to do with metaphysics. Accordingly, Melville scarcely mentions the word *nature* in *The Confidence-Man*, although when he does, it is in the context of a private rather than of a public mythology. The brief specific attention Melville gives to nature occurs during a discussion between the Confidence Man and Pitch, the hard-headed Missourian. Although the Confidence Man victimizes an old miser by playing on the presumed benefits of nature, Pitch knows the natural world too well to be tricked on that subject, although, like the rest, he is at last tricked. Throughout the argument on nature, the Confidence Man affirms its goodness. In seeking to trap the Missourian, he assures him that "'you have just as much [confidence in nature] as I have'" (p. 122). He does indeed have confidence that it is inimical to man. At this point both have left the nature of America's garden and have entered into an examination of the metaphysics so disturbing to O'Brien. They speak of a nature only partly geographical.

The mythological region explored in *The Confidence-Man* scarcely leads to O'Brien's nature, to the nature of America's garden, however much Melville may have tied his story to a national idea of the West. This "nature" of Melville's, not primarily of the forest, or the ocean, or the sky, and certainly not of railroads, canals, and steamboats, was part of the demonic world that long ago had haunted the mind of Cotton Mather, whose *Magnalia Christi Americana* (celebrating the triumphs of Christ in America) Melville had been investigating just before he wrote his novel of the new incarnation who haunted Mammon's Cave, America's new garden.[19]

5

Causeways Over The Moon

Although the major writers generally ignored America's westward journey as a setting for literary enterprises, they nevertheless found in it a useful image. In some instances the application was indirect, as in Hawthorne's *The Blithedale Romance.* Here, the story follows the form of a journey to nature for gain, although Coverdale actually goes in an eastern direction. In other cases, references to the West refer almost exclusively to the archetypal *West* of death or union with God. Such descriptions are often mistaken for references to America's West, as perhaps Shelley's "Ode to the West Wind" might today have been perceived by some as a comment on the regenerating force of the frontier had he been an American. But this kind of "West" belongs to romantic myth rather than to national history. It is the archetypal "West," for example, toward which the *Pequod* drives in the "Needle" chapter of *Moby-Dick*. The geographical direction Ahab finally achieves for his ship after discovering the distortion of his compass does not change his truest direction, since he and his crew are ineluctably headed west.

But writers could and did take an American image of the West and transform it into varying versions of romantic myth. Whitman's "Lilacs" and his "Passage to India" both comment on the American West, even as the poems speak finally to ideas that transcend the geographical journey. Less reverentially, in the face of America's gold fever of 1849, Poe employs in "Eldorado" the

word so often associated in his day with the material potential of
the West. In doing so, he moves toward a region outside the context of America:

> 'Over the Mountains
> Of the Moon,
> Down the Valley of the Shadow,
> Ride, boldly ride,'
> The shade replied,—
> 'If you seek for Eldorado!'[1]

A similar, though far broader use of this journey idea occurs in
Thoreau's "Walking," a particularly significant example because
of the traditional close identification of its author with nature. In
what is perhaps the most famous line of the essay, Thoreau states
that "the West of which I speak is but another name for the Wild;
and what I have been preparing to say is, that in Wildness is the
preservation of the World."[2] But Thoreau, as we know, was no
wild man, no hermit of the woods in spite of his brief sojourn in a
cabin within easy walking distance of his home, toward which he
sometimes walked for dinner. His "West" and his "Wildness"
represent something other than a walk in the forest. Thoreau
finds his "wild" experience as easily in *Hamlet* as in "nature,"
although not even Shakespeare is "wild" enough.[3] Thoreau
seeks an interior perception, a mystical way of knowing. However
much he genuinely loved trees and flowers, his "wild" world
represents a different phenomenon, and his walk is archetypal
rather than geographical. "I am alarmed," he writes, "when it
happens that I have walked a mile into the woods bodily, without
getting there in spirit."[4] Thoreau's spirit must transcend the
physical world to reach an ineffable religious experience. Nor can
he often achieve or sustain this, since his entrance into the
mystical world of "nature" is "occasional and transient
. . .only."[5] This nature has nothing to do with the Mississippi
Valley, nor can it be reached as easily. In Emerson's words:

> There is in woods and waters a certain enticement and flattery,
> together with a failure to yield a present satisfaction. This

disappointment is felt in every landscape. I have seen the soft-
ness and beauty of the summer clouds floating feathery
overhead, enjoying, as it seemed, their height and privilege of
motion, whilst yet they appeared not so much the drapery of
this place and hour, as forelooking to some pavilions and
gardens of festivity beyond. It is an odd jealousy, but the poet
finds himself not near enough to his object. The pine-tree, the
river, the bank of flowers before him does not seem to be
nature. Nature is still elsewhere.[6]

Thoreau pursued this distant nature, the glimpses of which
were so "occasional and transient." Toward this "place," the
same region free from the "unnatural" world Whitman had
described, Thoreau journeys in "Walking":

Unto a life which I call natural I would gladly follow even a
will-o'-the-wisp through bogs and sloughs unimaginable, but
no moon nor firefly has shown me the causeway to it. Nature is
a personality so vast and universal that we have never seen one
of her features.[7]

Coming from a man who was a brilliant student of natural life,
this might seem like babbling, as most of what he wrote struck his
non-transcendental contemporaries.[8] Thoreau is not babbling, of
course, because he is not writing about the world of physical appearance associated with nature; he is not in search of a world
defined by the "moon" or by a "firefly." Perversely, he scorns
the very "moon" that poets of "nature" conventionally
celebrated.

As in Dana's panegyric on the American journey, Thoreau's
prose poem leads westward. And in the course of his spiritual
quest he does *seem* to celebrate the movement away from Europe
toward the American geographical West. Concluding, however,
that Thoreau's compulsion to "walk toward Oregon" primarily
concerns a geographical journey misses the whole metaphorical
thrust of the essay.[9] "Oregon," like "America," had been
transformed into Thoreau's private spiritual realm. As Thoreau
records in his journal in 1855, several years before the publication of "Walking,"

Men rush to California and Australia as if the true gold were to be found in that direction; but that is to go to the very opposite extreme to where it lies.[10]

In the savage contempt he expresses toward the American journey in a letter (February 27, 1853) to his friend Harrison Blake, Thoreau reveals his feelings about the American geographical West:

The whole enterprise of this nation, which is not an upward, but a westward one, toward Oregon, California, Japan, etc., is totally devoid of interest to me, whether performed on foot, or by a Pacific railroad. It is not illustrated by a thought; it is not warmed by a sentiment; there is nothing in it which one should lay down his life for, nor even his gloves—hardly which one should take up a newspaper for. It is perfectly heathenish—a filibustering *toward* heaven by the great western route. No; they may go their way to their manifest destiny, which I trust is not mine.[11]

But in spite of this contempt, or perhaps because of it, in "Walking" Thoreau exploits America's sense of the West by turning the idea of a westwardly moving pioneer into one of the key metaphors of his essay, in much the same way that in *Walden,* under the rubric of "Economy," he transforms America's commercial interest into a religious statement. In "Walking," he writes,

Every sunset which I witness inspires me with the desire to go to *a* [my italics] West as distant and as fair as that into which the sun goes down. He appears to migrate westward daily, and tempt us to follow him. He is the Great Western Pioneer whom the nations follow. We dream all night of those mountain-ridges in the horizon, *though they may be of vapor only* [my italics], which were last gilded by his rays.[12]

This is not *the* West of America, but *a* West. This is the romantic journey to nature, however intangible a place that may be.

Though this region may be illusory, "of vapor only," Thoreau must attempt the journey. He understands the archetypal meaning of the West; he knows the biblical location of Eden. So it is in the "wildness" of his own spirit that he hopes for some return to an older garden, far removed from that constructed in America: "Yes, though you may think me perverse, if it were proposed to me to dwell in the neighborhood of the most beautiful garden that ever human art contrived, or else of a Dismal Swamp, I should certainly decide for the swamp. How vain, then, have been all your labors, citizens, for me!"[13] In repudiating America's garden, Thoreau looks instead to the kind of "swamp" Whitman journeys to in "Lilacs."

Yet, to find the swamp, the transcendent world of "wildness," creates greater difficulties than even Thoreau's wonderful essay suggests. Too often, as he records in *The Maine Woods,* he is bafflingly tied to the temporal world. "I stand in awe of my body, this matter to which I am bound has become so strange to me," he writes. "I fear not spirits, ghosts of which I am one [for he is not in his "natural" world],—*that* my body might,—but I fear bodies, I tremble to meet them. What is this Titan that has possession of me? Talk of mysteries!"[14] Attributing this kind of experience to sexual maladjustment serves as a function only if one explains all mysticism that way. Whatever the meaning may be of man's attempt to escape the confines of the flesh—to seek the "wild"—it predates New England Puritanism; for that matter, it predates Christianity. And however much the clouds may have been "of vapor only," Thoreau made the bold attempt to find another order of being.

In "Walking" he asked Americans to follow him into "the immaterial heaven" he sought,[15] although he knew that his countrymen wished to travel in a different direction. So in calling for a "crusade. . .to go forth and reconquer this Holy Land from the hands of the Infidels,"[16] Thoreau fully understood how remote his own vision of nature was from the more prevalent one of his society. Indeed, some three decades earlier in a strikingly

similar metaphor of "crusade" and "infidel," Francis Grund
had already defined the nation in a way alien to the quest Thoreau
would enunciate with the same trope. Grund had written,

> Business is the very soul of an American; he pursues it, not as
> a means of procuring for himself and his family the necessary
> comforts of life, but as the fountain of all human felicity; and
> shows as much enthusiastic ardor in his application to it as any
> crusader ever evinced for the conquest of the Holy Land, or the
> followers of Mohammed for the spreading of the Koran.[17]

If both Thoreau and Grund too easily stereotyped a whole nation,
both correctly understood that the "Holy Land" in America was
closer to a world of business than to metaphysical swamps.
Thoreau's "infidels" clearly possessed America in a way alien to
the crusader from Concord. By the time he embarked on his crusade,
the "infidels" had won. As in all crusades, the only question was
whether the Holy Land could be reconquered.

The victory of these "infidels," however, and not Thoreau's personal quest, gave us the great saga of America's triumph in the
past geographical West: Cooper's Leatherstocking series.
Thoreau registered his complaint about the "infidels" in the year of
his death, 1862. But he had been only ten years old when Cooper
recorded the death of Natty Bumppo—history even then.
Thoreau spent his life vainly seeking an audience to hear his particular quarrel with the infidels, while Cooper, sharing the very
aspirations of that group, emerged as America's most respected
contemporary writer, because he managed what no other writer
could, or wished, to achieve. Conforming to the paradigm of
economic gain through westward journeys, Cooper's
Leatherstocking stories sanctified America's frontier triumphs as
almost religious events, while sentimentally lamenting from the
distance of history whatever injustices may have happened along
the way. At the same time, he created the wonderful fantasy of
Natty Bumppo in never-never land. It was no small accomplishment, this reconciliation of history and myth.

In giving Cooper full credit for his artistic triumph, one must not assume that he compromised his principles. He was deeply committed to the triumph of civilization that he described. All of Cooper's modern critics have understood that he faced a dilemma in not being able to have a world belonging both to Natty Bumppo and to civilization. But this problem, which did not go unresolved, rests more with modern assumptions about the past than with any anguish we may imagine Cooper felt. In spite of the problems between Natty and the civilization that nature is shaping, the fictional world of the Leatherstocking novels does put Cooper's position solidly on the side of the "infidels." The value of civilization, of law and order, had to prevail. Even Natty Bumppo, as a driven Peter Pan, never quarrels with this assumption. Cooper's fantasy world explores the genuine sadness of civilization defeating Natty's ending childhood world. But Cooper himself could never endorse any deviation from the grand American image of civilization blooming from the wilderness. As with most of us, he could tolerate social outcasts or peculiar visionaries in small numbers. Cooper could even write a poetic version of their history. One Natty Bumppo on Marmaduke Temple's legally owned land made for much sentimentality about a dispossessed old man haunting the estate like a ghost from the past, sentimentality about the land belonging to God, Natty, and everybody else. But when many people claimed the land as common to them all—and not the exclusive property of rich squires—the sentimentality ended, and the claimants emerge— not as dear Natty Bumppo—but as the ugly rent-strikers of Cooper's novels, *The Chainbearer* (1845) and *The Redskins* (1846). Natty has the decency to leave the squire's land and accept the legitimacy of society's privileged people. Had there been only one, a token Natty in these other novels, Cooper could have tolerated the refusal to pay rent, or at least he could have been sentimental about it. Likewise, the Indians, who obliged civilization by leaving the wilderness, were "good." Those who resisted were "bad."

Unlike Thoreau, Cooper not only endorsed the victory of the "infidels," but he defined the basic issues in the context of the

very tangible world of America, rather than in Thoreau's
metaphysical realm. The categories of thought differed fundamentally. No sense of Thoreau's nature—the ''occasional and transient'' place beyond the moon toward which the poet
journeys—appears in Cooper's fiction. His novels do not contain
Thoreau's nature as a place ''so vast and universal that we have
never seen one of her features.'' Nor does Cooper present any of
the metaphysical terror found in Melville's story of the West,
The Confidence-Man. Cooper's Indians appear in the clichés of
America's demonic metaphors, but they have nothing of the
devil in them. They kill, but are vulnerable; they mutilate the
flesh, but have no capacity to touch the spirit. Their threat ends
on the last page of the novel. These Indians, like Natty and like
Cooper, do not find in the moon something separate from nature.
Cooper needs no ''causeway'' to nature.

Even the apocalyptic rhetoric Cooper sometimes uses does not
really suggest a terror in nature beyond immediate physical
dangers. When he writes in *Satanstoe* (1845), in his stunning
description of the potentially disastrous breaking up of the ice,
that ''spring had come like a thief in the night,'' we always
understand that the threat is of this world rather than of some
other. Cooper masterfully describes the breaking up of the ice in
Satanstoe, but he gives nothing more than a brilliant use of nature
to generate a reader's excitement. Cooper's ice is only frozen
water; it is quite different from Melville's iceberg, with its ''dead
indifference of walls,'' symbol of a threat in nature beyond the ice
itself.[18] Cooper's ice exists in much the same way that it does in
Uncle Tom's Cabin (1852), as something for Eliza to cross, or
that it does in Mrs. Anne MacVicar Grant's *Memoirs of an
American Lady* (1808)—an often-reprinted book containing a
description of ice breaking up on the Hudson which Cooper may
very well have used as his source. Cooper's nature titillates rather
than terrorizes because he presents no horror inherent in it. The
springing animals or falling trees of his fictional world represent
physical terrors of America's nature. They signify nothing more
frightening. When Heyward in *The Last of the Mohicans* (1826)

offers money in return for help, Natty replies: " 'Offer your prayers to Him who can give us wisdom to circumvent the cunning of the devils who fill these woods.' ' "[19] These are Flint's "devils," not Melville's, and the reader knows that Natty, God willing—and he almost always is in Cooper's world—will find the way. With splendid certitude, Cooper follows the pattern of America's journey to nature and civilization.

Only once, I think, does Cooper approach something genuinely frightening in nature, as he describes man's diminutiveness and vulnerability before an undefinable power. This occurs in *The Prairie* after Ishmael Bush has condemned his brother-in-law Abiram to death. Bush feels "for the first time. . .a keen sense of solitude. The naked prairies began to assume the forms of illimitable and dreary wastes, and the rushing of the wind sounded like the whisperings of the dead.' '[20] Cooper has other descriptions as vivid as this, often in his sea fiction, but nowhere else do they as forcefully juxtapose the frightening enormity of forces beyond man with an individual as genuinely human as Ishmael Bush. Unfortunately, the scene is ruined by the reader's temptation to speculate how Abiram White, "his arms bound at the elbows behind his back" can find the "consolation" from the "fragment of the Bible" sent by his sister and "placed in his hands" (p. 448).

However distracting this description may be, Cooper's atypical hint remains of man's existence in a universe where nature might be manifestly evil, or merely different from the moon. But Cooper stops at this hint. His writings simply do not engage a universe where the moon, as in "Walking," does not correlate directly with nature. Cooper's commitment to a tangible nature makes him representative of his society in a way that Melville or Thoreau could never be. Although his fictionalized perception of the Indian or his literary regret at the passing of the wilderness had no serious place in American thought outside the realm of art, he did see nature as part of this world rather than of another. He wrote from a perspective closer to his society's than that of any other major American writer of his time. Cooper's heroes—at least his civilized ones, such as Oliver Effingham in *The Pioneers* (1823), Duncan Heyward in *The Last of the Mohicans* (1826), Duncan Middleton in *The Prairie* (1827), and Jasper Western in *The Pathfinder* (1840)—go into the wilderness, and, in accordance with an American paradigm, eventually find material success in a civilized world. Although these heroes play minor parts as Cooper's drama of a western wonderland unfolds, in the end the land or the economic triumph is theirs, along with what passes for a woman. The capacity of these characters to emerge from nature into civilization conforms to Cooper's full commitment to America's crucial premise that nature tended toward that direction.

As for Cooper's great hero, Natty Bumppo, his ideas on nature derive from the same premise held by the returning civilized heroes. Natty appreciates and understands his milieu in a way that no other white man can, and this makes his relationship to nature special, although very different from that of Thoreau or Melville. Natty loves nature, so he mourns pigeons wantonly slaughtered, good Indians passing from the American scene, and game no longer plentiful. He mourns, too, the physical world with its manifold beauty being consumed by an advancing civilization that is questionable in its wisdom at times, but never in its destiny or in its legitimacy. For Natty, nature is tangible—something the eye can see and never an "occasional and transient" place. Although Natty argues with civilization over *how* the commodity is to be used and *whose rights* to it are preeminent, the disputants share an identical assumption that nature is commodity. The basic argument between Natty and Marmaduke Temple concerns the proper utilization of commodity. Would the land remain with those who first found it, or would it pass to a legislating civilization? Although Natty finally runs from the society of Cooper's ideal squire—as Huck runs from his society in Twain's treatment of a somewhat similar theme—Cooper, unlike Twain, has his hero leave a social order defined as "good," however alien to Natty. In the good society benevolently directed by Marmaduke Temple, in the time before democratic scoundrels spoiled

Cooper's America, the quarrel over commodity—that persistent theme in Cooper's writings—lent itself to nice solutions. Thus, when Cooper began his frontier myth in *The Pioneers,* the most insistent questions related to commodity. Will Oliver get the land that is really his? Will Natty lose the land that he inhabits by " 'natural right?' "[21] Will Temple preside over the proper distribution of property, as well as the destiny of the region? These are the basic problems of the book, and we all know their solutions, right down to the portioning off of the judge's daughter to Oliver, whose merits are clarified only after he gets rid of his wild ways, which are, after all, a pose. Natty obligingly goes away, not in anger, but with tender love for those who now possess the land. With Natty wandering toward the sunset, America can live happily ever after—at least while people obey the interchangeable wills of Marmaduke Temple, James Fenimore Cooper, and God.

Although the adventures of Cooper's western stories are more likely to attract readers than are less exotic matters, the subject of commodity will not go away. It turns up in Cooper's most disparate adventure stories: in the utopian world of *The Crater* (1847), ruined by people who will not be guided by Cooper's landed squire; in his finest nautical story, *The Sea Lions* (1849); even in his last novel, *The Ways of the Hour* (1850), the very unexotic tirade against all that he saw as wrong in democratic America. These stories and others reveal an obsessive concern with the appropriate channeling of land, money, or social arrangement. His nature—whether in America's past, or in the volcanic land of *The Crater* (which is really America), or in the antarctic region of *The Sea Lions*—offered a concrete region in a non-metaphysical world. Presenting exciting possibilities for adventure, that world remained securely anchored in the assumptions about nature held by an American society whose manifest destiny accorded with God's scheme of the world. Unlike "Walking" or "Passage to India," Cooper's fiction, in hewing closely to an American paradigm, kept the journey's definition in the tangible world of linear history.

This is not to say that romantic writers consistently lived in some other world. On the contrary, they had to contend with "moon nature" (the physical world), and either accept the inimical aspects it often revealed or transform them through the power of their vision to another order of understanding. Such transformations could lead to beatific visions or moments of profound horror, depending on the ulterior discoveries found beyond the moon. Whatever one finds in this other nature, however, out of the search for it emerges Emerson's *Nature,* Thoreau's *Walden,* Melville's *Moby-Dick,* and even at times the nature poetry found in writers such as Longfellow, Bryant, and Whittier. On the other hand, "moon nature"—the environment of the "external world"—often suggested the chimeras that private myths of nature sought to slay. Romantics had few illusions about what "moon nature" might be, and they generally comprehended it in the context of contemporary scientific assumptions. Certainly every educated person in early nineteenth-century America knew the same "facts" about nature that later in the century would be codified by Herbert Spencer in his theory of "social Darwinism." These facts about the internal struggles in nature could be found in the well-known theories of Jean Lamarck or in works growing out of his studies, or in simple empirical observation.

The discovery that all was not sweet harmony in a nature that was dissociated from myth obviously predates the nineteenth century, but the notion of God in some wise way manipulating the universe, as in Cooper's world, served to minimize fears—at least theoretically—of nature acting irrationally against man. In a world where God is called into question, however, nature's threats take on more serious proportions. Despite one's religious beliefs, the idea of nature as potentially threatening was real, even to the most rhapsodic praisers of the natural world. This potentially inimical nature—the one that Tennyson in the fifty-sixth poem of *In Memoriam* called "red in tooth and claw"—was as immediate to someone like William Cullen Bryant as it was to Herman Melville. I single out Bryant here because, along with other nature poets who have received little serious attention, he is deeply identified with a frequently held modern idea of nineteenth-century America as a place particularly defined by faith in the goodness of nature. I choose him to stress the profound divisions between nature of transcendent poetry and nature of empirical observation; between nature of romantic myth and nature of history.

Bryant repeated the joys of nature with such persistence that even his most distinguished critic, Tremaine McDowell, observes that for Bryant "nature is a serene temple for worship and a reservoir of health and joy to which he continually invited his reader to escape." Bryant, the argument goes, was a man whose "affection for the physical world" was so great that he "closed his eyes" to its "despoilings."[22] This is the Bryant most of us imagine when we think of him, if at all, and I only use Professsor McDowell's description because he has taken Bryant more seriously than have most readers. Moreover, there is surely ample evidence to support Professor McDowell's well-documented view of Bryant. But another Bryant also exists, just as another nature does: the same writer who composed poetry to that "reservoir of health and joy" also wrote such stories as "The Whirlwind," which was told with quite an open eye to the "despoilings" of nature. The text of Bryant's "Skeleton's Cave" might well have received nodding approval from Herbert Spencer or Theodore Dreiser:

We hold our existence at the mercy of the elements; the life of man is a state of continual vigilance against their warfare. The heats of the noon would wither him like the severed herb, the chills and dews of night would fill his bones with pain, the winter frost would extinguish life in an hour, the hail would smite him to death—did he not seek shelter and protection against them. His clothing is the perpetual armor he wears for his defence, and his dwelling the fortress to which he retreats for safety. Yet, even there the elements attack him; the winds overthrow his habitation; the waters sweep it away. The fire, that warmed and brightened it within, seizes upon its walls and consumes it, with his wretched family. The earth, where she seems to spread a paradise for his abode, sends up death in exhalations from her bosom; and the heavens dart down lightnings to destroy him. . . .[23]

This prose reflects a not-uncommon view among ''nature'' poets and must not be construed as inconsistent with Bryant's praises to nature. As with other poets, in celebrating the sublimity of his natural environment, in finding a wonderful beauty in the world around him, he portrayed the experience of a moment, captured it in the timelessness of art. The same writer could at varying times celebrate the landscape with rhapsodic language and define a world of Spencerian strife. Indeed, an individual could be indifferent to nature in one moment and find aspects of it a petty nuisance in the next. These differing perspectives stem partly from human caprice and partly from shifting metaphorical applications. In *Walden,* nature belongs primarily to romantic myth; in Cooper's wilderness, Bryant's fire and lightning, and Thoreau's ''moon,'' it belongs to history.

The moon of Thoreau's ''Walking''—that which does not belong to nature because it exists in history rather than in myth—is the same part of the world containing the black flies Thoreau vainly battled in the Maine woods. Indeed, if we take Thoreau's word, his trip to Mt. Ktaadn, where he experienced one of his most moving and terrifying glimpses into ''nature,'' might very well have been prevented by some pesky insects—creatures quite remote from the nature on the other side of the moon. ''I was fortunate also in the season of the year,'' he writes in *The Maine Woods,* which contains his description of climbing Mt. Ktaadn, ''for in the summer myriads of black flies, mosquitoes, and midges, or, as the Indians call them, 'no-see-ems,' make traveling in the woods almost impossible; but now their reign was nearly over.''[24] Such forms of nature did not promise to redeem man. Similarly, Emerson had no theology of nature in mind when he contended against the bugs in his garden. ''An Orientalist,'' he writes in his *Journal,* and one can only wonder whether it was Thoreau,

who was a Hercules among the bugs and curculios, recom-
mended to me a Persian experiment of setting a lamp under the
plum tree in a whitewashed tub with a little water in it by
night. But the curculio showed no taste for so elegant a death.
A few flies and harmless beetles perished, and one genuine
Yankee spider instantly wove his threads across the tub, thinking that there was likely to be a crowd and he might as well set
up his booth and win something for himself. At night in the
garden all bugdom and flydom is abroad. This year is like
Africa or New Holland, all surprising forms and masks of
creeping, flying, and loathsomeness.[25]

Emerson's misadventure in the garden, along with Thoreau's
confrontation with insects in the Maine woods, calls attention to
how remote the natural world might be from a visionary
literature of nature. Far from offering a call to some new
mythology, the world of physical nature could be as dangerous as
it was to Bryant, or even as dull as it was to Thoreau, as he
observed in a statement reminiscent of the complaint lodged in
Godey's Lady's Book: "The most stupendous scenery ceases to
be sublime when it becomes distinct, or in other words limited,
and the imagination is no longer encouraged to exaggerate it. The
actual height and breadth of a mountain or a waterfall are always
ridiculously small; they are the imagined only that content us.
Nature is not made after such a fashion as we would have her. We
piously exaggerate her wonders, as the scenery around our
home."[26] There is nothing strange in this view of nature by the
man so associated with a special commitment to it. In moon
nature one could only be expected to find something less than "a
fashion as we would have her," something smaller than might be
"imagined." All readers of *Walden* know that Thoreau never
hints, never dreams that man should behave the way ants do in
his description of their memorable battle. Nature obviously exists
here as a metaphor describing the worst in man. In using nature
for such metaphors, romantic writers were treating it as their
culture did—as a plastic, malleable element of language, not
strictly bound by any cohesive theory of the day nor consistently
defined within the formulations of any given writer. What set

romantic use of nature apart from the more prevalent employment of it was the way writers chose to "fashion" it. In the statement about the dullness of scenery, Thoreau affirms that "we
would have her" far more wondrous than the physical world
around us. And at times one could, as in the brief moments of
"Walking," or in the apocalypse of Emerson's *Nature*. These
moments, however, are internal. They reflect an interior perspective, a way of "seeing" past the scaffold falling in America, and
past the distance of the "moon" to the interior world of private
vision. A scene that is at one moment dull may in the next be
transformed to the place beyond the moon.

Thus, in the same work where Thoreau described the scenery
as so unexciting, he found in nature a transcendent image: "May
we not *see* God? Are we to be put off and amused in this life, as it
were with a mere allegory? Is not Nature, rightly read, that of
which she is commonly taken to be the symbol merely?"[27] Yes,
he implies, although never suggesting that he read it wrong in finding the scenery dull. Nor was he being hypocritical or obtuse in
failing to address an apparent discrepancy, since none really existed. Dull scenery belonged to the everyday world of man in
historical time. Redemptive nature belonged to a mythology
formed by one's inner perceptions.

Moreover, such inner perceptions could also suggest man's
dislocation in the universe, and, accordingly, a less joyous
mythology. In Thoreau's "The Cliffs and Springs," for example,
the poet awakens from a transcendent moment in nature to a
sense of loss rather than discovery:

> When breathless noon hath paused on hill and vale,
> And now no more the woodman plies his axe,
> Nor mower whets his scythe,
> Somewhat it is, sole sojourner on earth,
> To hear the veery on her oaken perch
> Ringing her modest trill—
> Sole sound of all the din that makes a world,
> And I sole ear.
> Fondly to nestle me in that sweet melody,

And own a kindred soul, speaking to me
From out the depths of universal being.
O'er birch and hazle, through the sultry air,
Comes that faint sound this way,
On Zephyr borne, straight to my ear.
No longer time or place, nor faintest trace
Of earth, the landscape's shimmer is my only space,
Sole remnant of a world.
Anon that throat has done, and familiar sounds
Swell strangely on the breeze, the low of cattle,
And the novel cries of sturdy swains
That plod the neighboring vale—
And I walk once more confounded a denizen of earth.[28]

In the world of this poem, presented in its entirety, Thoreau surely finds an ''occasional and transient'' moment of wondrous
discovery in nature, but when the moment passes he again
becomes the ''confounded. . .denizen,'' the alien cut off from his
spiritual source. Melville used the metaphor of an orphan in
Moby-Dick to describe the same phenomenon, though without an
earlier entrance into Thoreau's briefly entered beatific world.

Although the search for the place beyond the moon defined
romantic theology, nature on this side of the moon remained
morally neutral. There is no intrinsic malice in Cooper's springing panther, in Bryant's lightning, or in the fish-hawks that
Thoreau observes threatening the fish, as they in turn are
threatened by the bald eagle.[29] In moon nature, strife carries no inherent moral significance, only a rhetorical one. Events in nature
are seized upon by writers to make any point they wish, as
Thoreau does in having his ants show us how not to behave.
Ironically, this very process of using the internal struggles in
nature to exemplify human baseness offered to a later generation
of American businessmen moral truisms to justify similar
behavior.[30] The great child of America's commercial vision and
our archetypal industrial giant, Andrew Carnegie, legitimized his
momentous economic triumphs through the sanctification of
nature, while Thoreau, America's archetypal nature devotee,
condemned the triumph of the strong over the weak by showing

how base the process is in nature. This wonderful irony cannot be explained by any theory implying some "development" or "degeneration" of the "American mind." Long before American industrialists justified their activities by Spencer's rule of "survival of the fittest," nature was teaching the same lesson to others. For example, while watching small fish falling victim to larger one, Francis Parkman observes: " 'Soft-hearted philanthropists,' thought I, 'may sigh long for their peaceful millenium; for, from minnows to men, life is incessant war.' "[31] This view of nature, a cultural commonplace found in the writings of authors as diverse as Timothy Flint and Emerson,[32] offered the neutral event in nature from which one could draw whatever moral lessons one's particular world view required.

Since the moral neutraility of nature was constant, its usage for exemplary purposes served many ends. Thus, although in his description of the ants Thoreau tells us not to imitate nature, elsewhere he affirms that "nature never makes haste. . . .Why, then, should man hasten as if anything less than eternity were allotted for the least deed?"[33] Here, he wants his reader to imitate nature. He appreciates having nature teach him what he already believes. Only in this sense is nature really a teacher, as it is for Emerson when his brother asks him whether one could properly "make use of animals." Emerson answers affirmatively, supporting his argument with an anecdote about a Laplander who killed a reindeer in order to obtain certain necessities of life. "Does any mind question," asks Emerson, "the innocence of this starving wretch in thus giving life and comfort to a desolate family in that polar corner of the world?" The answer is no, and the lesson is that "there is a whole *nation* of men precisely in this condition, all reduced to the alternative of killing the beasts, or perishing themselves." The matter ultimately reduces itself to whether "the tender-hearted" will "make the beasts *his* food, or be himself *theirs*. . . ."[34] Such a view seems to place Emerson on the side of Andrew Carnegie in the lesson he learned from nature. But Emerson was not "learning" anything, and he certainly did not mean to make such struggles in nature models for human behavior. Once, when it rained until he wearied of it, Emerson wryly observed that ''the good rain, like a bad preacher, does not know when to leave off.''[35] Here, the lesson in nature teaches us what not to emulate. No hypocrisy attends such shifting uses of nature, since no moral commitment to a figure of speech exists.

An American society accustomed to protean uses of nature could readily comprehend such plastic usage. Less recognizable was the employment of nature to symbolize a new way of spiritual knowing, the kind revealed in Emerson's *Nature,* Thoreau's ''Walking,'' or *Walden.* But more typically, when used as a spiritual trope in America, nature was identified with a natural world that revealed a familiar, traditional God, the kind made manifest to Cooper in a leaf or a tree, as he described in *Oak Openings* (1849).[36] Thus, when Cooper sends his civilized heroes into the wilderness, where they hear Natty speak of one's closeness to God in a world of nature, his fiction conforms to the general belief that a traditional God and an American society share a common enterprise. It was perfectly Christian for Natty to find God in nature, just as it was perfectly Christian for the civilized heroes to return to their world and to financial success. It all made sense to America. But *Walden,* though it followed this paradigm of an individual going into nature, finding gain, and returning, could only be a cultural oddity. Thoreau's nature in this enterprise on the other side of the moon did not reveal a recognizable God, and it condemned the whole idea of what nature generally meant in America. It even suggested at times a mythology devoid of redemption.

Indeed, for all the promise of salvation that Walden *seems* to offer the awakened man, Thoreau never constructed a simplistic world where one could assume the inherent goodness of the universe. In *Walden* Thoreau reminds us that ''most men, it appears to me, are in a strange uncertainty about it [life], whether it is of the devil or of God. . . .''[37] Although Thoreau does not claim that the universe is malign, *Walden* and other works by him imply the possibility. If most men will not awaken to the new world of ''nature,'' and Thoreau assures us in the conclusion of *Walden* that this will probably be the case, what remains other than a fallen world—without a redeeming deity—from which a handful might arise? And what made this world fall? Although Thoreau opens these questions, he obscures them within a vision of his own awakening world. Yet most men, Thoreau tells us over and again, fail to awaken. As in the days of the Puritans, most do not achieve salvation. Those outside of Thoreau's new day, therefore, live in what might be seen as his analogue for hell—the spiritual darkness within. Implicit in *Walden* is the prophecy that most of humanity may expect this destiny. True, Thoreau holds out to his reader a better future, but so also did Jonathan Edwards. Both knew, however, that most people would fail to overcome an inner perversity that kept them from the promised kingdom. Offering no certainty of God, Thoreau's theology of nature generally promised spiritual darkness. To a few, it offered moments of illumination, without which there would remain the blackness we find in Melville's world—a universe perhaps "of the devil." The mythology of nature always bordered on this other possibility. The questing hero seeking to build a better world risked discovering on the other side of the moon the dark side of Western civilization's dualistic vision.

The Western tradition of contending spiritual forces was not to be abolished in one mere century of "rationalism," nor in a bright, romantic myth of nature—even if the vocabulary changed. Thus, it was the ancient dualism Thoreau confronted one morning in looking at the broken bodies of men destroyed in an explosion. The human carnage suggested to him "an avenging power in nature."[38] That power, described by him in another context as "the west side of any mountain,"[39] was different from America's West and different from the "west" he reached in "Walking." But the morning after Thoreau examined the broken bodies, he relished the wind on his cheek and the beautiful sun in the sky. Because of this apparent incongruity between nature's savage fury and its unspeakable beauty, he asks a rhetorical question: "Are there not two powers?"[40] The answer is yes—not in moon nature, but in the nature into which one's entrance is "occasional and transient.'' Thoreau is expressing the enduring belief in what has sometimes been called the ''devil.'' All of Western tradition, despite Christianity's persistent attempt to merge the contending powers into one, affirmed this duality that would not be removed by a new vision of nature. The universe continued to contain the force that, according to Emerson, ''has not only helps and facilities for all beneficial operations, but fangs and weapons for her enemies also.''[41] This defines not merely ''nature, red in tooth and claw''—at least as the phrase is associated with strife in the natural world—but it also characterizes nature as the force that may devour our very self, our soul, and bring the terror that Whitman describes:

> Now I am terrified at the Earth, it is that calm and patient,
> It grows such sweet things out of such corruptions,
> It turns harmless and stainless on its axis, with such
>   endless succession of diseas'd corpses,
> It distills such exquisite winds out of such infused fetor,
> It renews with such unwitting looks its prodigal, annual,
>   sumptuous crops,
> It gives such divine materials to men, and accepts such leaving
>   from them at last.[42]

This, too, is part of romantic nature. Bryant calls it ''A power. on the earth and in the air/From which the vital spirit shrinks afraid.''[43] While Emerson, often the serenest of men, or so he seems, writes in anger:

> O Sun! I curse thy cruel ray:
> Back, back to chaos, harlot day!

Provoking this wrath were the ''two faces''[44] of nature, Thoreau's ''two powers,'' the dualism that persisted in intruding upon visions of benevolent unity.

Although writers in visionary moments might very well perceive a universe where duality becomes unity, where nature reveals order instead of contention, where the god-man is awakened to a new and higher form through the world-redeeming power of his new myth, they could not sustain endlessly such experience. If art momentarily brought their world together, the duality inherent in their metaphysical systems continued to reaffirm itself. The conception of man as a fallen being separated from his spiritual source persisted, and the new myth of nature had the power to reunite them only during "occasional and transient" moments. Often faced with a world that would not conform to their myth, writers sometimes asked the questions Thoreau poses: "*Who* are we? *where* are we?"[45] Man, he feared, might exist in the fallen sphere described in his "Epitaph on the World":

> Here lies the body of this world,
> Whose soul alas to hell is hurled.
> This golden youth long since was past,
> Its silver manhood went as fast,
> And iron age drew on at last;
> 'Tis vain its character to tell,
> The several fates which it befell,
> What year it died, when 'twill arise,
> We only know that here it lies.[46]

This corrupted earth, as he writes in "I am a Parcel of Vain Strivings Tied," is alien to him, for he was designed "For milder weather." From some divine world, from "fair Elysian fields," he has been plucked along with "weeds and broken stems," and he has been placed as a stranger on earth with "no root in the land."[47] If before the poem is over he begins to sense some purpose in his visit to earth, he still remains the uncomprehending alien in it. Do we not recognize Melville's orphan in this strange world? Or Whitman's poetic journeyer in the "unnatural" place?

The sense of dislocation often found in a mythological nature was not curious to American writers, although it was surely curious to the general American public searching for its own garden in the sure realm of God. The sense of dislocation that appeared grew logically out of religious temperament set loose from its traditional moorings, and it certainly did not stem from political or economic alienation. Romantic problems were more important than that. Thoreau's questions, "*Who* are we? *where* are we?" echoed across Europe, as in the comment of Goethe's Werther "that adults, too, like children, stumble about on this earth of ours and do not know where they come from or where they are going"; or as in Shelley's image of people "All hastening onward, yet none seemed to know/Whither he went, or whence he came, or why."[48] Or as Melville askes in the "Gilder" chapter of *Moby-Dick,* "Where lies the final harbor, whence we unmoor no more?"[49] This lack of knowing reflects the same rootlessness that Mary Shelley's monster feels as he compares himself to Adam, "apparently united by no link to any other in existence"; it is behind the questions he asks himself (which he perhaps found in the copy of *Werther* he had read): "Who was I? What was I? Whence did I come? What was my destination?"[50] The distance between Frankenstein's monster and Melville, Thoreau, Shelley, and Goethe is not quite as great as it might appear, nor should the parallels be examined as matters of "influence." Who said it first matters little. For some, all mankind seemed newly created now that their old eschatological assumptions were fading. The monster and Thoreau and others were "a parcel of vain strivings"—new, dislocated, and fallen Adams in the "new" world of America and in the "old" world of Europe. Each asked who he was. It was the romantic question of the age, and to believe that American writers found anything other than an "occasional and transient" answer in nature is to misunderstand them.

The "religion of nature"—and for a few it sometimes approached being that, although trees were certainly not the temples—formed its outlines from Christianity's theme of fall and redemption. But the concept of nature as Christianity has obvious limitations that grow in proportion to the seriousness with which the idea is taken. In imposing the religion of Christianity upon nature, one mixes theology with poetic metaphor, as Emerson does when he asks for a sign from nature, some signal from "the tree, the mountain, the lake," that they "knew the man who was born by them."[51] This particular plea is marked by an utter sense of futility at the refusal of nature to work the miracle that, if it had happened, would have stunned Emerson into disbelieving his own perceptions. As Emerson writes in a calmer moment, "If Nature relented at all from her transcending laws, if there were any traces in the daily obituary that the yellow-fever spared this doctor or that Sunday School teacher, if any sign were that a 'good man' was governing, we should lose all our confidence, the world all its sublimity."[52] To request a sign from nature is to deny this rationalistic perception of the world, though the tragedy of Emerson was that his rationalism kept getting in the way of the new myth he sought to define. He did not find the sign in nature that he was seeking, but his heart could not stop searching for the "good man" that his mind told him did not exist. It was the irony of more than one writer's life that attempts to locate the self more permanently in the "occasional and transient" place called nature began with the "rational" view of the world that had turned them from their old religion in the first place.

Only through the power of art would chaos and order seem to be merged for such individuals into one transcendent, unifying vision—surely a tribute to those like Emerson, Whitman, and Thoreau, who, in the magic of their literary craft, succeed at times in bringing us with them to their special visions of nature. It is also a tribute to their humanity that they continued to question the meaning of that nature. And we may wonder how often in the tension between these conflicting modes of thought they sensed the presence of the cosmic joker of *The Confidence-Man,* that deity Melville suggested earlier in the "Hyena" chapter of *Moby-Dick:*

There are certain queer times and occasions in this strange mixed affair we call life when a man takes this whole universe for a vast practical joke, though the wit thereof he but dimly discerns, and more than suspects that the joke is at nobody's expense but his own. . . .And as for small difficulties and worryings, prospects of sudden disaster, peril of life and limb; all these, and death itself, seem to him only sly, good-natured hits, and jolly punches in the side bestowed by the unseen and unaccountable old joker.[53]

More succinctly, if less poetically, Emerson, who had promised man a world "beyond his dream of God," expressed the opinion that life might after all be an affair for *Punch*.[54] Such "queer times and occasions" may have been only as "occasional and transient" as Thoreau's entrance into nature. But these moments were part and parcel of the romantic quest in "nature," which took more than one route past America's "garden" and beyond the "moon."

6

Adam Once More

Whereas Emerson's perception of the world as a joke was surely atypical of him, the whole romantic quest for nature risked such a discovery. Central to the idea of the quest was the notion that the world might be met anew; figuratively, the new man might be the new Adam. Although in one sense the roots of this metaphor are found in the Puritan idea of America as the geographical nexus for world regeneration, by now the "new world" was two centuries old. Neither the social arrangements nor the theologies of America had brought the world to a new garden, other than the one growing from railroads and canals. In spite of lingering hopes by some Romantics that democracy would yet bring spiritual transformation, for the most part the recovery of an original relation to the world seemed to lie outside of politics or history. Thus, the romantic Adam of the nineteenth century was "new" primarily in private, spiritual terms that had little to do directly with the new garden of America. An Adam in this American garden would have little reason to perceive the world as a joke, for in spite of the many private failures, most Americans could generally feel that the national journey West had brought with it the transformation of the wilderness into the garden of nature. The romantic exploration of nature, however, took a fundamentally different course, since the distinguishing characteristic of the romantic Adam was his metaphysical attempt to begin anew a spiritual discovery of the world. For romantic writers, the metaphor of Adam did not belong so much to the newness of America as to the newness of their search for a belief to replace the theology that no longer seemed plausible to them. Private myths had to be constructed, new beginnings postulated. But new myths carried the inherent possibility of new failures—new disillusionments that might indeed suggest a cosmic joke. At the end of the new journey, Adam might find that Eden always led to the Fall, or perhaps that there was no Eden at all. No honest explorer could exclude these contingencies.

There is no need here to define fully the ''Adamic'' idea, since R. W. B. Lewis, Roy Harvey Pearce, and others have examined it so carefully. I need only emphasize that this myth is not tied simply to explicit statements about Adam, as in Hawthorne's comparison of Donatello with the primal man. The myth has its equally important implicit dimension, which manifests itself whether Adam is mentioned or not, whenever a new spiritual beginning is pursued or examined. Thus, the seminal work of American Romanticism, Emerson's *Nature,* employs what modern scholars have quite usefully defined as the ''Adamic myth,'' although this particular work by Emerson does not depend on an explicit metaphor of Adam. In Emerson's fable—for *Nature* is far more poetry than systematic philosophy—the poetic voice journeys through the bewildering, seemingly contradictory definitions of nature, arriving at last with the knowledge that allows the absolute transformation of the poetic hero from a ''god in ruins'' to a ''god'' rightfully restored to his lost powers. This is the special triumph that inspired Thoreau, Whitman, and who knows how many lesser writers. It is the apotheosis of the poet, the symbolic return to Eden, where the devil may be refought and this time defeated. One scarcely can say with enough emphasis, though, that the poet is not the *innocent* Adam before his first small step out of Eden, for nothing was more fundamental to the romantic idea of Adam than that he was a fallen being. Emerson was certainly not reluctant to state that fact. ''Man is fallen,'' he writes in 1844 in the essay ''Nature,'' which appeared in his *Essays Second Series.*[1] It is hard to be more direct on such a point.

In that same collection he writes the sentences given such prominence by Roy Harvey Pearce: "It is very unhappy, but too late to be helped, the discovery we have made that we exist. That discovery is called the Fall of Man."[2] Again, it is difficult to be more explicit than this. Nor will it do to say that these statements, coming as they do in 1844, represent some change in Emerson's perspective. For whether Emerson had or had not become more pessimistic between 1836, when *Nature* appeared, and 1844, the premise on which his essay, *Nature,* hinged was that man is a "god in ruins." He must find his way back to Eden from the condition Thoreau describes in *Walden:* "we are such gods or demigods only as fauns and satyrs, the divine allied to beasts, the creatures of appetite, and that, to some extent, our very life is our disgrace."[3] Whatever the psychological meaning of this beast may have been, romantic salvation lay in the victory of the divine part of the self over it, in the restoration of the fallen soul—no longer in harmony with nature—to its prelapsarian innocence, to a rediscovered harmony with the universe. The goal is achieved in the artistic triumph of works such as *Nature* or *Walden,* but no important writer—or any unimportant one I know of—saw himself as Adam *before* the Fall.

Thus, the new idea for those Romantics who sought the promise of redemption in nature was not that man had changed from his fallen state, but rather that this same fallen man could regenerate himself in a universe that could be made better than it appeared to the unseeing eye. Salvation could be found outside of historical Christianity, even while the ideas of *fall* and *redemption* hewed closely to the older theology. The way for this new Adam, burdened with his old humanity, would be through the vague conceptualization of nature, more rhapsodic than intellectual in its texture; more poetic than theological in its canon. The path to nature would at the same time lead backward toward the idea of recovering a lost Eden, and forward toward some future way of abolishing temporal disorder. The redeemed Adam of tomorrow would find the divinity in himself, in the universe around him; but he would also understand that in some mythological sense, in the time of Adam before the Fall, man had been better than he was now. The world had been better. This is why the goal would be not so much to create a new man—the use of such rhetoric notwithstanding—as it would be to rebuild the old "god in ruins."

The journey to this way of knowing was interior. "That is," as Thoreau puts it, "Man is all in all, Nature nothing, but as she draws him out and reflects him."[4] One difficulty with this idea is that man existed in history, in the physical world of "moon nature" that had to be part of the equation. The natural world could not really remain as "nothing." So, ineluctably, this marriage of types—"moon nature" with "redemptive nature"—led at times to linguistic incest. As a further complication, the romantic quest was taking place at a time when scientists were proclaiming evolutionary changes in the nature remote from romantic mythology. The emerging science of evolution was common knowledge to the very writers who looked to nature for a world of stable meaning. Supposedly, their spiritualized nature offered permanence in an otherwise transient universe. But the scientific vocabulary of nature as changing process intruded into "redemptive nature," partly from the confusion one may expect when one word is describing fundamentally different things, and partly from some genuine uncertainty about just how bright man's prospects were for redemption. Thus, doubts about the possibility of finding in spiritualized nature a redemptive force led almost predictably to the imposition of temporal characteristics on what was supposed to be perceived as a transcendent idea. The ominous perceptions of science's nature intruded into the myth of nature and sometimes overwhelmed it, as in Emerson's "The Poet," where man is not quite the god-man that he is in *Nature:*

> . . .The stars are glowing wheels,
> Giddy with motion Nature reels. . .
> Change acts, reacts; back, forward hurled. . .
> Discrowned and timid, thoughtless, worn,
> The child of genius sits forlorn:
> Between two sleeps a short day's stealth,

'Mid many ails a brittle health,
A cripple of God, half true, half formed,
And by great sparks Promethean warmed,
Constrained by impotence to adjourn
To infinite time his eager turn.'

It is this similar fear of man's and the world's transience that
Hawthorne describes in his "Hall of Fantasy," where he retreats
from the stance of an ironic, Olympian observer to that of an
oedipal supplicant. Pleading to "our Mother Earth," the narrator asks for "her great, round, solid self to endure inter-
minably, and still to be peopled with the kindly race of man."[6]
Now the idea of man swiftly passing from the earth was scarcely
new. It was very old when Chaucer used it in "The Knight's
Tale" in the lament of Egeus that "this world is but a
thoroughfare full of woe,/And we are pilgrims passing to and
fro."[7] The idea of the world's end is also older than the magnificent description in the vision of St. John. What gives these ideas
their special definition in a nineteenth-century romantic context
is the attempt to regenerate the world through one's own inner
divinity but without the external aid of God. Even Hawthorne,
who believed less in regeneration than most, pursued this myth of
private salvation, as in "Earth's Holocaust":

> The Heart—the Heart—there was the little, yet boundless sphere,
> wherein existed the original wrong, of which the crime and
> misery of this outward world were merely types. Purify that in-
> ward sphere; and the many shapes of evil that haunt the out-
> ward, and which now seem almost our only realities, will turn
> to shadowy phantoms, and vanish of their own accord.[8]

For all his mocking of transcendentalism, Hawthorne too was seeking a way by which the "shadowy phantoms"—Emerson's
"sordor and filths of nature"—could be made to "vanish"—the
identical word Emerson used. "Purify" the self, and "the many
shapes of evil" will "vanish." Surely that is what *Nature* and
Walden say in the new myth they seek to construct.

The romantic hero, however,—particularly in pursuing the goal through some idea of nature—could not always find his way through the net of contemporary scientific thought. Emerson's idea of redemption through nature presupposed a golden Adamic time to which man might return, but this postulate existed concurrently with Emerson's rational belief in the evolutionary process of nature as physical phenomenon relentlessly moving into the future after man's "short day's stealth." The scientific nature, as evidenced in "The Poet," persistently intruded into the mythic one, and in the quest for the golden age of Adam, the romantic journeyer had to pass the dragons of scientific findings. Posed agaist the dream of recreating the ideal realm in which Adamic man once walked remained the counter image of Emerson's "cripple," anything but the god-man. The very findings that were offering Western civilization a "death of God" ideology assaulted the theologies of nature almost as quickly as they arose to supplant the weakening religion of historical tradition.

Ironically, the day of doom predicted in the Bible was becoming an article of scientific faith at the very time the new theology of science was undermining that of scripture. No less a "nature devotee" than John Greenleaf Whittier became absorbed by this inimical potential of nature that science had revealed. "Very serious and impressive," he writes, "is the fact that [the end of the world] is not only predicted in the Scriptures, but that the Earth herself, in her primitive rocks and varying formations, on which are lithographed the history of successive convulsions, darkly prophesies of others to come."[9] Whittier shied away from the implication of what he saw and took the position, in spite of his geological observation and his religious beliefs, that the earth would, after all, endure. The crux of the matter was not whether the earth would go up in flames the next day (for even science had given man eons to put his affairs in order), but rather the implication that nature revealed the same impermanence of earthly things described in the Bible, though without the simultaneous promise of salvation. Although fears of an imminent end of the world had little impact on those with a modicum of psychic equilibrium, the very notion of transience in nature seriously weakened the basis for a mythology positing a new Adam in a metaphysical garden. Even a stable present might seem out of reach, to say nothing of an ideal past. When Hawthorne writes of holding on to his ''Mother Earth,'' or when Emerson describes himself as helpless in a world of nature that is ''Giddy with motion,'' each is reflecting a yearning at least to hold on to the present even while assuming a linear thrust of time toward an uncertain future. ''As I have written long ago,'' writes Emerson in 1849, ''the universe is only in transit, or, we behold it shooting the gulf from the past to the future.''[10] Only in the golden past, or in the resurrection of it, could Adam and the original relationship with nature be found again, but those in search of this past lived in a world ''shooting the gulf from the past to the future.'' No acceptable resolution to this dilemma existed, except in the creation of a nature totally divorced from the physical world, in those ''occasional and transient'' moments when the world became private vision. Although such moments did seem to occur at times, when they passed a more familiar world of ''sordor and filths'' quickly returned. Nor did any of the writers ever attempt to live out all their lives in the apocalypses of their own minds. In emerging from those ''occasional and transient'' moments one still encountered a natural world becoming less coherent with the passing of time. One moved increasingly away from the Adamic return.

Over and again this sense of loss was given expression in the metaphor of a separation from ''nature,'' itself the metaphor for the separation of Adam from the garden, which in turn is the metaphor for things perhaps too deep to know. In the privacy of his *Journal,* Thoreau documents the loss by asserting that ''once I was part and parcel of Nature; now I am observant of her.''[11] This, two years before *Walden* was published and five years after he left the pond. Nature simply receded from its questing pursuer. ''She always retreats as I advance,'' Thoreau writes in 1842.[12] The theme was a common one. Whittier describes it as

''Beauty that eludes our grasp,/Sweetness that transcends our taste.''[13] Emerson, in one of many places, relates the retreat in ''The World-Soul'':

> Alas! the Sprite that haunts us
>   Deceives our rash desire;
> It whispers of the glorious gods,
>   And leaves us in the mire.
> We cannot learn the cipher
>   That's writ upon our cell;
> Stars taunt us by a mystery
>   Which we could never spell.[14]

Melville embodies it in the symbol of the receding Yillah, using the metaphor of ''woman'' rather than ''nature.'' So also, Hawthorne presents it as a female apparition in ''The Vision of the Fountain.'' Such women are not to be understood as creatures of the flesh. They are incarnations of the ''feminine'' principle in the universe, whether manifested as woman or as nature. It is the very balancing feminine aspect of the universe that Ahab almost finds in the ''Symphony'' chapter of *Moby-Dick,* where the feminine and nature blend into one. It may even be what the whiteness represents at the end of Arthur Gordon Pym's journey. Since the complex correlation of nature with the feminine has been investigated extensively elsewhere,[15] it is sufficient to say here that in the romantic quest, nature or the feminine, in their beatific manifestations, were metaphors for the indefinable, transcendent experience of ''occasional'' moments.

But while the rewards of the mystic union with the feminine or nature might lead one beyond the kingdom of God to something inexpressibly glorious, the corollary remained that visionary journeys might instead reveal the horrors of the world, as in *Moby-Dick.* Although the rewards of the reunion with nature were great indeed, the threat also existed that nature was not to be ''caught,' or even that there was nothing but chaos to catch. Under such circumstances ''redemptive nature'' offered no escape from the threats located in ''moon nature.'' Nor could myriad exaltations prevent from surfacing the deep, frightening possibility that nature, as myth or history, might be monstrous.

A segment of Emerson's *Journal* titled "Vision" vividly exemplifies this alternative possibility to what the new Adam sought in nature. Emerson describes a cottage in the forest, a "magnificent" moon, and "breathless solitude." Only an occasional sound intrudes upon "Nature" at her magnificent best. "Here is her Paradise, here is her throne." He describes the sky, the forest, the flowers, and he refers to "the worshipping enthusiast [who] stands at the door of his tent mute and happy. . . ." Suddenly, everything changes.

> A cry in the wilderness! the shriek and sudden sound of desolation! howl for him that comes riding on darkness through the midnight; that puts his hand forth to darken the moon, and quenches all the stars. Lo! where the awful pageantry rolleth now to the corners of the heaven; the fiery form shrouds his terrible brow behind the fragment of a stormy cloud, and the eyes of Creation gaze after the rushing chariot. Lo! he stands up in the Universe and with his hands he parts the firmament asunder from side to side. And as he trode upon the dragons, I saw the name which burned underneath. Wake, oh wake, ye who keep watch in the Universe! Time, Space, Eternity, ye Energies that live—for his name is DESTRUCTION!—who keep the *Sceptre* of its eternal order, for He hath reached unto your treasuries, and he feeleth after your sceptre to break it in pieces. Another cry went up, like the crash of broken spheres, the voice of dying worlds.[16]

In this macabre apocalypse, one's eyes open only to the dream of nature as nightmare. Emerson ends his "vision" with a wry comment suggestive of a nice return to the equanimity we associate with him. But the nightmare vision had nevertheless been told. Nor does the vision define an aging Emerson losing the optimism of his youth, since he was only eighteen at the time and years away from essays such as "Fate" or "Experience."

The continuing difficulties with the new myth, in fact, usually had little to do with a writer's age or "development." They

resulted from perceptions shifting between the concepts of nature
as science's phenomenon ''shooting the gulf'' and the Adamic
notion of nature stably situated in mythic time. Though Emerson
never could find his way through this problem, he understood its
existence very well: ''Are beasts and plants degradations of man?
or are these the prophecies and preparations of Nature practising
herself for her master-piece in Man? Culminate we do not; but
that point of imperfection which we occupy—is it on the way *up*
or *down?*''[17] As he so often did, Emerson had faced the problem,
although an answer here eluded him.

Any nature on the way ''up'' is scientific nature, that which
moves along the evolutionary scale toward perfection. But if one
waits for the world to be perfected by evolutionary process, the
apotheosis of the self must await external and uncontrollable
forces. Viewed scientifically, nature denies the mythic version of
a retrievable and once perfect nature that fell with the fall of man.
Yet the Emersonian idea of perfection through some redefined
relation with nature turns on the idea of restoring a prior perfection. This genuine dilemma of two versions of nature pointing in
opposite ways offered no clear resolution unless nature became
some version of the self—a way of perceiving, rather than a
phenomenon to be defined in the ordinary arrangement of logical
categories. This is why Emerson defined *nature* as inner vision.
''The problem of restoring to the world original and eternal beauty is solved by the redemption of the soul,'' he says in the passage
that all Emersonians have memorized. ''The ruin or the blank
that we see when we look at nature, is in our own eye. The axis
of vision is not coincident with the axis of things, and so they appear not transparent but opaque. The reason why the world lacks
unity, and lies broken and in heaps, is because man is disunited
with himself.''[18] As long as Emerson or any other writer engaged
in the same enterprise could keep the ''axis of things'' aligned
with the ''axis of vision,'' the ''vision'' could remain intact. But
to do so one had to posit a world of ''things'' contrary to one's
own experience. This was no easy task, and Emerson more than
once knew the blurred ''vision'' that he recorded in his *Journal*

one year after the publication of *Nature:* "Whilst I feel myself in sympathy with nature, and rejoice with greatly beating heart in the course of Justice and Benevolence overpowering me, I yet find little access to this me of me. I fear what shall befal [sic]: I am not enough a party to the great order to be tranquil. I hope and I fear. I do not see."[19] Unlike those Americans who could "see" past the wilderness to their "garden," Emerson could never be so sure that his own eye would see the particular structure he was after.

Having nature emanate from the internal regions of the self implied an acceptance of some version of the "ideal theory," the view that the world exists in the mind of God. But without God as traditionally conceived, the world was left to reside in the mind of man. One need not catalogue all the problems inherent in such a view, and Emerson's first impulse in *Nature* was to belittle the problem and affirm in the section "Idealism" that whether or not nature existed "only in the apocalypse of the mind, it is alike useful and alike venerable to me."[20] Unfortunately, while this nicely straddled the issue, the matter was too basic to avoid. Emerson, as usual, came around to facing the problem. Before the chapter ended he was indeed holding to the view that nature had to exist "in the apocalypse of the mind." Only in such a realm could the myth he was formulating have any degree of coherence. "It appears," he writes, "that motion, poetry, physical and intellectual science, and religion, all tend to affect our convictions of the reality of the external world. But I own there is something ungrateful in expanding too curiously the particulars of the general proposition, that all culture tends to imbue us with idealism." As man becomes more civilized, Emerson is saying, more truly learned, he comes to understand that nature is within him. For this view he apologizes, even as he insists on it:

I have no hostility to nature, but a child's love to it. I expand and live in the warm day like corn and melons. Let us speak her fair. I do not wish to fling stones at my beautiful mother [that is, the "feminine"], nor soil my gentle nest. I only wish to indicate the true position of nature in regard to man, wherein to establish man all right education tends; as the ground which to attain is the object of human life, that is, of man's connection with nature. Culture inverts the vulgar views of nature, and brings the mind to call that apparent which it uses to call real, and that real which it uses to call visionary. Children, it is true, believe in the external world. The belief that it appears only, is an afterthought, but with culture this faith will as surely arise on the mind as did the first.[21]

The compelling fact from his perspective, although he presents his views in the context of some vague belief in an external God, is that Emerson defines *nature* as in some way an extension of man in a relationship bordering on a metaphysical symbiosis. But in his quest for "this me of me," Emerson faced some impeding philosophical incongruities. For if nature is an extension of the self, it will not unaided lead man back to his golden past of mythic time. It will only go there with him, as he leads it. And to be "on the way up"—to move toward self-perfection, harmony with the universe—is to be on the way *back,* to deny scientific evolutionary theory, which is what Emerson was suggesting in his question about "beasts and plants" being "degradations of man." When Emerson asked his question, he boldly confronted the contrasting claims of science and myth with the full awareness that all he so wanted to believe in hinged on the resolution of a problem he could not solve. He had to reject scientific history if he were to retrieve a past golden age of man and nature. But as Emerson understood all too well, he was a very rational man who accepted the science of his day. In spite of Emerson's quest for a unifying vision of man and nature in some newly won "Adamic garden," the single world kept splitting into two. "Ah, wicked Manichee," he exlaims in that much-quoted passage. "A believer in Unity, a seer of Unity, I yet behold two," and he adds the question that could not be answered affirmatively: "Cannot I conceive the Universe without a contradiction?"[22]

Atlhough Emerson certainly found more than one contradiction, the basic duality of myth and history carried a possibility even more serious than the destruction of a poetic vision. For if myth collapses before scientific inquiry, as theological history seemed to have done, what remains is a barren "moon nature." If this nature is not "practising herself for her master-piece," or if it cannot be described teleologically, or, indeed, if it is going "*down,*" what hope is there for man? Only one, assuming the exclusion of God. This was the individual's capacity to make the world conform to his best idea of it. Given this condition, if there were going to be any redemption involving nature, *it would be its redemption by man, as he redeemed himself.* "Whatever we study in Nature," writes Emerson in 1857, " 't is always found to be the study of man"[23] It always came back to this, to the individual's capacity to perfect himself unaided by external forces. If this process failed, as Emerson feared it might, then only the mindless world described in his early journal entry, "Vision," would remain. The physical apocalypse to come, as well as the indwelling self, might finally exist in a meaningless context. Implicitly, the whole idea of an internal, redeeming relationship with nature drove toward the polarities of man redeeming the world on one hand, and facing the void of receding faith on the other. And in the latter case, nature could only be the vast, impersonal, even terrifying force we associate with a later generation of "naturalists." Such a world, which Emerson and some of his contemporaries at times perceived well before that generation, leaves man a diminutive being—helpless and alone. He is indeed Adam again, only with no prospect that the fruit of some future seed would triumph over the serpent.

Precisely this implication of "Emersonianism" struck Horace Bushnell in *Nature and the Supernatural* (1858), where at one point he calls Emerson "mephitic."[24] Bushnell was keenly aware of what Emerson's philosophy implied about man's location in the universe. Since he never took seriously the possibility that man could redeem himself in a world without the divine Christ, Bushnell saw rather clearly what remained in Emerson's assumptions. He saw the implication of "blackness" in Emerson that even Melville did not entirely grasp in the man he both ridiculed

and admired. What Bushnell observes about the Emersonian view
is that

> if there be no such thing as a divine supernatural agency, then
> . . .[w]e exist as a solitary party. Nature is our cage, and the
> nearest approach we get to a recognition, is to find that we are
> shut up in it. Is it so? Do any of us think it is so? Did we really
> believe it, what could our existence be but a conscious defeat
> and mockery, a longing that is objectless, a breathing without
> air?[25]

Or, as Emerson calls it in ''The World-Soul,'' ''the cipher. . .writ
upon our cell.'' For Emerson, indeed, understood to what degree
man might exist in ''defeat and mockery'' if nature took the im-
prisoning direction it always threatened. In 1838, Emerson had
envisioned even more vividly than Bushnell a world without God:

> Meantime, as unlovely [as tradition-bound religion], nay
> frightful is the solitude of the soul which is without God in the
> world. To wander all day in the sunlight among the tribes of
> animals unrelated to anything better; to behold the horse and
> cow and bird, and to foresee an equal and speedy end to him
> and them. No, the bird as it hurried by with bold and perfect
> flight would disclaim his sympathy and declare him outcast; to
> see men pursuing in faith their varied action, warmhearted,
> providing for their children; loving their friends; performing
> their promises;—what are they to this chill, houseless,
> fatherless, aimless Cain, the man who hears only the sound of
> his own footsteps in God's resplendent creation? To him, it is
> no creation. To him, these fair creatures are hapless spectres.
> He knows not what to make of it.[26]

Emerson at that time was assuring his audience that there really
was a God, while concurrently defining which children of Adam
they were if God did not exist. He was recoiling from the vision
that Horace Bushnell would see as implicit in the whole enterprise of Emersonian nature. While we will never be able to say
how often Emerson felt that loneliness, we know that at times he

did. In grieving for his lost and beloved first wife, Ellen, he freely
admitted his vulnerability to the "suggestion that, as C. said of
Concord society, 'we are on the way back to Annihilation,'—only this threatens my trust."[27] Certainly, this was a time of crisis, but
it is precisely in such times that one may put to the rigorous test
a particular dream. No doubt Emerson was usually surer of the
universe than in such moments. Yet the logic of his particular vision always had a certain thrust in the bleak direction Bushnell
saw in Emerson's philosophy of nature.

Others felt the same loneliness and portrayed it in their works.
It is the rediscovery of Adam's terrible isolation that Melville
defines in *Mardi,* when his hero Taji, adrift on the ocean, senses
"what a mere toy we were to the billows, that jeeringly
shouldered us from crest to crest, as from hand to hand lost souls
may be tossed along by the chain of shades which enfilade the
route to Tartarus."[28] We expect Melville, the genius of
"blackness," to evoke such images, but we find the same sense
of diminutiveness, of man's fragility in an awesome universe, in
Thoreau's description of his "little egg-shell of a canoe tossing
across that great lake, a mere black speck to the eagle soaring
above it!"[29] And we have no reason to be surprised when Emerson observes that "a man is but a bug, the earth but a boat, a
cockle, drifting under" the stars[30]—"drifting," not steering.
Sometimes the myth simply could not contain the universe.

Remarks expressing man's loneliness in the universe were
common enough, in spite of some modern claims about an earlier
age of romantic innocence. Before Stephen Crane found Zola (if
the Frenchman were indeed his "source"), Emerson and others
had already drifted in an "open boat." Imaginations capable of
molding gods from nature could, however reluctantly, also con-
jure devils. Indeed, the new Adam at times carried a lonely
burden that the old one never felt. The first sinners knew whom
they had offended. They were never quite as alone as, for example, Thomas Cole depicted them in his important graphic
representation of the expulsion of Adam and Eve from the
Garden of Eden. The distinguishing characteristic of Cole's "Ex-

pulsion'' (1828) is the incredible diminutiveness of the lonely pair as they leave their fallen home. Pictorially, he offers his sense of their awesome loss, redefined and intensified in his day. This painting can very easily be dismissed as one more example of an obsession with the landscape, for unlike the traditional Expulsion paintings, its subject is the grotesque world of nature into which the sinners step, rather than the forms of Adam and Eve. It is also true that in other paintings Cole, himself a reasonably traditional man in his religion, presents nature as large and man as small. This was part of the aesthetic wonder in the ''new world'' that some artists did indeed find. But after all this has been conceded, Cole's ''Expulsion'' remains as an iconographic depiction of Thoreau's vivid questions, ''*Who* are we? *where* are we?'' For Cole did something that to my knowledge no other painter had ever done with the Expulsion. He presented a diminutive Adam and Eve entering a grotesque nature, and at the same time he showed the wonderful beauty of the Eden they had lost. In representations from Michelangelo to Blake, nothing resembles this. Only as one moves toward Cole's own era can anything comparable be found, for others were also suspecting Adam's new plight. Nature loomed large and ominous as man's significance diminished. So John Martin also deemphasized Adam and Eve—although not to the extent that Cole did—and Doré depicted Eden as lush, although neither one juxtaposed it against a fallen world. Regardless of Cole's motives, he gave graphic form to the same idea behind Melville's conception of man as ''a mere toy''; or Emerson's description of man as ''a bug''; or Thoreau's sense of man adrift, ''a mere black speck to the eagle soaring above''—a tiny ''egg-shell'' in a gigantic world. An indifferent and possibly meaningless nature dominated diminutive man.

From this harsh, forbidding physical world, the poet could withdraw into an interior myth of nature. The inner self could project upon the outer world a redefined image. But what if the inner self failed, or concluded that the interior world was itself no more than a physical place? What if the ''axis of vision'' *was* correspondent with the "axis of things" and both were monstrous? Then the world would participate in Melville's "blackness," a region recognizable in Emerson's interior journey to nature in the poem "Monadnoc."

At some point in his life—the exact date is not known to us—Emerson wrote "Monadnoc," a symbolic poem about a mountain that was literally a looming presence in his landscape.[31] As an aesthetic expression, "Monadnoc" may not be Emerson's best work of art, although in revealing his fragmented typology of nature it is cast in gold. In "Monadnoc," a poet awakens to the beckoning mountain's potential to teach man "the lordship of the earth."[32] The "I" hero sets out on his journey toward the mountain, along the way confronting disappointment, confusion, doubt, even horror. Ultimately, the hero approaches the borders of understanding, although he never quite crosses them. The wonderful mystery of the universe, "though the substance us elude,/We in thee [Monadnoc] the shadow find" (p. 74). Although lacking the stunning apocalyptic vision found in *Nature,* the poem more intimately reveals the difficulty of entering Emerson's remarkable "kingdom" described at the end of that essay.

At the beginning, the uncomprehending poet is invited to discover a nature that already reveals its duality:

> Let not unto the stones the Day
> Her lily and rose, her sea and land display.
> Read the celestial sign! (P. 60)

We immediately recognize a vocabulary of Christianity. The "lily" and the "rose" ("return of happiness" and "beauty," respectively, in the flower lexicon of the day[33]), traditionally symbolize the Church, Mary, Christ; the "stone" symbolizes death, which the Son of God in His resurrection removed. Although Christian symbolism is expected in the myth of nature, we may nevertheless wonder why "the Day" should not reflect its glory on "the stones." Are not life and death integral to the unified vision of nature? At this point in the poem the answer is clearly no, although we have not yet, with the poet, read "the celestial sign."

With this implicitly dual vision, the poet moves toward the mountain of inspiration "which God aloft had set/So that men might it not forget" (p. 61). The poet seems to walk in a world where God is separate from him; "Monadnoc" does not yet hint that it is the poet who contains God. Looking for a redemptive message in "Nature," the disappointed poet only discovers how mean man's life is, even in the shadow of the mountain:

> 'Happy,' I said, 'whose home is here!
> Fair fortunes to the mountaineer!
> Boon Nature to his poorest shed
> Has royal pleasure-grounds outspread.'
> Intent, I searched the region round,
> And in low hut the dweller found:
> Woe is me for my hope's downfall!
> Is yonder squalid peasant all
> That this proud nursery could breed
> For God's vicegerency and stead? (P. 62)

The disappointment increases as the mountain, "God's vicegerency," fails to offer the revelatory role sought in it.

> Is this colossal talisman
> Kindly to plant and blood and kind,
> But speechless to the master's mind? (P. 63)

Nature, the poet had believed, would lift him to infinite spheres of knowing; instead, the poet only finds grubby mountain folk residing in a coarse tavern-like atmosphere.

At this point, the poet looks to a better "axis of vision." In the reconsidered and superior way of seeing, churlish mountain folk now appear as busy, productive workmen in some way under the aegis of "The World-Soul." They "Bridge gulfs, drain swamps, build dams and mills,/And fit the bleak and howling waste/For homes of virtue, sense and taste" (p. 65). Here is familiar stuff indeed—American workmen attacking the ''howling waste,'' converting wilderness to civilization, to the true form of N. P. Willis' description. The ''scaffold'' of Dana is dropping, as the poet, at this stage of the journey, is on solid American ground. Beyond that, the American builder of civilization has become apotheosized within a teleological scheme of nature. Historical and mythological nature become one. Emerson has brought us in ''Monadnoc'' to the same threshold of knowing to which he led us in *Nature;* only now, instead of an ecstatic promise from a certain ''poet,' we shall have the revelation from a mountain. Monadnoc becomes a speaking voice.

The mountain first addresses the presumption of the poet, who would go where so many had gone before him in ''summer,'' but where so few have come ''To see strange forests and new snow'' (p. 67). Do you dare, in effect asks the mountain, ''be my companion/Where I gaze, and still shall gaze,/Through tempering nights and flashing days,/When forests fall, and man is gone'' (p. 67)? That man will pass while the mountain endures was perhaps not quite what the poet had sought to find in his quest. But we are to be surprised if we expect that on the mountain top a way will be found to transcend this reaffirmation of mortality. Indeed, the mountain—the beckoning presence which the poet had hoped would dissipate the world's mystery—is after all only a process in it.

> 'Let him heed who can and will;
> Enchantment fixed me here
> To stand the hurts of time, until
> In mightier chant I disappear.' (P. 68)

Explicating this ''mightier chant,'' the mountain describes the process of cosmic order from atom to sun, of which the mountain is but one part. And then comes this statement:

> 'Monadnoc is a mountain strong,
> Tall and good my kind among;
> But well I know, no mountain can,

Zion or Meru, measure with man.
For it is on zodiacs writ,
Adamant is soft to wit:
And when the greater comes again
With my secret in his brain,
I shall pass, as glides my shadow
Daily over hill and meadow.' (P. 69)

The mystery is thus locked in the mountain; the mountain
alone knows it; but the mountain, which is no measure for man,
cannot reveal it. Only the knowing man can, the man who
already contains the secret before he reaches the mountain. The
poet has therefore gone to the mountain to be told about a force
that can bring forth the music, a force revealed as the poet himself.
Once again, the richness, the meaning and majesty of nature, is in
man. Man contains ''Reason'' (p. 68). The mountain, which had
beckoned the poet, must itself ''await the bard and sage,/Who, in
large thoughts, like fair pearl-seed,/Shall string Monadnoc like a
bead'' (p. 70). This is the continuing revelation of nature—for
Emerson at Monadnoc, for Thoreau at Walden, for Melville in
the endless chase, or for Whitman in ''Song of the Rolling
Earth.'' Whether expressed in the most exultant poetry or encountered in the most tragic stance, nature in the romantic quest
becomes in some way the measure of man's knowing. For the
poet in ''Monadnoc'' this knowledge suddenly seems to become
a boundless range, an opportunity for visions never seen before.
The vastness of geography becomes ''Dwarfed to measure of his
hand'' (p. 71). We seem to be at home again with the Emerson
who wrote *Nature*. Then the mountain suddenly states explicitly
what had always been implicit in the view of man as the final location of being. We are back at once to the horror of Emerson's
''Vision.'' The mountain first quotes itself and then speaks
directly to the poet

''See there the grim gray rounding
Of the bullet of the earth
Whereon ye sail,

Tumbling steep
In the uncontinented deep.''
'He [man] looks on that, and he turns pale.
'T is even so, this treacherous kite,
Farm-furrowed, town-incrusted sphere,
Thoughtless of its anxious freight,
Plunges eyeless on forever;
And he, poor parasite,
Cooped in a ship he cannot steer,—
Who is the captain he knows not,
Port or pilot trows not,—
Risk or ruin he must share.
I scowl on him with my cloud,
With my north wind chill his blood;
I lame him, clattering down the rocks;
And to live he is in fear.
Then, at last, I let him down
Once more into his dapper town,
To chatter, frightened, to his clan
And forget me if he can.' (P. 72)

With Monadnoc having spoken, there remains only for the poem to give some meaning to this now-familiar look at man, the ''cripple'' in nature. But there is little to tell. The secret mined from its ''granite'' reveals only the knowledge that Monadnoc is a ''Firm ensign of the fatal Being'' (p. 73), the time-trapped revealer of our own ephemeral condition. This knowledge in the mountain was, after all, the power of ''Reason,'' which was the knowing man. In the sublime tautology of the poet's vision, he has found himself alone in the universe, alive on ''the bullet of the earth,'' and plunging like the mountain and all else toward chaos. This Adam has seen himself as a very new kind of god, with all the loneliness that such a role contains. Meanwhile, time moves inexorably, as the poet brings his ''insect miseries'' (p. 73) to this particular altar of nature.

All that remains to console the poet is that he shares this experience with the world around him, with the very Monadnoc that had seemed to promise him the elusive and the ''stable good/For which we all our lifetime grope'' (p. 74). This ''stable good'' implies no banal moral code; it represents the unchanging ''good man,'' the world order yearned for in the midst of possible chaos. Emerson's obsessed poet continues to seek this ''formless'' thing. He only finds its ''shadow,'' found in nature, which is found within the god-man self. Only this ''shadow'' keeps us ''sane'' (p. 74). Only the ''shadow'' contains the promise the poet had sought when he journeyed toward the mountain. But the shadow also contains the threat. With this, the poem ends. ''Monadnoc'' and *Nature* have taken us to the same point, although one work leaves us helpless at the mountain while the other transports us to places far over the moon. Yet both take place in the imaginative location of nature.

The great spoofer of Emerson's nature was Herman Melville, which is in a way unfortunate, since Melville's treatment of his contemporary suggests a greater visionary difference than actually existed. Careful readers, however, aware of the similarities these writers shared in their theological plights, have never been surprised by Melville's stated admiration for Emerson—his various parodies of transcendentalism notwithstanding. A few years before Melville published *Pierre*—where his own Adam faced a mountain—he made a particularly important statement on Emerson, apparently to deny that he himself was a transcendentalist, as some of his contemporaries assumed. ''Nay,'' writes Melville to Evert Duyckinck in a letter dated March 3, 1849, ''I do not oscillate in Emerson's rainbow, but prefer rather to hang myself in mine own halter than swing in any other man's swing. Yet I think Emerson is more than a brilliant fellow. Be his stuff begged, borrowed, or stolen, or of his own domestic manufacture he is an uncommon man. . .[sic] for the sake of the argument, let us call him a fool;—then had I rather be a fool than a wise man.—I love all men who *dive*.''[34] As Melville said, his ''halter'' was his own, so I do not insist in the ensuing discussion that he was Emerson's twin but only suggest the common ''nature'' they explored.

A few years after this tribute to Emerson, Melville offered in *Pierre* his own definition of nature: ''Say what some poets will,

Nature is not so much her own ever-sweet interpreter, as the mere supplier of that cunning alphabet, whereby selecting and combining as he pleases, each man reads his own peculiar lesson according to his own peculiar mind and mood.''[35] Read one way, the observation fulfills Robert Baird's insight into the imaginative potential nature held for literary use in America. But more important, the passage evokes an ''Emersonian'' correspondence with man and nature. It suggests a dependence by nature upon man; it defines a nature that exists almost entirely in the ''mind and mood'' of man. Although the quotation alone will not carry the whole burden of this meaning, the novel does reflect how the outside world is contingent upon the way the inner man ''sees.'' Such a method for Melville is not unique to *Pierre.* It appears in the ''Doubloon'' chapter of *Moby-Dick,* where Ahab imposes the same equation but uses the doubloon rather than nature. Ahab affirms that '' 'this round gold is but the image of the rounder globe, which, like a magician's glass, to each and every man in turn but mirrors back his own mysterious self. Great pains, small gains for those who ask the world to solve them; it cannot solve itself.' ''[36] ''The ruin or the blank that we see when we look at nature, is in our own eye,'' we recall from Emerson. ''The reason why the world lacks unity, and lies broken and in heaps, is because man is disunited with himself.''[37] Is that not implicit in what Ahab says? Of course this is only Ahab's view, and not one that he always holds. Nor is it always Melville's, who at times inclines to the view that a separate and malign power exists. But to invest in his most compelling character such a particular vision is to suggest at the very least a fascination with the idea, which in *Pierre* becomes more sharply defined through the use of nature rather than through a doubloon.

Melville's definition of the ''cunning alphabet'' comes almost at the beginning of the ''Enceladus'' section in *Pierre,* where Melville clarifies the meaning of the book's dedication to Mount Greylock. The dedication—its rich irony notwithstanding —establishes from the outset a separation between ''his Imperial Purple Majesty,'' Greylock, and the individual dwelling at

its base. One of Pierre's tasks is to ''climb'' the mountain. This
is quite explicitly explained as Pierre sits high in the temple of the
apostles, just before hearing ''tidings from the meadows,'' that
place where he had once seemed to be nature's special child.
Pierre

> did not see, that. . .all was but one small mite, compared to
> the latent infiniteness and inexhaustibility in himself; that all
> the great books in the world are but the mutilated shadowings-
> forth of invisible and eternally unembodied images of the soul;
> so that they are but the mirrors, distortedly reflecting to us our
> own things; and never mind what the mirror may be, if we
> would see the object, we must look at the object itself, and not
> at its reflection.

To show the ''object'' rather than the ''reflection,'' Melville il-
lustrates his point with metaphors of mountains. We keep in
mind that this mountainous world of nature about to be entered is
only the ''mirror'' of the incomprehensible self, what Emerson
calls ''this me of me.'' Melville writes:

> But, as to the resolute traveler in Switzerland, the Alps do
> never in one wide and comprehensive sweep, instantaneously
> reveal their full awfulness of amplitude—their overawing ex-
> tent of peak crowded on peak, and spur sloping on spur, and
> chain jammed behind chain, and all their wonderful battalion-
> ings of might; so hath heaven wisely ordained, that on first
> entering into the Switzerland of his soul, man shall not at
> once perceive its tremendous immensity; lest illy prepared for
> such an encounter, his spirit should sink and perish in the
> lowermost snows. Only by judicious degrees, appointed of
> God, does man come at last to gain his Mont Blanc and take an
> overtopping view of these Alps; and even then, the tithe is not
> shown; and far over the invisible Atlantic, the Rocky Moun-
> tains and the Andes are yet unbeheld. Appalling is the soul of a
> man! Better might one be pushed off into the material spaces
> beyond the uttermost orbit of our sun, than once feel himself
> fairly afloat in himself![38]

The ''appalling'' prospects notwithstanding, Melville explores these "mountains" in *Pierre,* as Emerson does in "Monadnoc."

In such moments of self-exploration, Melville's hero has become Melville himself, as Ishmael is similarly appropriated in *Moby-Dick.* I take this as self-evident, although true believers in "new criticism" obviously would not. Between the meadow and the mountain, Melville himself is in the peculiar position of climbing higher and higher from the deceptive Eden of "Saddle Meadows" to a paradoxically deeper and deeper abyss of consciousness. The journey to the mountain, ironically recalled from the heights of the temple of the apostles where Pierre lives, is no different in character from Emerson's own search for the indwelling consciousness, the "god," deep within the self that he seemed to find in *Nature.*

Melville, though, could find no similar redemption. Greylock—like Monadnoc the emblem of the self—reveals the validity of Melville's warning that the mysteries of the self place in mortal danger the "illy prepared" individual who seeks them. One may josh about Greylock in a dedication, but not when the mountain becomes transformed into the deadly "Mount of Titans" that Melville in his guises of Pierre or Enceladus seeks to climb. As Henry A. Murray in his classic edition of *Pierre* notes, the "Mount of Titans" is Greylock transposed.[39] It is also—as Melville writes in the same paragraph where he gives his definition of nature as "that cunning alphabet"—formerly the "Delectable Mountain," the fool's summit seen from the innocence of Saddle Meadows. The problem for Pierre, who now sees more deeply, is that by climbing the mountain he knows that the amaranths growing on it—symbolic of immortality in the contemporary flower lexicon Melville used—in fact represent the lie of immortality. They mock Pierre's whole complex quest, defined at one point by the juxtaposition of two plants: "The catnip [a form of mint, which in floral lexicon is "virtue"] and the amaranth!—man's earthly household peace, and the ever-encroaching appetite for God" (p. 345). This can be a dangerous appetite, as Pierre discovers after casting off from the meadows, from the peacefulness of the self at one with nature, from the unity at Saddle Meadows that was only an illusion. In comprehending this irony, Pierre becomes Enceladus, "wrought by the vigorous hand of Nature's self" (p. 346). The transformations of Pierre to Enceladus and of Greylock to the Mount of Titans represent more than artistic manipulation. They define the "mirror" of Melville's climbing self; they point to a dark myth of man and nature as one. Seen this way, nature does indeed tell the innermost thoughts of man. It becomes vision, separate from birds, stars, trees, or the moon. It is where Emerson and Melville meet at the peaks of Monadnoc and Greylock in moments of self-discovery after having begun in each of the works as fresh children of nature, and having ended within the self, the romantic counterpart to the culminating city of the American journey to nature.

7

The Oceans of America

Exploring Monadnoc and Greylock was akin to seeking the interal region described by Thoreau in *A Week on the Concord and Merrimack Rivers* (1849): "The frontiers are not east or west, north or south; but wherever a man *fronts* a fact,"[1] he writes, transforming the image of America's frontier into a private metaphor. Although any geographical setting potentially was sufficient for encounters with such "facts," the sea, as it has since the time of Odysseus and before, offered a location for mythic explorations of the kind Melville offered in his masterpiece of American literature, *Moby-Dick.*

But the sea—perhaps because the American West was so particularly identified as a "garden"—also gave more popular writers a particularly inviting setting for tales of adventure and suspense, for manly exploits, for rescuings of imperiled ladies. In constructing stories of the sea, writers did not have to worry about the plausibility of Indians as "noble savages" or as demonic incarnations. Cooper, in a setting away from America, could tell his adventure stories without Indians and without the West. From the sea, as Thomas Philbrick has reminded us, Cooper found the material for more than a third of his fiction.[2] As a body of literature, Cooper's tales carried the values and subscribed to the patterns of the "external world" rather than of romantic myth. His fiction owed its allegiance to America's image of nature.

Cooper sends his heroes to an American sea. Their journeys lead to places in "moon nature," and the pattern of their voyages conforms to and draws its basic conditions from America's broad perception of nature as offering material gain in historical time. His novels, flaws and all, offer the best of the genre that America produced. If his tales lacked the slickness that later books and movies would bring to the American sea story, he nevertheless created the genre. He found in American culture an alluring image, and he gave it form, as he did in shaping the legend of the lonesome man in the West with his faithful dark companion. No major writer came close to Cooper in shaping popular American art.

This does not mean that Cooper invented the sea novel. Claiming this, as is often done, perhaps underestimates and distorts his genuine accomplishments. Just as heroes always had faithful companions—as Beowulf had in Wiglaf before Natty took a dark one to his side—heroes had long been at sea. They simply had not been Americanized. Anyone who claims that Cooper invented the sea novel is perfectly aware that Smollett preceded him. The argument is that Smollett's novels are not "truly" sea novels, that they primarily give us tales of manners rather than adventures at sea. It is a fair distinction. But once the differentiation has been made, once Cooper's idea of a sea novel becomes the norm against which the genre is measured, the implications have to be accepted; the conclusion has to be extended further. Melville's sea fiction, since it is obviously not spun from the ship battles and love affairs out of which Cooper weaves his stories, is as different from Cooper's as the latter's is from Smollett's. Cooper certainly did give the sea novel a new and influential form, but he surely did not inspire Melville's exploration of his metaphysical sea. At issue here is not the relatively trivial matter of determining who wrote the first sea novel. Rather, it is a matter of defining two fundamentally different uses of art that happened to employ similar geographical settings and of maintaining the distinction between Cooper's American nature and the "nature" of the romantic quest. Inside the framework of cultural preconceptions, Cooper found within his imaginative range an ideal setting in the sea—a place that conformed to his particular concerns. His real invention was the formula for incorporating America's idea of nature into the conventional European romances, exemplified by Scott, and forming from this amalgam the American sea novel of adventure, action, and financial reward. It was no small accomplishment.

In his impressive number of sea stories, Cooper chose his times and places with remarkable versatility, although he rarely deviated from the imaginative premise of creating a historical moment when a hero finds some gain in nature. His formula is remarkably consistent, and although it is unfair to any artist's achievements to look only at the outlines of his work, I do so here to show the force of America's image of nature on Cooper's art, rather than primarily to make aesthetic judgments. Cooper's sea stories—and in the following sense they are not very different from his land stories—generally present us with an ''archly'' smiling young lady, either eighteen or nineteen years of age, under the care of a guardian male with no wife or a guardian female with no husband. (A slight deviation occurs in *The Two Admirals* [1842], where the ''mother,'' though married, is actually not the true mother). Generally, this girl is an orphan who will find her way onto a ship, have her life threatened by the elements, and be rescued by a supremely honorable hero, who, after having gone to sea, will come home with or to the bride. He also in some way gains wealth. In *The Water Witch* (1830), Alida de Barberie is the woman and Captain Ludlow the man, although another pair—Eudora and Skimmer of the Seas—reject both the land and the financial gain that come to Eudora when she is reunited with her father. Eudora and Skimmer of the Seas represent Cooper's nautical version of the idea, incarnated in Natty Bumppo on land, of aliens from society. *Afloat and Ashore* (1844) and *Miles Wallingford* (1844) stretch one story over two novels and narrate how Miles Wallingford wins Lucy Hardinge subsequent to many adventures Miles has at sea. After much disappointment—including disaster at sea, the unfounded idea that Lucy might love someone else, and the demise of Grace Wallingford in what may be the longest death scene in the history of fiction, extending as it does over two novels—Miles wins Lucy and a fortune. Cooper works his theme well. The depiction of Grace's death would not embarrass Dickens, and the deceptive natives who attack the hero's ship in *Afloat and Ashore* give us quite as much adventure as Poe did in the fascinatingly similar situation in *Pym,* from which Cooper may have taken the idea. Leaving his happy childhood at Clawbonny with his darling Lucy and his darling sister Grace (did Melville parody this in *Pierre?*), Miles Wallingford sets out upon the world, finds its rewards, and completes the circle to his ancestral home, to bride and wealth. The journey to nature has brought the hero to the reward of civilization.

Neither the time nor the place chosen by Cooper changes this basic strategy. He tells it in *Mercedes of Castile* (1840), where the formula yields nothing less than the discovery of America, as the love affair between Luis de Bobadilla and Mercedes de Valverde actually precipitates the journey of Columbus, who is even present at the wedding of these lovers. *The Two Admirals,* set in the mid-eighteenth century, though yielding less than America, brings marriage and wealth to young lovers, along with the usual sea battles. All the plots do not bear repetition, but the formula is likewise at work in *Red Rover* (mid-eighteenth century to the American Revolution), *Jack Tier* (1848, Mexican War), and *The Pilot* (1823, American Revolution). The only significant departure from the basic strategy appears in *The Wing-and-Wing* (1843), set in the Napoleonic era. The hero, Raoul Yvard, dies without marrying the heroine, a nineteen-year-old virgin named Ghita Caraccioli, who becomes eighteen as the novel progresses. Aside from its deviation from the formula, *The Wing-and-Wing* commands attention as one of Cooper's favorite books among those he had written. While Cooper may not have been fair to his own talents in this judgment of the novel, he seems even more deter-

mined in his moralizing than usual; he is intensely concerned
with the problem before him. The story insists that in a world of
conflicting theological ideologies human beings can find
themselves in moral confrontations that are finally unsolvable.
The bridge between the rational Yvard, child of the French
Revolution, and the Catholic Ghita Caraccioli is uncrossable—even
by love. Therefore Yvard dies, and Ghita goes to a convent. But
even in this story, Cooper does not abandon entirely the idea of
gain, since in his dying moment Yvard finds God, although not in
Ghita's Catholic Church nor in the Anglican one Cooper favors.
However, since finding God is the greatest reward that the book
describes, the story keeps faith with the idea that the sea brings
gain. Even in *Ned Myers* (1843), the ostensibly true story
''edited'' by Cooper, the hero, after many decadent years at sea,
emerges to find Christ. Gain from the sea journey, generally
material, though in a few cases religious, is absolutely predictable
in Cooper's world.

Another motif in Cooper's sea stories may have some bearing
on what our beliefs about Natty Bumppo ought to be. This is the
death of old men, a recurring event that should be taken into account when considering the implication of Natty's moving death
scene in *The Prairie*. The sadness evoked may not be entirely
because of the end of the frontier or the end of a much-loved individual. Old men die regularly in Cooper's sea stories. *The Two
Admirals, The Red Rover, Jack Tier, The Water Witch, The
Pilot,* and *Miles Wallingford* present, respectively, and with varying degrees of sentimental effectiveness, the deaths of Admirals
Bluewater and Oaks, the Rover, Stephen Spike, Ben Trysail, Colonel Howard and Tom Coffin, and Moses Marble. Included in
this list are the good and the bad, though the tendency in the
deaths of Cooper's old men is for them to share in religious unor-
thodoxy. If the recurrence of these deaths merely represents an
artist's bid to win his audience with tears, then we may have
made some bad assumptions in defining Natty's death primarily
as symbolic of the passing frontier. While this traditional judg-

ment may not necessarily require revision, another aspect of Cooper's thinking must appear in the equation. The death of Natty draws part of its power from Cooper's relentless insistence upon the inexorability of time and history. The young lovers, who witness the many deaths of old men in Cooper's fictional world—and Cooper usually insists that they observe these deaths—are characters in the same linear world, married not merely to themselves but also to history. Thus, America's public triumphs in the Leatherstocking series and the small triumphs of private loves are consummated with a memento mori. Cooper was a moralist infatuated with this message, which very well may explain why he thought so highly of *The Wing-and-Wing*. There, in bringing death even to the young hero, he makes little concession to happy endings. Yvard's death has a message, as Natty's does, but like Yvard's death, the Leatherstocking's may not have been most importantly tied to a local event. Rather, the larger implication may have been a lesson in historical necessity. This is a potentially tragic theme, although Cooper does not quite fit it into that mode, partly because of his artistic limitations and partly because he always affirms that God takes care of good people. Accordingly, though the sea has much to do with death, in Cooper's fiction the old men who remind us of our own mortality finally belong to the benign and reassuring province of God, as does Natty and the land he inhabits. Cooper's sea always holds this assumption, which is one reason why he could participate so easily in America's temporal journey into nature rather than the one others were seeking with less certainty about the God—or the "good man"—Cooper always knew was there.

The formula of the sea that Cooper had worked for so many years finally came to its conclusion in 1849 with the publication of *The Sea Lions,* a book which ironically appeared in the same year that Melville in *Mardi* sent Taji on the quest for redemption. In a sense, both writers were discovering the possibilities of symbolism, although for Melville it was a beginning while for Cooper the end was near. Since the basic symbolic structure of *The Sea*

Lions has been explained by Thomas Philbrick, there is no need here to repeat his excellent analysis.[3] However, the extent to which this most ambitious of Cooper's sea novels fits into his enduring conformity to America's image of nature requires some examination. For whereas Cooper offered in *The Sea Lions* a more imaginative literary technique than he had used before, his use of symbols remains directed at his old formula: nature is part of the historical process where men of this world find either their wealth or Cooper's God—whose existence is never in doubt—and return enriched to civilization. Cooper's symbolic adventure, rooted in his firm knowledge that divine blessings are always available to the person who subordinates his will to God's, tells a story radically different in its rationale from Taji's less certain enterprise.

Since Cooper knew God was in heaven, and since he knew His will, *The Sea Lions,* in conveying this information to the reader, emerges as unabashedly polemical, its premise finely articulated in the preface:

> In this period of the world, in enlightened countries, and in the absence of direct idolatry, few men are so hardy as to deny the existence and might of a Supreme Being; but, this fact admitted, how few really feel that profound reverence for him that the nature of our relations justly demands! It is the want of a due sense of humility, and a sad misconception of what we are, and for what we were created, that misleads us in the due estimate of our own insignificance, as compared with the majesty of God.[4]

The "insignificance" of man that Cooper insists upon throughout the novel is the antithesis of Taji's "insignificance" in a world threatening to be meaningless. Cooper's sailors who find themselves adrift in the sea have only to reach for the sure rudder of God. Their earthly home, Cooper's primary fictional concern, belongs to the very Serenia that emerges as the land of Sirens for Melville's questing hero. Unlike Taji, Cooper's hero, Roswell Gardiner, is finally humbled, and if chronology did not make the idea impossible, one could almost call it self-evident that Cooper and Melville were responding to each other in their novels of 1849. What *is* chronologically possible, however, is that Cooper had in mind the Emersonian notion of man's limitless possibilities. This was an idea that Cooper severely attacked, although he did so in the specific context of rationalism rather than of transcendentalism. "We hear a great deal," Cooper writes "of god-like minds, and of the far-reaching faculties we possess; and it may all be worthy of our eulogiums, until we compare ourselves in these, as in other particulars, with Him who produced them. Then, indeed, the utter insignificance of our means becomes too apparent to admit of a cavil."⁵ How Roswell Gardiner comes to accept Cooper's truism by relinquishing reason for a faith strongly bolstered by right reason is the religious story Cooper tells.

At first, Gardiner's commitment to reason prevents him from accepting Christ as the Son of God. The woman Gardiner loves is Cooper's standard virgin, although this time given the special name Mary and born of a man called Israel. She will have Roswell as a husband only if he accepts Christ. With this premise, Roswell Gardiner goes on his sealing trip to the Antarctic, has some bad times, but armed with his Bible given to him by Mary and having had selected passages prepared for him by her, he finds the true Christ. He is aided in his task by the wisdom of one Stephen Stimpson, like Tom Coffin in *The Pilot,* a sea-going Natty Bumppo of simple faith, marvelous American skill, and unerring judgment. With these advantages Gardiner finds the true God, brings home a fair prize in cash value, marries Mary—who brings a much larger price—and finally settles down at a wheat mill in the "el dorado of the west" (p. 490). Cooper has sent his hero on the American journey to nature and civilization, and it would almost defy the wits of man to write a book more in conformity with the cultural faith in nature as the giver of tangible gifts.

I specifically say "tangible" because, for all its polemics against material attachments to this world, Cooper's story ultimately endorses their value. Cooper's polemics against materialism, to put it bluntly, are profoundly at odds with the values presented in *The Sea Lions,* as the ring of hypocrisy sounds through his novel. Cooper's own commitment to things of this world persistently intrudes into his attack on materialism and undermines his stated theological intentions. Yet the possibility for subordinating man and his material possessions to the providence of God surely arises in the awesome scenes—moments of what were then called ''the sublime''—that confront the reader with lyric invitations to redefine one's place in the universe, as, for example, in the following passage:

> The ocean has many of the aspects of eternity, and often disposes mariners to regard their fellow-creatures with an expansiveness of feeling suited to their common situations. Its vastness reminds them of the time that has neither beginning nor end; its ceaseless movement, of the never-tiring impulses of human passions; and its accidents and dangers, of the Providence which protects all alike, and which alone prevents our being abandoned to the dominion of chance. (Pp. 137-38)

In such a world, the subordination of the self, of one's material interests, to the all-consuming embrace of God becomes the highest ideal—Taji's refusal to submit, the worst of sins. Gardiner, of course, does submit, but if God wants him to marry Mary Pratt and get rich, why then who should question His will? In the context of Cooper's story this thought is not in itself at odds with the message, even in the face of vitriolic attacks on the love of wealth. But Cooper gives the game away, ironically, in his angriest attacks on greedy mankind. For Cooper's quarrel, as we know, or should know, was not with wealth but with usurpers who wanted to take away a man's justly accumulated possessions. In Cooper's sermon on Roswell Gardiner as a kind of modern allegorical figure led by the hand of Stephen Stimpson, who, as it were, plays Virgil to Cooper's Dante in the pilgrimage toward Christ and Mary Pratt, the author finds time to attack the rent strikers (p. 291), the injudicious ways that judges settle wills (pp. 329-30), and the nasty New York State laws that divide estates with methods and outcomes so outrageous to his monetary sensibility that he proclaims that America is headed toward the fiscal decadence of Turkey—Cooper's example of the worst of financial worlds (pp. 461, 484). He makes it hard to keep one's mind on Christ. One misses the "expansiveness of feeling."

More is at stake here than Cooper's artistic problems, for in his country God and money had much to do with each other. To tell a good story of one in an American context could very well be to tell a good story of the other, and Cooper did this well in *The Sea Lions*. He kept faith with a national trinity of money, God, and nature. Although Mary Pratt certainly does not have a greedy bone in her, as with most of Cooper's women, she does not have a human one either. Roswell Gardiner, however, whose quest carries the novel's message, risks his life for wealth—which he would have gained only in moderation, if at all, had he not found Christ on the journey to nature. By accepting Christ he survives the voyage, wins Mary, and becomes a wealthy man. All the advantages were with accepting Christ, and though Gardiner did not pursue God with that cynicism, the linking of nature's bounty, God's blessing, and Mary's board and bed were all part of the same event.

By coincidence or otherwise, this last of Cooper's sea novels, appearing in 1849, was reviewed by Melville, who, as we recall, published *Mardi* that same year. Although Melville's review seemed to be a favorable one, in 1849 he was already a master of the ambiguity and rhetorical equivocation we associate with his best works and that require us to approach his praise of Cooper's novel with care. At the outset, Melville gives Cooper some well-earned appreciation for "the grandeur of many of the scenes here depicted."[6] He also describes with reasonable objectivity the adventurous aspects of the book, and he ends his review with the assertion that "upon the whole, we warmly recommend the Sea Lions." Indeed, Melville even defends Cooper, who was then so embroiled in his public controversies—in financial, legal, and political quarrels—that "fashion's sake," as Melville puts it, leads many to turn against Cooper. Not that Melville takes a position here on any of the controversies. He simply says that even those who are unfriendly to Cooper, "will in this last work [*The Sea Lions*], perhaps, recognize one of his "happiest" literary efforts. It is all very nice praise until one thinks about what Melville has applauded, or what he has not. For although Cooper himself affirmed the book to be primarily about the struggle for Roswell Gardiner's religious self-definition, Melville defines the whole enterprise of converting Gardiner as "one of the subordinate parts of the book." And of that sea-going Natty Bumppo, whose pieties Cooper lavishly served to the reader, Melville offers this memorable analysis:

> Then we have one Stimpson, an old Kennebunk boatsteerer, and Professor of Theology, who, wintering on an iceberg, discourses most unctuously upon various dogmas. This honest old worthy may possibly be recognized for an old acquaintance by the readers of Cooper's novels. But who would have dreamt of his turning up at the South Pole?

No doubt Melville had Natty Bumppo in mind, although he seems to aim at Cooper himself. But the richest equivocation is reserved for the love story, the religious intentions of which Melville burlesques. "Mary," he writes, at first with apparent praise for the lady, "we love for a fine example of womanly affection, earnestness, and constancy." By itself this is probably a nice thing to say, although the flattery slips away as Melville defines the quid pro quo whereby Gardiner gets Mary in return for accepting Christ. "And as the reader will perceive," Melville observes, "the moist, rosy hand of our Mary is the reward of his orthodoxy. Somewhat in the pleasant spirit of the Mahometan, this; who rewards all the believers with a houri,"—which is really what Cooper's book tells us, although it is surely not the sermon he tries to preach. Having thus praised Cooper, Melville concludes the review with his defense of Cooper against those who were attacking "our national novelist."

What remains is a review that applauds the book in general while gently mocking its most important premises. In the year of

Mardi, Melville knew the difficulties of a religious quest; he understood how different the oceans Taji sailed were from the ones used by the ''national novelist'' in a book that on its own terms was indeed worthy of some kind words and surely superior to writings by other authors who also imposed America's special vision of nature upon the sea.

This became a common vision. Joseph C. Hart, for example, perhaps to the astonishment of no one, opens his *Miriam Coffin, or the Whale-Fisherman* (1834) with a panegyric to the commercial potential of the Mississippi Valley, even though this story touches on that region only in its premise that ''the men of America are devoted to business.''[7] *Mocha Dick* (1839), like *Miriam Coffin* a source for *Moby-Dick,* concludes with a ditty celebrating the skill of Yankee whalemen and with a tribute to their unprecedented commercial success.[8] *Symzonia* (1820) takes the narrator to a utopian world in the South Pole where acquisitiveness is not part of the social order. Even as he lauds this ideal society, the narrator steals some pearls and vows to keep the existence of the newly discovered world a secret in the hope that his future opportunities for commercial exploitation will not be threatened.[9] Joseph Holt Ingraham's *Lady of the Gulf: A Romance of the City and the Seas,* which appeared a few years before *Moby-Dick,* tells of a young man, Harry Hastings, who, like Ishmael, goes to sea as an alternative to suicide. Happily, he finds adventure, beautiful women, marriage, wealth, and of course, civilization. The pattern of this American journey, whether followed by Cooper or his lesser contemporaries, remained relatively constant.

Employing this basic pattern—although turning it to his own ends—Melville fashioned *Moby-Dick.* In its outline the formula is obvious enough. Like Harry Hastings, Melville's hero substitutes a sea journey for suicide and embarks on a ship preparing for an ostensible commercial voyage. Although the enterprise fails to achieve this purpose, as it atypically failed in *Miriam Coffin,* the hero returns to the world of civilization, represented by the *Rachel.* To the extent that Melville followed this pattern he was ''implicated'' in his country's history, in its assumptions about the sea. To the extent that he shaped his art into the mythic form in which the book emerged he escaped that history to explore a region where the self-reliant man casts off the restraints of society and seeks new categories of understanding.

The Emersonian phrase, *self-reliant,* has long been applied to Melville by perceptive critics. Stephen Whicher drew the fine comparison with Emerson's idea when he wrote that ''Melville was to create the archetype of such radical self-reliance in the fated voyage of the Pequod and its ungodly Godlike captain against the White Whale.''[10] Although Melville did not write *Moby-Dick* to test Emerson's theory of the universe, he certainly projected upon nature the idea that in some way it might dissolve the internal disorders of his questing hero Ishmael. In its manifestation as the sea, nature defined another order of being or knowing into which the hero might journey, as he did in the archipelago of *Mardi,* and as he would in the holy land of *Clarel,* or in the sea of *Billy Budd.* Whether Melville found his answers at the end of his own voyage may be debated elsewhere, but in *Moby-Dick* the hero passes through nature having gained much experience, but without having discovered what lay behind the pasteboard mask Ahab confronted.

For reasons that elude me, some readers of Melville—a dwindling number admittedly—cling to the idea that Ishmael is ''saved,'' that he returns with some cure for the spiritual affliction that sends him to sea in the first place. What that cure is remains a mystery. However, since Ishmael's experience importantly defines the way Melville worked with an Emersonian idea of nature as one of the potential alternatives to a world that otherwise promised only the void, the matter of salvation must be addressed. Certainly, Ishmael seeks it. His purpose in *Moby-Dick* is to enter that aspect of nature called the sea, commit a form of ritual suicide, and return spiritually reborn. Melville has sent his hero to find again the comforting certitude suggested, though not without irony, near the end of *White-Jacket* (1850):

And believe not the hypochondriac dwellers below hatches, who will tell you, with a sneer, that our world-frigate is bound to no final harbor whatever; that our voyage will prove an endless circumnavigation of space. Not so. For how can this world-frigate prove our eventual abiding place, when, upon our first embarkation, as infants in arms, her violent rolling—in after life unperceived—makes every soul of us sea-sick? Does not this show, too, that the very air we here inhale is uncongenial, and only becomes endurable at last through gradual habituation, and that some blessed, placid haven, however remote at present, must be in store for us all?[11]

In such a world orphans apparently come home to their parents, as in Cooper's fiction. The trouble with reading such a resolution into *Moby-Dick*—at least most obviously—is that though it may satisfy some pious longing for a moral, it minimally ignores the very grammar of Ishmael's narrative, as has been pointed out in a significant essay by Ted N. Weissbuch and Bruce Stillians.[12] At an indefinite point in time, *after* the destruction of the *Pequod,* Ishmael is giving an historical account of a past experience. Presumably, if he had been "saved," the spiritual disorders would be matters of history. But this is not the case. The Ishmael who relates the story is *now* in the same state of spiritual disorder described in the first chapter of *Moby-Dick*. Melville is not coy in presenting this fact. "Some years ago," he has Ishmael say, "I thought I would sail about a little and see the watery part of the world," but in the passage where Ishmael's ritual suicide is suggested Melville lets us know that the disorders remain. Going to sea for Ishmael

is a way I *have* of driving off the spleen. . . .Whenever I *find* myself growing grim about the mouth; whenever it *is* a damp, drizzly November in my soul; whenever I *find* myself involuntarily pausing before coffin warehouses, and bringing up the rear of every funeral I *meet*. . .then, I account it high time to get to sea as soon as I *can.* This *is* my substitute for pistol and ball.[13] (My italics)

In view of such observations by Ishmael *after* the destruction of the *Pequod,* the most that one could reasonably argue would be that if some form of salvation had occurred, its conditions were only transient. Yet Ishmael obviously seeks more than a respite from some temporarily disturbing malady. He pursues that "final harbor" described in *White-Jacket,* the redemptive place beyond Thoreau's moon. This is a place not to be found in *Moby-Dick.* We know it from the beginning, since the Ishmael who has lived to tell about the experience responds to the sea in precisely the same way as did the Ishmael who "some years ago" went on a particular journey. The experience is circular. Ishmael, with his "hypos," has become that very "hypochondriac" described by Melville in *White-Jacket;* the denial in that novel "that our voyage will prove an endless circumnavigation of space" becomes the affirmation of *Moby-Dick.* Because Ishmael's experience is circular, his comparison at the end of the novel with Ixion is chillingly appropriate. With no real way back from his empty state, Ishmael goes round and round in his hell, as Ixion had.

The failure of Ishmael to achieve anything in nature other than the possibility of trying again is presented to the reader in a world no less dream-like than the allegorical region of *Mardi,* which Melville had conjured a few years earlier. Thus, like those who accompany Taji, the crew of the *Pequod* may be understood as the sum total of Ishmael's psychological alternatives, from the hopelessly Promethean Ahab to the ineptly submissive Starbuck. In *Moby-Dick* these aspects of possibility are subsumed under the pervasive metaphor of man as an orphan in the universe. Ishmael does not merely represent one spiritual orphan picked up by the wrong mother at the end of his sea journey. All of us, Melville is saying, are Ixions turning in the circles of cosmic mystery; all of us are unable to find repose with that divine source cast in parental metaphors. Melville almost seems to be writing a reply to the apparent promise offered in *White-Jacket,* since in *Moby-Dick* the "hypochondriac" is now to be believed after all. Thus, in the "Gilder" chapter, Melville writes:

There is no steady unretracing progress in this life; we do not advance through fixed gradations, and at the last one pause:—through infancy's unconscious spell, boyhood's thoughtless faith, adolescence' doubt (the common doom), then skepticism, then disbelief, resting at last in manhood's pondering repose of If. But once gone through, we trace the round again; and are infants, boys, and men, and Ifs eternally. Where lies the final harbor, whence we unmoor no more? In what rapt ether sails the world, of which the weariest will never weary? Where is the foundling's father hidden? Our souls are like those orphans whose unwedded mothers die in bearing them: the secret of our paternity lies in their grave, and we must there to learn it. (Pp. 486-87)[14]

This is the voice of one who remains as cut off from his "parents" as Adam from his Father.

The journey in *Moby-Dick* is in part depicted within this idea of parental metaphor—a search for parentage that should indeed lead to rebirth and salvation. But Ishmael is an orphan. And instead of leading him to divine parentage, the voyage takes Ishmael on a journey, significantly marked by nine gams, that almost parodies the idea of spiritual rebirth. The ninth gam is the grotesque encounter with the *Delight,* whose appearance had been prefigured in the crucial speech of Father Mapple:

Delight,—top-gallant delight is to him, who acknowledges no law or lord, but the Lord his God, and is only a patriot to heaven. Delight is to him, whom all the waves of the billows of the seas of the boisterous mob can never shake from this sure Keel of the Ages. And eternal delight and deliciousness will be his, who coming to lay him down, can say with his final breath—O Father! (P. 48)

With the appearance of the *Delight,* juxtaposed in the reader's mind against this sermon by Father Mapple, one sees clearly enough the ironic direction of Ishmael's quest. Unlike Father Mapple's ideal spiritual journeyer, Ishmael cannot "say with his final breath—O Father!" The last word of the novel is "orphan," the very condition of Ishmael at "the beginning," "middle," or "end" of the spiritual center around which he turns. The last scene of the novel, though not of Ishmael's circular journey, is of Ixion's wheel giving birth only to a lost orphan clinging to a coffin, as the old man would one day in *The Confidence-Man* cling to his "life-preserver." And as Ishmael clings to this thing of death, the *Rachel* closes in to take aboard the child who is not hers. The implicit evocation of the biblical Rachel sets the final mood of *Moby-Dick:*

> A voice was heard in Ramah, lamentation, and bitter weeping; Rahel weeping for her children refused to be comforted for her children, because they were not. (Jeremiah 31:15)

Nor was Melville comforted, as he remained a resident of the "step-mother world" that Ahab for a moment felt would at last embrace him. "That glad, happy air," says Melville of Ahab in the "Symphony" chapter, where the masculine and the feminine in the universe seem to unite for a passing moment, "that winsome sky, did at last stroke and caress him; the step-mother world, so long cruel—forbidding—now threw affectionate arms round his stubborn neck, and did seem to joyously sob over him, as if over one, that however wilful and erring, she could yet find it in her heart to save and to bless" (pp. 533-34). In this chapter, the last before the three-day chase of the white whale, "the feminine air" joins with "the masculine sea" (p. 533) in the cosmic marriage of unity in nature. One might even call it an "occasional and transient moment." But it passes swiftly, and Ahab goes to his doom.

The failure of *Moby-Dick* to sustain this union is not an artistic flaw. By denying Ishmael or Ahab or anyone the symbolic union with the divine parents, Melville defines his nature as a place that does not yield spiritual renewal or understanding. The monstrousness of nature is stronger than the Promethean side of Ishmael's (Melville's) consciousness—Ahab—which attempts to slay it in the symbolic embodiment of a whale. Thus, *Moby-Dick* is not to be understood as a novel that pits man against God, or even against "God's great, unflattering laureate, Nature" (p. 187, "moon nature"), but rather as a novel where the sea and nature generally exist as the symbolic region where matters of private consciousness can be revealed. Understood in the Emersonian vision, the monsters and storms are all within. The "sea" is in Melville before he gets there, just as a decade later the forest of "Walking" is in Thoreau before he reaches it. At the same time Melville holds to the belief in an external force—generally malign—just as Emerson too held his belief in an ulterior force, though in his case it was generally benign. But in each instance, the external force—malign or benign—continues to suggest that the "axis of vision is not coincident with the axis of things." Whether this resulted from man's disunity with himself or from conditions stemming from a world wrongly put together, the restoration of a unified vision where the "masculine" and "feminine" in the universe play the music of the spheres, or the "Symphony," remained elusive. The spiritual dislocations presented by Melville in *Moby-Dick* symbolized the disordered world Emerson hoped to rectify when he prophesied in *Nature* that the perfected self would bring harmony into a chaotic world. But the problem of the age, posed by Thoreau, stubbornly remained: "*Who* are we? *where* are we?" In search of an answer to this mystery in a world defined by Emerson as "broken and in heaps," Melville, who we may reasonably assume was "disunited with himself," sent Ishmael on the quest into nature which proved to be quite as "disunited."

Melville's choice of the sea for this particular journey may easily enough be explained in biographical terms. But other reasons also exist. One is that the sea's blankness gave Melville that plentitude of "sea-room" which an author needed "to tell the Truth in,"[15] to reveal perceptions uncluttered by the necessity of conforming to the normal restrictions of historical time and geographical space. Melville also had important historical precedent, since the sea in Western literature, though often a place of monsters and supernatural terrors, was more significantly an imaginative region of redemption. Indeed, historically Melville's story of the whale departs in its dark implications from the brighter ones of other sea narratives extending in time from Homer to Coleridge. The horrors encountered by Odysseus, for example, reflect stages along the way of knowing that culminate in the newborn self emerging from the sea a better man than the one who first set out for Troy. His return to Penelope, to his son, to his father, and to his kingdom after terrifying adventures at sea, symbolizes not only the fulfillment of himself, but, more significantly, the bringing together of an ordered world. The sea often made this promise, as in the Anglo-Saxon poem *Andreas,* where the hero passes through the nightmare world of the sea to accomplish his divine task after a journey where God had been with him. In the Bible itself, whether in the tale of Jonah's salvation by way of the whale's belly, or of Christ on a ship in the Gospel of Mark teaching His disciples, who listen from the land (4:1), or in the Gospel of John where He suddenly appears to them on the sea (6:19), the watery realms are places of redemption. Even where the promise holds less than this, ways of knowing emerge from the sea, as in the case of the Ancient Mariner or the narrator of the poem told long ago, *The Seafarer.* One would be hard put to find basically symbolic or allegorical stories of the sea, at least before the nineteenth century, where heroes return with as little to show for their journeys as Ishmael does.

Although Melville was one of the earliest to bring this historical turn in perception to the sea, he was certainly not alone among the Romantics. Thoreau, for example, found in the sea his vocabulary for retelling the medieval reminder of the worms that will in time pass through caskets to devour our remains. He used a ship for his ''corpse,'' though, and he gave no promise that God would make it all right if we only believed.

> The vessel, though her masts be firm,
> Beneath her copper bears a worm;
> Around the cape, across the line,
> Till fields of ice her course confine;
> It matters not how smooth the breeze,

How shallow or how deep the seas. . . .
Far from New England's blustering shore,
New England's worm her hulk shall bore,
And sink her in the Indian seas,
Twine, wine, and hides, and China teas.[16]

These lines are from a poem by Thoreau in *A Week on the Concord and Merrimack Rivers,* in part written as an elegy to his brother. In a book significantly dependent upon metaphors of time, the medieval postulate of linear movement toward death—though now without God—becomes a warning that the deeply lamented loss of his brother might signify that journeys ended only in geograpical places and that no new myth could finally rescue the romantic creator from history. Nor did the return to an older theology seem to promise much, as Thoreau suggests elsewhere in the book, wryly commenting on a biblical passage. "True," he writes, " 'not a sparrow falleth to the ground without our Heavenly Father's knowledge,' but they do fall, nevertheless." [17] As we all shall fall, he is saying in the poem about one particular voyage that ends in history rather than myth. In this little poem about the "sea," Thoreau, like Melville, finds no redemption in the journey to nature.

Others responded in similar ways. Even such a religious man as John Greenleaf Whittier found in the sea a metaphor for whatever religious doubts he may have harbored. In his poem "Hampton Beach" (1843), Whittier tells the story of a walk to the sea by a troubled individual—Whittier himself, we may assume. On first encountering the waters, he seems to find a happy resolution to the quest:

Ha! like a kind hand on my brow
  Comes this fresh breeze,
Cooling its dull and feverish glow,
  While through my being seems to flow
The breath of a new life, the healing of the seas![18]

The word *seems,* however, is the reader's clue that something else will happen. It does, but only after the poet gives a litany of all the benefits he apparently receives, including an end to "Pain and Care," a triumph over "Time's veil," and the defeat of "all we shrink from now." He even experiences a temporary abandonment of the self, not merely a private removal from a pejoratively described civilization, but a surrender to the universe quite reminiscent of the moment in the "Quarter-Deck" chapter of *Moby-Dick* when Ishmael is almost lulled into losing his identity to a Platonic pantheism. Whittier writes:

> In listless quietude of mind,
>   I yield to all
> The change of cloud and wave and wind;
> And passive on the flood reclined,
> I wander with the waves, and with them
>   rise and fall. (P. 143)

But quite as prudently as Ishmael, or perhaps as undaringly, depending on how one regards the experience, the poet draws back. The sea holds something to which one must after all not surrender the self. It has a "shadow," one at least as dark as that which Emerson seemed to suspect at Monadnoc; it also has a "night-wind" that abruptly warns the poet away. He heeds the advice, returning to the despised civilization he had left in search of the redemptive water. Promising that he will long remember the experience, the poet has nevertheless made it impossible for the reader to forget that the sea's promise is only a siren call, as it is to Ishmael.

The argument here is not that Whittier held Melville's doubts about the certainty and benevolence of God. On the contrary, Whittier's reasonably steady faith allowed his return to civilization and its traditions with relative ease, even after he flirted with dissolving his ego into the universe. His very belief promised him safety from the egolessness to which he momentarily yielded in "Hampton Beach." Melville, on the other hand, was forced to continue the quest, whether in the circularity of Ishmael's journey or in the subsequent stories that played on a similar search. What Whittier did share with Melville in "Hampton Beach" was a rhetorical identification of the sea as a metaphysically threatening place.

Even Whitman, who more than any other romantic writer found in the sea a vocabulary of redemption, equated the sea with death. In "Out of the Cradle Endlessly Rocking" he succeeds in merging the discovery of death with his personal poetic rebirth. This poem belongs with *Nature* or *Walden* as a literary occasion for the triumph of private myth. But its assumption remains based upon the typical romantic association of the sea with death, and in "As I Ebb'd with the Ocean of Life," Whitman gives the other side of what that might mean. Here the poet feels his presumption in supposing that through art he could find meaning. Rather than being the god-man, he resembles more closely Emerson's "cripple":

> I too Paumanok,
> I too have bubbled up, floated the measureless float,
>   and been wash'd on your shores,
> I too am but a trail of drift and debris,
> I too leave little wrecks upon you, you fish-shaped island.[19]

Or perhaps he evokes Melville's Pip in asking the sea to "cry for your castaways."[20] Whatever the reason for what Gay Wilson Allen calls "the morbidity of the 1860 *Leaves*,"[21] Whitman found in the sea his metaphors for a disunited world, whether in the image of men as helpless "drifts" at the "feet" of whatever force moves the universe, as in "As I Ebb'd. . . .," or more bluntly in the poem "Tears," the tone of which is revealed in the title. If his "Sea-Drift" poems vacillate between the poetic apotheosis of "Out of the Cradle" and the near despair of "As I Ebb'd," they all dwell hauntingly on death, on "morbidity."

Why writers as apparently diverse as Melville, Thoreau, Whitman, and Whittier should employ the sea to symbolize their doubts or fears can be explained in various ways, perhaps even by virtue of the simple fact that they lived in a country having some experience with the sea. One did not have to be a metaphysician to know that ships sank there. But when all the obvious explanations have been offered, when the rubric *gothicism* has been dutifully invoked, one still confronts the fact that such rhetorical identifications of the sea were commonplace among our major writers, as well as among minor ones such as Whittier. Indeed, the following equation emerges: the land is life and the sea is death. Such a formula is obviously not absolute or immutable. Doubtlessly, examples exist where the equation is reversed. But generally it holds, since the sea often becomes the metaphysical equivalent of what the wilderness was for America in general— an inimical place that one sought to transform, as Cooper succeeded in doing. But in the mythic realms of the romantic sea, man's art did not triumph as the nation did in the geographical region of America's nature. Among our major writers only Cooper discovered in the sea a genuine and continuing place of gain. Others found doubts about the universe.

Examples abound. Poe's Arthur Gordon Pym has the horrifying vision of being alone in a ''limitless'' world, suggestive of what Melville's Pip experiences in the ''intense concentration of self in the middle of such a heartless immensity.''[22] Emerson tells of how one hurries across the sea, ''as through the valley of the Shadow of Death''; Irving describes how the sea ''severs'' one from the land and sets him ''adrift upon a doubtful world,'' while Richard Henry Dana records ''a feeling of loneliness, of dread, and of melancholy foreboding.''[23] The women in Whittier's ''Skipper Ireson's Ride'' wait for the wrecked ship and look ''for the coming that might not be,''[24] which may imply some momentary doubts going beyond the ''coming'' of a ship. In moments of doubt, death seems to mediate the condition of the sea, as nature becomes for Thoreau ''naked Nature,—inhumanly sincere, wasting no thought on man''; the sea contains for Emerson ''hints of ferocity in the interiors of nature''; while for Hawthorne it emerges as '' 'that wide and nameless sepulchre.' ''[25] So alien was the sea as an idea of regeneration that unlike nature in its traditional feminine role, the sea at times takes a masculine gender, as in the "Symphony" chapter of *Moby-Dick* or even in Richard Henry Dana's *Two Years before the Mast* where "the genius of the place [Cape Horn, which the ship was rounding] had been roused at finding that we had nearly slipped through his fingers, and had come down upon us with tenfold fury."[26] And in a strikingly masculine simile, Thoreau describes the uncontrollable of the sea. "This gentle ocean," he writes, "will toss and tear the rag of a man's body like the father of mad bulls."[27]

Against a temporal shore, the sea of death pushed relentlessly. The "mortally intolerable truth" that Ishmael suggests in the "Lee Shore" chapter appears as a metaphor of the elements pushing ships to destruction against the land. The sea becomes an irresistible force: "No mercy, no power but its own controls it. Panting and snorting like a mad battle steed [cf. Thoreau's "father of mad bulls"] that has lost its rider, the masterless ocean overruns the globe."[28] "The ocean," writes Thoreau, "is a wilderness reaching round the globe, wilder than a Bengal jungle, and fuller of monsters, washing the very wharves of our cities and the gardens of our seaside residences."[29] In this particular "Wildness" one would not find "the preservation of the World."[30] The song from the ocean, "sweetest" though it may be, which comes "Out of the cradle endlessly rocking," is death. One could perhaps come to terms with this, as Whitman did in his poem, or one might mourn it as Poe did in setting his "Annabel Lee" by the watery kingdom. But the equation held. The vast, empty sea offered a perfect metaphorical region for projecting a similar emptiness within.

No convention of the English language, however, required that the sea hold this meaning. For example, a few years before Whittier wrote "Hampton Beach," Frederick Marryat, England's best-known novelist of the sea, had written his *Three Cutters* (1836), a sea-going comedy of manners quite remote from any ideas of redemption or threats to the self. That same year he published his much better known *Midshipman Easy,* an essentially comic tale of the sea. However, when Marryat uncharacteristically turned the sea into a symbolic, metaphysical region, as he did in *The Phantom Ship* (1839)—a novel very important to Melville[31]—he took the Flying Dutchman legend and wove from it a tale of absolute redemption at sea, victory over death, and a restoration of nature's inner harmony. No American writer of the sea turned that region to such purposes, simply because the Romantics did not identify the sea in that way and because others were telling their stories in conformity with the nation's paradigm of the quest into nature for material gain. Such writers could find in the sea a place of adventure, as Marryat did in his *Pirate,* or as Walter Scott had done in his novel of the same title (1822), although as Cooper accurately noted, Scott's novel had very little to do with the sea. The sea might also be the location for such sentimental stories as *The Wreck of the Golden Mary* (1856) by Charles Dickens and Wilkie Collins. Even in this story, where an adorable little girl dies—as they often do when Dickens gets hold of a pen—in the end a kind of resurrection occurs that leaves the sea a much less threatening place than the book at times suggests.

The one major British work that does have an affinity with American romantic uses of the sea is Coleridge's ''Rime of the Ancient Mariner,'' written over a period of many years. Without a discussion of the complex history and meaning of the poem, one may observe simply that however this story of a supernatural journey toward the polar regions of the South is defined, the mariner returns with an insight he lacked before the journey began. Whatever doubts Coleridge may have had about nature were not sufficiently compelling to prevent this ultimate gain that emerges from the poem. But no gain emerges from Arthur Pym's journey to the same polar region.

Poe's story, which perhaps presented as many problems to him as it has to his critics, offers us in the first paragraph of Chapter I the American subject absent from Coleridge's poem—money. As Poe's story proceeds, the hero finds himself involved in a sealing expedition just prior to the final, apocalyptic adventure that leads to the white figure, just as the whaling expedition would lead the

Pequod to its encounter with whiteness.[32] Poe, as Melville would, and as Coleridge obviously did not, was framing his story within the assumptions of American culture. He was sending his hero to sea in a story where financial gain contributes to the structure of the tale, as in *Moby-Dick*, however insignificant it may be thematically. Although Poe did not resort to invocations of the Mississippi Valley, some obeisance to America's idea of nature seemed almost obligatory in *Pym*. But Poe's larger interests in this story were not wedded to a commercial ideal, which brings one to the much stickier problem of just what Poe was attempting in this story, where he assumed the sea to be a place of death, a region where questing heroes find nothing.

Although Poe's religious predilections are somewhat anomalous, many of his tales, as Edward H. Davidson cogently observes, "were ways of making a fractured and dismembered world obtain some form."[33] But Pym could find a resolution no more satisfactory than Ishmael's. Unlike Melville, Poe defines the disordered world through the very chaos of art itself, rather than through a coherent metaphor or orphans and parents. While some readers have quite persuasively argued that the white figure which appears at the end of *Pym* represents a mother image, the story nevertheless does not develop around a coherent maternal metaphor. Rather, the white apparition thrusts itself upon us at the end of a tale, the very disorganizations of which reflect Poe's "fractured and dismembered" perception of the world, his own "axis of vision." The incoherence of the story's ending becomes "logical"—if that word is appropriate—in the context of the sustained chaotic way that the work unfolds. In other words, the structure defines the story's meaning of the impossibility of knowing or finding anything at the journey's end.

Paradoxically, the motif of disorder and chaos holds the story together. This strange formulation begins with the preface, signed "Pym." But the preface is nothing more than a delicious exercise in purposeful distortion. "Pym" credits "Poe" of *The Southern Literary Messenger* with having urged "Pym" to publish his story, which is listed in the *Messenger's* contents

under the name of "Poe" for the purpose of duping the public into believing the story is fiction. However, "Pym" tells us that
the plan backfired, giving as evidence the claim that letters were
sent to Mr. P. ("Poe," we *assume*) indicating that the story was
not received as fiction. "Pym," the reader is told, then decided to
tell the "facts" of his narrative, presumably this very preface, so
that the story could reappear without any danger of the public
doubting the story's *truth;* this, after the elaborate explanation of
how readers saw through the hoax that presented the story as *fiction.* At this point in the preface any logical arrangement of facts
has already ended, a prefiguring of what is to follow. Poe also offers some exquisite double talk on the authorship of the story.
First of all he presents the "real" Poe, who has written the entire
tale, then he gives us a "Poe" in this fiction, who edited the
Messenger, which the "real" Poe did. And he creates "Pym,"
who, having announced that the authorship of the story was his,
proceeds to tell us in the final paragraph of the preface that the
story is only partly his. Lest there be any confusion on this point,
this paragraph of the preface "clarifies" it all:

> This *exposé* being made, it will be seen at once how much of
> what follows I claim to be my own writing; and it will also be
> understood that no fact is mispresented in the first few pages
> which were written by Mr. Poe. Even to those readers who
> have not seen the *Messenger,* it will be unnecessary to point
> out where his portion ends and my own commences; the dif-
> ference in point of style will be readily perceived.[34]

One may only guess how many people fought their way through
that involuted prose, which in its duplicity must surely have been
a labor of love.

Nor did the chaos of authorship end there, since Poe picked it
up again in the "Note' at the end of the story, which is once
more to "clarify" the situation. "Pym," the author tells us, has
died, as everyone has heard by now. We, therefore, cannot have
the final chapters of the story. Moreover, "Poe" will not fill
them in, says the author, since "Poe" does not believe "in the

entire truth of the latter portions of the narration'' (p. 852).
Whereupon the author, who is now neither ''Poe'' nor ''Pym,''
proceeds to demonstrate the accuracy of those ''latter portions''
about the mysterious cave formations and the words they form.
And it all ends with a cryptic quotation, quite biblical in tone,
though not from the Bible at all. We are left to ask who the final
''author'' is, who wrote what part of the story in the elaborate
game called *Pym,* what the biblical-sounding quotation means,
and what we are to make of the world of natives and whiteness
that at last emerges. But most important, we are forced to wonder
whether we can believe *any* internal fact in the story. For Poe's
game goes beyond that of authorship and apparitions, as may be
illustrated in the following example, only one of many that the
careful reader will find in a story that questions the whole concept
of reality and of plausibility in perceived events.

At one point Augustus sends a note to Pym, who is hidden
below the deck. Augustus, writing in blood, of course, sends his
note on the back of the first draft of a forged letter. Happy is the
reader who can go on to follow Poe's adventure tale without pausing to consider that something terribly wrong has happened. For
a few pages earlier, before the ''explanation'' Augustus gives to
Pym as to how the letter was sent, Pym had with great ingenuity
guessed that the paper was a note from Augustus. After finding a
method of reading in the dark ''which seemed rational'' (p. 743),
Pym discovers the paper to be blank. The ''rational'' approach
having failed him, he tears the paper to bits before realizing that
he had examined only one side of it. Nothing is really ''rational''
in this tale that Poe constructs, but Pym continues his
''rational'' approach. With his sometimes faithful dog Tiger he
pieces the letter together, and in the dim light he manages to
catch a fragment of the words, as cryptic to him then as the
''biblical'' inscription is to us at the end. And as Pym is left to
wonder in the darkness what those words mean, the reader is left
to wonder how a piece of paper can have a forged letter on one
side, a note written in blood on the other, and a side that is blank.

Such puzzles run through Poe's story, and they will not be

solved by readings focusing on one organizing image. For example, the apparition at the end may very well be a mother figure,
but we do not find throughout *Pym* the clear language of parentage Melville gives us in *Moby-Dick*. Or, to give another example, the end of the story in part clearly suggests America's South
and its problem of slavery; the natives seem to symbolize, among
other things, the nightmare possibility of slave rebellion. But the
book as a whole is certainly not about slavery or the South or
America. The "answer," unless we are to believe Poe's claim
that the story is simply "silly,"[35] may be that the very incoherence of all these events and authors is a type for the incoherence of the world. The art that defines this particular quest
into nature seems to reflect the incomprehensibility of the world
it seeks to know. And the "biblical" inscription, which is not
from the Bible at all, may give the story's final testimony to the
ambivalence with which this "fractured and dismembered"
writer perceived his world. In the end, even the word upon the
rock is suspect. From that suspicion the Romantics constructed
both sides of their dualistic myth.

8

The Urban Garden

When Cooper's heroes completed their quests at sea and returned
to stability and prosperity—whether in the "el dorado of the
west" where Roswell Gardiner and his bride settled, or in any
other geographical region—readers of the day were seeing in fictional form the logical culmination of a journey to nature. For
Cooper, as for the nation that found him its finest novelist, the
"el dorado" of civilization that emerged for the Roswell Gar-
diners symbolized the fulfillment of a national destiny. As the
travel writers had found the city the culminating expression of
nature, so also did America's "national novelist" suggest in
symbolic form the same outcome.

Writers exploring the region of romantic myth also often
brought the conclusion of their journeys to civilization, or,
sometimes more specifically, to the city. When Thoreau writes of
the "ocean. . .washing the very wharves of our cities and the
gardens of our seaside residences"[1] he evokes an image of the
waters threatening to overwhelm civilization, to flood the
"gardens" America had built. Since Thoreau certainly had no
fears of the ocean literally flooding America, the waters clearly
suggest a symbolic meaning, either of death or of spiritual emptiness. But his concern, which he shared with other Romantics in
their relentless representation of the sea as inimical, was not as
much directed to the spiritual fate of America as to the spiritual
fate of the self. Romantic solutions were private, not collective;

salvation tended to be for the individual, not for the group. In matters of the spirit, the Romantic tended to see himself as alone.

Therefore, when romantic writers appropriated for their own literary ends the image of civilization or the city emerging from nature, they transformed the ''city'' as radically as they transformed ''nature.'' As they had brought the natural world to a representation of the self, so they brought the world made by human hands to a similar signification. Romantic destiny, as well as national destiny, directed itself toward some idea of a city. This image remained the constant center toward which the hero of American culture or of romantic myth gravitated, the place where journeys to sea or journeys to land ultimately concluded.

Before pursuing further the ways in which writers turned a national idea of the city into private myth, I want to emphasize the power of that idea on the ''external world'' of America, since modern preconceptions about the early nineteenth century as anti-urban offer formidable barriers to the recovery of romantic typology in regard to the city. Romantic writers were familiar indeed with the American city that would emerge when Dana's ''scaffold'' fell; they knew the place that could be seen by the penetrating eye of a Willis. The Romantics understood that the culture in which they were ''implicated'' had a deep allegiance to its urban vision.

Although anti-urban rhetoric appears frequently in early nineteenth-century America, the attacks are mainly against the faults of cities rather than against the desirability of their existence. Whether or not America's destiny lay with them was not much of an issue, even though attachments to the old Jeffersonian ideal of a rural America clearly existed. Although evidence of an important urban vision in America is certainly plentiful, a particularly compelling and persuasive example of this vision was presented by one of the great intellectual leaders of the so-called ''agrarian'' South, Thomas Roderick Dew. This brilliant polemicist taught at William and Mary, the very heart of the old South's intellectual life, where one might least expect to find a widely heralded celebration of urban America. Dew is best known to historians as one of the architects of the South's fascinating intellectual defense of slavery, but he was also generally appreciated in his own day as one of the region's leading intellectuals, and, for whatever it may be worth, he was a political hero of Edgar Allan Poe.[2]

In March of 1836, the year of Emerson's *Nature,* when Poe was editor of *The Southern Literary Messenger,* Thomas Dew was too ill to deliver a scheduled speech before the Virginia Historical and Philosophical Society. Accordingly, one G. A. Myers, recording secretary of the society, received instructions to send Dew's address to the *Messenger* for publication. That month, the *Messenger* appeared even later than usual, since the presses literally stopped while Poe and his publisher Thomas White awaited Dew's address, the inclusion of which created the longest issue of the journal that the public had seen. The response to Dew's prepared address, if Poe has given us a fair sample in his Supplements to the April and July issues of the *Messenger,* was laudatory, to say the least. Significantly, most of the uniformly favorable reviews came from Southern journals, where one might expect to find particularly strong sentiment for an agrarian ideal. But in view of the consistent praise lavished upon Dew's essay, the discovery that he passionately lauds cities reflects significantly upon Southern values of his day. The dirtiest word in Dew's lexicon is not *abolitionism,* as one might expect, but *agrarianism.*

Before examining just what Dew said that was so fondly received throughout the South, I want to play fairly with this word *agrarianism,* which was an obscenity in its time and quite comparable to the word *communist* in its disreputable connotations today, or even to the onus it held at the height of American political turmoil in the 1950s. *Agrarianism* carried such offensive connotations that even James Fenimore Cooper attacked it, to give one example, in his satirical *The Monikins* (1835).[3] A particularly incisive definition of *agrarianism* is provided by C. C. Hazewell in an essay appearing in the April 1859 edition of *The Atlantic Monthly.*[4] As did Cooper and Dew, Hazewell passionately believed in private ownership of property as the basis of

American society—indeed, as the "ordinance of God." He was fiercely opposed to "Socialists, Communists, Fourierites, and so forth."' But his fervid principles did not prevent him from calmly understanding that politicians often labeled their opponents with the dirty word *agrarianism,* even though the epithet was rarely deserved. Since agrarianism, as Hazewell himself believed, was a worse sin than atheism because all agrarians were by definition atheists and opposers of private property (atheists at least could believe in private ownership), he would be the last person to defend agrarianism. It stood primarily for redistribution of land, and no believer in private ownership of property could be happy with such a policy. Hazewell, however, as a man with faith in America, minimized the threat, believing that all radical movements—and even non-radical ones—were loosely tagged "agrarian" to discredit them. While holding agrarianism to be a vile notion, he felt certain that it was not nearly as widespread as unscrupulous politicans would have people believe.

One's first reaction to Hazewell's clarification of agrarianism might be to say that Dew, Cooper, or any number of social theorists were attacking a concept that actually had little to do with the idea of an agrarian society. Yet such a reaction leaves open the reasonable question of why people chose the word *agrarian* to define such an odious political idea as land redistribution. Why were the two notions linked, and what does this union reveal about views on a rural America? Perhaps the most important answer is that in spite of the outrageously unfair uses of the word, its identification with an *agrarian* America, as the term is generally understood today, was the actual source of the hostility to it. Although the whole history of agrarianism and its European origins cannot be examined here, the idea probably came to America in its most significant way through Thomas Paine's *Agrarian Justice* (1797). Although Paine's study was not confined to farming, he was saying that if we were to have an agrarian society (here, of course, not in any pejorative sense) land would have to be equitably redistributed. Paine's logic was simple but forceful: there cannot be a nation of farmers unless ordinary people own farms. What he was saying, what Dew and others understood perfectly, was that an agrarian society could not possibly emerge without a continuing redistribution of property. Whether this was true or not is something about which political and economic theorists may debate. But it was believed to be true. Consequently, the attacks on agrarianism, however wildly they may have been employed, were indeed attacks on that very idea of an agrarian America that many theoreticians envisaged at the time of the nation's birth. When Thomas Dew attacked agrarianism (as when Cooper attacked it), he aimed directly at the idea of a basically non-technological, non-commercial, non-urban American society with an agrarian base. In the North and in the South the ideas expressed by Dew on agrarianism—if not always on slavery and governmental structure—were as safely nationalistic as waving a flag.

Dew conceived his essay as a theoretical, massively documented disquisition on the excellences of America's present form of decentralized government, particularly in relation to the furtherance of literature. The vastness of America provided an opportunity for a large population, with all the benefits associated with this and with none of the disadvantages. Geographical space was large enough to prevent isolated despots from stopping the flow of ideas, and technology was sufficiently advanced to link the sprawling nation into the loosely unified sphere necessary for greatness. "The canal and the rail road," writes Dew, invoking some of America's favorite icons, "the steam boat and the steam car, the water power and steam power, constitute in fact the great and characteristic powers of the nineteenth century—they are the mighty civilizers of the age in which we live."[6] Although Dew venerated Jefferson, one scarcely sees the old agrarian dream held prior to his fellow-Virginian's realization that America's destiny lay elsewhere. Dew did not pretend that Jeffersonian agrarianism was a factor in America's future. America's West, in Dew's vision, did not even seem to incorporate a cotton kingdom. Indeed, the models for the West—and for Virginia itself—were to be the industrial, urban centers of the

East. "New York and Pennsylvania," writes Dew, still celebrating railroads, canals, and now also cities, "have already executed works which rival in splendor and grandeur the boasted monuments of Egypt, Rome or China, and far excel them in usefulness and profit." In his utilitarianism a veritable Ben Franklin (at least as we often think of him), Dew went on to affirm that "the states of the south and west too are moving on the same noble career." And "Virginia, the *Old Dominion,* has at last awakened from her inglorious repose, and is pushing forward with vigor her great central improvement, destined soon to pass the Blue Ridge and Alleghany ranges of mountains, and thus to realize the fable of antiquity, which represented the sea-gods as driving their herds to pasture on the mountains" (p. 267). Here was America's technological, commercial vision—shared by Northerners and Southerners—promising fruition in a plethora of urban centers. It is hard to imagine a dream more remote from that perceived by the "agrarians" of the 1930s, some of whom even included Dew as an anti-industrialite hero; so also it is difficult to reconcile our myriad fables of America's supposed anti-urbanism with representative statements such as Dew's. The extent of that urban dream becomes apparent in Dew's cold-eyed recognition of the dangers inherent in cities, even as he insists that they contain our national destiny:

> One certain effect of our great systems of improvement must be the rearing up of large towns throughout our country. I know full well that great cities are cursed with great vices. The worst specimens of the human character, squalid poverty, gorgeous, thoughtless *luxury* [Dew's italics], misery and anxiety, are all to be found in them. But we find, at the same time, the noblest and most virtuous specimens of our race on the same busy, bustling theatre. Mind is here brought into collision with mind—intellect whets up intellect—the energy of one stimulates the energy of another—and thus we find all the great improvements originate here. It is the cities which constitute the great moving power of society; the country population is much more tardy in its action, and thus becomes the regulator of the machinery. [To what a function has the agrarian

ideal descended!] It is the cities which have hurried forward the great revolution of modern times, ''whether for weal or woe.'' It is the cities which have made the great improvements and inventions in mechanics and the arts. It is the great cities which have pushed every department of literature to the highest pitch of perfection. It is the great cities alone which can build up and sustain hospitals, asylums, dispensaries—which can gather together large and splendid libraries, form literary and philosophical associations, assemble together banks of literati, who stimulate and encourage each other. In fine, it is the large cities alone which can rear up and sustain a mere literary class. When there shall arise in this country, *as there surely will* [my italics], some eight or ten cities of the first magnitude, we shall then find the opprobrium which now attaches to us, of having no national literature, wiped away; and there are no doubt some branches of science which we are destined to carry to a pitch of perfection which can be reached no where else. Where, for example, can the great *moral* [my italics], political, and economical sciences be studied so successfuly as here? (P. 267)

But a reptile lurks in the urban garden, and Dew vigorously warns his audience to beware of ''the deadly crocodile'' called ''agrarianism'' (p. 276). As I have indicated, although Dew attacks agrarianism at length, nothing in his essay explicitly links it with rural society. Moreover, the specific threat of agrarianism—the redistribution of property—was urban as well as rural. Therefore, in calling attention to the widespread hostility toward agrarianism that Dew invoked, I do so with the emphasis on implicit connotations, with the lesson in mind taught by linguists, historians, anthropologists, and theologians alike: this lesson is the sheer power of *words* themselves. No society committed to an agrarian ideal will choose the word *agrarianism* as one of its most pejorative terms. The Dews, the Hazewells, the Coopers, and indeed those politicians described by Cooper as using agrarianism—along with other epithets—''to throw dirt at all opposed to them,''[7] scarcely would choose the national ideal as the label for tagging opponents and wooing constituents in the electorate. However sacred some old idea of agrarianism may have remained in America, even the South had placed above it an urban dream.

Dew's essay holds little else of importance, unless one has not encountered the pro-slavery rationale he and others formulated. Having assured his audience that "the frame work of our southern society is better calculated to ward off the evils of this agrarian spirit, which is so destructive to morals, to mind and to liberty, than any other mentioned in the annals of history" (p. 277) he proceeded to show why the institution of slavery offered the best defense against agrarianism. Dew's case need not be repeated here, since his defense of slavery may be found in any modern study of the subject. Yet one point remains to be emphasized. The hostility to agrarianism was not a euphemism for hostility to abolitionism. The threat of agrarianism had been felt in Europe and in the North, and the idea had been fully castigated in both places. Dew's defense of slavery at the end of this essay, moreover, was certainly not directed merely to members of the Virginia Historical Society. By tying the institution of slavery to a defense against agrarianism, Dew was telling the Northern propertied classes the South's way of handling a common enemy. Dew's strategy goes a long way toward explaining why the essay made such a stir, since Southern praise of cities in itself was so commonplace. That Dew's point at least found a forum in the nation's capital is clear from the appearance there of the portion of his essay on slavery as a defense against agrarianism in Duff Green's Washington newspaper, the *United States Telegraph* (April 6, 1836).

But pursuing further this tangled story of agrarianism and slavery moves us too far from what is most significant here in Dew's essay—its definition of the city as the fulfillment of America's destiny. Out of the vast region of inimical, uncultivated nature would emerge the flower of the city. Strained though this metaphor may seem, it defines the imaginative place of the city, or any commercial complex, in nineteenth-century American thought. Whitman, for example, could take this cultural metaphor for granted when making his poetic promise that "Through the new garden the West, the great cities calling," he would, as the "chanter of Adamic songs," present his offering.[8] Although most people never quite comprehended Whitman the mystic, they knew that cities grew in "gardens." The equation between the city and the journey to nature was so widely accepted that in 1832 James Kirke Paulding found it a subject for satire. In his *Westward Ho!* the new settlement is named Dangerfieldville because Colonel Dangerfield "had followed the fashion of the west, where, if a man has a name as long as that of Aldibirontiphoskiphornio, it goes hard but he will tack a *ville* to its tail when he lays the foundation of a city which is to become the great mart of the western world."[9] Cities were indeed arising in the West, and in perceiving their flowering from nature a writer could say without fear of ridicule, as Robert Montgomery Bird says in *Peter Pilgrim* (1838), that "as if magic ruled the day, as soon as an oak falls to the ground, a city sprouts up from its roots."[10]

Bird's metaphor represents more than American boosterism. The cities that were "springing up on all sides as if by magic," in the words of Michael Chevalier in 1839,[11] symbolically represented the promise made to America that nature would complete its transformation. Thomas Farnham made perfect sense to his contemporaries in 1841 when he observed that "government" (by which he meant white civilization imposing its will on the Indian) gave more happiness than man "could enjoy in the *natural* state," [my italics] a fact that was "the ordination of nature."[12] Or, as the case had been more directly stated as far back as 1793 by Judge Nathaniel Chipman, civilization is man's "ultimate state of nature."[13] The city, civilization's ultimate form, might very well be described as the grotesque environment found in the familiar comments about urban horror, or it might be defined as Elisha Ayers described Washington in 1847:

Here shall wealth, and power, and empire, fix their home—
Give thee unbounded sway, and make government and commerce
thy own.[14]

Or it might be the utopian place of Cooper's *Crater* (1847), albeit a utopia in danger of sinking if poorly managed. But however they might appear in the myriad visions of them, the cities of America were to be the inevitable flowering of nature. And more often than not, the flowering of the city appeared as a happy event for Americans not yet seriously concerned with the warnings about conservation suggested, for example, by Cooper in his *Pioneers,* or more directly and deeply by George Marsh in America's first important ecological treatise, *Man and Nature* (1864). The sinking of Cooper's utopia in *The Crater,* or nature overrunning civilization in Cole's ''Course of Empire'' (1836) may have represented actual fears, but such concerns remained peripheral, particularly those written by Marsh about America's abuse of its environment.

Indeed, ironically enough, before Marsh's classic work began to change environmental premises, one of the particular blessings America saw in its destruction of the wilderness was the emergence of the city as a generally invulnerable haven. Cities springing from the wilderness literally and symbolically represented the security gained over the hostile forces in the wilderness, whether manifested by ''savages'' or by ''miasma.'' We have to remind ourselves that to be safe from air pollution in the nineteenth century, according to the conventional wisdom of the day, one looked to the city for security. There, those deadly ill-nessess stemming from ''miasma'' were remote, since the diseases were thought to come from the vegetation of the wilderness (although some people really did suspect mosquitoes, even before Dr. Reed's famous studies). Not even the occasional plagues in cities held the consistent threat that ''miasma'' did. All Americans could appreciate the utopian feature Cooper gives his island paradise in *The Crater.* ''There were no exhalations from decayed vegetable substances or stagnant pools, to create miasma, but the air was as pure and little to be feared under a placid moon as under a noon-day sun.''[15] Just as it was in the fairy-tale region of Natty Bumppo's West, in the place where one did not have to assume about the wilderness—as some people actually did—that rotting wilderness caused earthquakes as well as disease.[16] And if one adds to such concerns the potential insecurity about natural phenomena that might be expected in a society whose founders came from Europe's relatively controlled environment to a vast, unknown place, it is not at all surprising that some special attachment to the material comforts associated with urban living would emerge. One struggled for ordinary creature comforts in a way understandably accentuated by the special circumstances of America's emergence. This almost obsessive concern for material comfort was readily observed by various travelers to America, most notably Tocqueville:

> In America the passion for physical well-being is not always exclusive, but it is general; and if all do not feel it in the same manner, yet it is felt by all. Carefully to satisfy all, even the least wants of the body, and to provide the little conveniences of life, is uppermost in every mind. . . .The love of well-being is now become the predominant taste of the nation. . . .[17]

Clearly, places other than cities could fulfill the desires Tocqueville observed and that are so easily recognizable today. While comely farms or scrubbed villages could do as well, in nineteenth-century America this ideal of material comfort took its fullest form in the ultimate transformation of nature—the city. America had other ideal locations, but the city remained a central one. Symbolically, the city of nineteenth-century America was the descendant of what Catherine Sedgwick had called, in reference to the first settlements, "illuminated spots, clear and bright lights, set on the borders of a dark and turbulent wilderness."[18] This puritan dichotomy of light and darkness representing civilization and wilderness never quite deserted America. What changed was the feeling that whatever remained of demonism in nature would yield before the emerging "illuminated spots" that came to be the cities. And from this deeply felt imaginative relationship came one fictional portrayal after another manifesting the hero's discovery of wonderful things in nature, accompanied by the relentless insistence on a return to the city where the fruits of triumph could be enjoyed.

As early as Charles Brockden Brown's *Arthur Mervyn* (1799) this formulation appears. For all the grotesqueness of Philadelphia, for all the innocence and joy to be found with the country girl Eliza and her rural environment, Brown's hero chooses a destiny in the city, plagues and all. But the complexities of Brown's novel, which will not be reduced to a simple city versus country motif, and Brown's relative obscurity in his time, make his work less than an ideal example for illustrating the ways in which fiction might follow an American pattern of the city emerging from nature. Far more suitable is William Starbuck Mayo's *Kaloolah* (1849), largely because of the artistic simplicity of the story and the enormous popularity of the novel, pandering as it did to some of America's fondest imaginings and deepest aspirations.

Kaloolah contains a feast of cultural myths. Perry Miller, for example, in his great service of bringing this forgotten book to our attention, cites it as being ''suffused'' with ''the religion of Nature,'' and places it in evidence as a cultural document supporting the theory that America had a widespread ''cult of Nature.''[19] Although Professor Miller seems to have overstated the case by calling the work ''suffused'' with some theology of ''Nature,'' he accurately points to the central celebration of nature appearing at the beginning of *Kaloolah*. The hero, Jonathan Romer, tells how,

> Often stretched at length upon the sunny bank of the most beautiful trout stream in the world, or seated upon some prostrate giant of the forest, I have turned with shuddering and loathing from the sight and sounds of the distant village, and have felt borne to my innermost soul the conviction that cant and rant are utterly inconsistent with the true worship of God. How soft, and low, and calm, yet deep and full of meaning and power are the hymns sung to His praise in the great temple of nature.[20]

Such a panegyric is familiar enough, although few stories are more in need of D. H. Lawrence's dictum: ''Never trust the artist. Trust the tale."[21] Mayo gave his obligatory chant to nature in the way Dwight or Flint gave it before getting on with their business, and then he wrote a novel richly defining the city in America as the fruition of nature, the city as the wonderful place Thomas Dew assumed it to be.

Kaloolah is about young Romer, immodestly described by himself as mentally and physically superb. Implausible as it may seem, he is even more a superman than Natty Bumppo, although like his more illustrious predecessor, Romer's individualism never denies society's legitimacy and his conquests in nature are tangible ones. In the course of his adventure he falls in with a slave ship, and after reaching the Congo he spots some naked slaves. One is a white woman. As frogs in fairy tales are in reality princes, this white pearl among black savages is indeed a princess and even looks like one after she is cleaned up and dressed. Enough of a hero to recognize the light in the darkness, Jonathan Romer begins his adventures with the newly found white goddess. He does not yet suspect that she will lead him to the brilliant city in the wilderness, that she in fact symbolizes that very city. Accompanying Romer on the journey is his dead mother, his spiritual companion and personal advisor, the wraith to whom he turns for advice in moments of crisis, since he never turns to nature, his opening invocation notwithstanding. The story leads Jonathan and Kaloolah to more separations and reunions than need be recounted here, to desperate adventures in the heart of Africa's wilderness, and finally to Romer's permanent reunion with the princess.

Mayo gathers in all the American clichés about nature, including such standard fare as the demonic Indian in the American woods, a nature rhetorically divided against itself, and an array of demonic imagery in nature touching on things as diverse as monkeys and storms. Against the terrors of nature the journey proceeds, although it is always Cooper's nature and never that of Emerson or Melville. Finally, in a magnificent city in the wilderness of another continent symbolic of America's West, set among *fifty* other cities, the journey ends in the wondrous city of

Kiloam. There Romer must decide whether or not to marry
Kaloolah. As he makes this decision, one does not expect him to
go to "the great temple of nature," which by now has been
forgotten; rather, for inspiration he seeks his mother, who scarcely would have him commune with nature, particularly since she
thinks of "transcendentalism" as such a silly thing. This level-
headed lady obligingly appears in a mist to the Yankee adventurer
and blesses the marriage, but Mrs. Romer's ethereal presence implies more than an author's aberration. Her dimensions are
mythic. She is hearth and home; she represents the calling back of
Jonathan (the) Romer to the world's settled institutions. She has
seen her son go through one initiation after another in the changing locations of nature, and now the moment is at hand for the
final rite of passage—true rebirth—since Mrs. Romer presides
over anything but Ahab's "step-mother world." Like the nation
he represents in the vintage American name he bears, Jonathan
will be reborn to his true American destiny. He and Kaloolah
literally descend into a tomb, are covered with a slab, and emerge
from their subterranean shrine married to each other. With the
experiences in nature now over, they have both been resurrected
into a world mediated by the city. Nature and Jonathan have been
reborn.

Just before Mayo gives us this resolution of the quest, his book,
with apparent abruptness—though quintessentially true to its implications—had suddenly appeared as an urban propaganda tract.
He had digressed from the basic plot to offer some serious con-
siderations on his urban ideal, represented by Kiloam. This city of
Mayo's imagination is filled with those beautiful flowers that so
many writers complained were missing in America. It is also a city predicated on the validity of Tocqueville's assumption about
America's passion for personal "well-being." The clean city of
Kiloam has indoor plumbing, an elaborate sewer system, air-
conditioning, and dehumidification. In its less utilitarian aspects,
the city is adorned not only by flowers but by the parks and
squares often lamented as missing from America. In the presentation of this ideal place, Mayo quite explicitly tells his readers to

build cities after the pattern of Kiloam. As for that "temple of nature" that he had written about in the beginning, it had been transformed into the city. The 623,000 people of Kiloam—large in its population, as cities of the American dream were to be—did their worshipping in urban temples. Jonathan Romer was now ready for the ideal city, a wife, and serious commercial schemes.

Though urban propaganda might seem odd to the modern reader encountering *Kaloolah,* we need not suspect that readers of Mayo's day would be disturbed by the shift from chasing a white goddess to a discourse on urban planning. The popularity of the book did not suffer. Readers approvingly understood that the city was the logical conclusion of America's own wilderness journey. At the end of the Cumberland Gap or the Oregon Trail or any of the roads west would be great and thriving commercial centers to match or surpass the cities of the East that had already magically grown from the wilderness. So profoundly accepted was this idea in America that even in the face of the most preposterous claims by land speculators who preyed on such faith, level-headed persons fully aware of pervasive frauds could be seduced by the lure of a "Kiloam." A marvelous example of this appears in some prose by Timothy Flint in which he castigates the "abomination" of speculators luring people to invest in towns of endless promise. Citing a comic advertisement appearing in St. Louis newspapers about an imaginary city, Flint notes that it is called

"Ne plus ultra." The streets were laid out a mile in width; the squares were to be sections, each containing six hundred and forty acres. The mall was a vast standing forest. In the centre of this modern Babylon, roads were to cross each other in a meridional line at angles, one from the south pole to Symmes's hole in the north, and another from Pekin to Jerusalem.

This advertisement was actually a "coarse caricature" of various enticements used to lure investors. Flint knew this, but he partook of his society's dreams, so after thoroughly attacking and mocking such claims he reflectively considered that possibly on one of these boundless plains, and contiguous to some one of these noble rivers, in view of these hoary bluffs, and where all these means of the subsistence and multiplication of the species are concentered in such ample abundance, will arise the actual "Ne plus ultra."[22]

Mayo knew his audience.

His moderate dispute with America in his urban polemics was not over whether cities would emerge like magic from the wilderness. Everyone knew that they would. What did disturb Mayo was the degree to which those cities would conform to his own urban ideal, which placed an unusual emphasis on city beautification. In his floral-decked city, where the flowers, not surprisingly, were coated with gold and silver, the nature that America loved might be most fully appreciated. Since one can scarcely believe that Mayo actually wanted his flowers gilded with precious metals, the image of those flowers is clearly symbolic. But Mayo was quite literal and scarcely out of harmony with his society when he saw in Kiloam the type of location that would embody the ultimate fulfillment of America, which he defined in Jonathan Romer's vision of what lay beyond even the city itself. For this "worshipper of nature," as we recall him in the beginning of the book, now sees his destiny "of civilizing barbarous tribes" and of "reclaiming from *rude* nature [as opposed to perfected nature] a large and fertile portion of the globe" (my italics, p. 449). The world was America's wilderness, and there were cities to build. Still the triumphant American individualist, Romer would bring to his "adopted land" a Yankee skill in making "gunpowder," which he believed to be "the greatest blessing to humanity, the supporter and protector of civilization, the spreader of true religion" (p. 448), which was anything but "nature." Romer had reached the American goal, albeit another city always remained to be built. He had discovered his magic urban place in the wilderness and he had attained wealth, power, and a bride—all this with flowers and indoor plumbing too.

Although *Kaloolah* charted more explicitly than any other novel the imaginative cartography whereby heroes are routed through the wilderness, pick up their gains, and emerge in the city, the basic outline was already an American fictional cliché by the time Mayo published his book in 1849. Paulding had worked the idea in 1832 when in *Westward Ho!* he described the transformation of the wilderness by "the 'wise white man,' who, wheresoever he goes, to whatever region of the earth, whether east or west, north or south, carries with him his destiny, which is to civilize the world, and rule it afterwards."[23] In 1829 Timothy Flint sent his hero George Mason to nature, from which he returned to civilization with his wealth, his bride, and his mother as well. In 1838 William Gilmore Simms exploited the theme in *Richard Hurdis,* as he did—though less directly—in his better-known *Yemassee* (1835) where adventures end in the security of the city of Charleston. But perhaps one of the most significant examples is to be found in a novel published in 1848, a year before *Kaloolah.* This is Charles Webber's *Old Hicks the Guide; or, Adventures in the Camanche Country in Search of a Gold Mine,* a story widely read in its time and even more direct in its association of the wilderness with wealth than *Kaloolah,* as one may guess from the title.

As with *Kaloolah,* Webber's once highly popular novel has been rescued from oblivion and brought to the attention of modern readers through the efforts of a distinguished scholar—in this case Henry Nash Smith—who in *Virgin Land* presented *Old Hicks* as developing a "primitivistic theory" and contrasting "the intuitive ethics of the wilderness with the bigotry of urban society."[24] Which it certainly did. But like *Kaloolah, Old Hicks* makes us turn to Lawrence's dictum; for the "ethics" of the wilderness presented by Webber are ultimately as unimportant to his ideology as is Romer's early hymn to nature. The subtitle of Webber's book, it turns out, may be trusted after all, even though the author makes other pretensions at times. The underlying motive of Webber's hero, as the tale unvaryingly tells us, is the search for gold. Therefore, after glorifying primitive values over civilized ones, the narrator of the novel wins the fortune in search of which he had gone west in the first place, and returns—to the surprise, I am sure, of none of his nineteenth-century readers—to enjoy it in the very urban city of New Orleans. As Professor Smith so accurately observed, Webber ''failed to construct an interpretation of the Western wilderness within the framework of primitivism.''[25] One may wonder whether he even tried, since America's attachments to urban society were too strongly held to allow a serious definition of the wilderness as a place where civilized people can accept ''primitive'' values. If Webber's hero learned some better ethical value, he treated it as contemptuously as Captain Adam Seaborn had when he encountered the polar hole in *Symzonia*. Indeed, in so directly bringing to our attention the insistence on civilized, urban values—those of New Orleans or other cities, even when one is offered a supposedly primitive paradise—Webber earns his important place as a commentator on his contemporary America.

In his fable of the West, Webber reveals the wilderness as a region where all the ethical values and blessings of peace conjured in his fairy tale land are subordinated to the American dream of nature yielding wealth, which is the book's main subject. Webber's fantasy of the West never goes so far as to insist that the hero should remain away from the city. As Emerson himself in one of his less poetic moments said, metaphorically capturing a generalized American belief, ''If God meant [man] to live in a swamp, he would have made him a frog.''[26] Webber's hero, although not at all lured toward a swamp, hastened to leave an attractive and exciting wilderness that had brought him a bride—who was the actual source of his financial gain—and some fine adventures that no doubt would make for excellent memories to be enjoyed in New Orleans. But the primitive values were never real. Even in the chapter where the hero pays his highest tribute to the noble savages and their primitive world, ''The Philosophy of Savage Life'' (albeit, in accordance with American assumptions about Indians, they are more savage than noble), the last paragraph brings readers back to the business at hand by describing the hero's plans to deceive the Indians into assisting in the quest for gold, the ''ultimate El Dorado of our

wild adventures.''[27] Gold mediated the quest and not the
''Edenic'' valley that an American hero wandered into—a valley
presided over, not surprisingly, by a decadent European count.
Given the fact that ''noble savages'' were a foreign invention, it
made some sense to place a European in Webber's fictional
valley, or so an American might have thought in 1848. *Old
Hicks* offers lavish praise of nature, a great deal of bloodshed in
the ''Edenic'' realm Webber describes, and a celebration of
primitivism on the journey toward wealth and respectable marriage in a great city, which happened to be New Orleans. The
famous Parisian bedroom syndrome described by D. H. Lawrence
was not exclusively Cooper's.[28]

The exact extent to which Mayo and Webber took seriously
their praise of nature along the way to the city is difficult to determine, although a fascinating insight into an author's own ap-
prehension of this formulaic American story is offered in a novel
that exploited the theme some two decades earlier. This is
Timothy Flint's *Francis Berrian,* published in 1826. Since fiction
was by definition fancy, Flint seemed perfectly at ease in offering a
fictional celebration of European fantasy about America that was
thoroughly at odds with his own recorded experiences and
understandings.

Francis Berrian, though differing in detail from *Kaloolah* or *Old
Hicks,* works the motif that would become a cliché in American
fiction. In this case, a young New Englander sets out for the
regions of the Southwest where he has numerous adventures, including an embroilment in Mexican revolutionary politics. The
difficult moments one expects in an adventure story appear, as
does the happy resolution whereby the hero wins his bride, a
Mexican beauty named Martha. She is quite an exotic creature,
sensual and Catholic, an extraordinary prize for a Protestant New
England boy to bring home to mother, although Francis does just
that. And why not, in the make-believe West Flint creates? Francis had set out in the first place to find his El Dorado, and if it
yielded love as well as gold, so much the better. In the alien world
he enters in search of some undefined fulfillment, he finds much

of his dream realized in the beautiful form of his Mexican bride.

In the midst of his innumerable adventures, however, Francis replies to a question by Martha with an answer that must make us pause. Why, she asks, had he come to Mexico in the first place?

> I answered, ''Such passages, particularly that, 'une belle nuit,' [from Chateaubriand's *Genie du Christianisme*]&c., gave me back more beautifully the image of my own thoughts. I was determined to converse with nature alone in those prairies, and those boundless deserts, that he so delightfully painted to my imagination. I could not hope to find these places, except in the western regions of my own country, and that part of yours contiguous to them.''[29]

This is remarkable rhetoric from Timothy Flint, who in his *Geography* belittled ''the pastoral dreams of Rousseau, or Chateaubriand.''[30] If Francis Berrian, whose infatuation with nature grew from his European readings, had been the victim of a delusion, Flint would have had a tidy parable. But Francis Berrian is not a European deluded by the West; he is an American lured there by a European fantasy that leads to a rewarding fulfillment. He is a fictional denial of the belief that Flint expresses in his *Geography.* Francis not only escapes being duped by the siren of Chateaubriand's America, but he validates the dream of America's promise that was born in European imagination. Francis discards the public advice of the Reverend Timothy Flint and, as conceived by novelist Flint, realizes his dream, flaunts the warnings of his staid New England family, rejects the love of a nice, bookish, sexless female of his own religious faith, and comes home with his exotic bride. While Flint dutifully interjects the moral that people should not go west seeking El Dorado, he spins a fable about how enjoyable it could be to ignore such advice. But in the end Flint returns to the American idea of what culminates from such journeys. It is not to the ''prairies'' or the ''boundless deserts,'' or even to any place in the unsettled West that Francis at last goes. Rather, he returns to the city—in this case Boston —that may not have had the attractions of Chateaubriand's imaginings, but that presented Francis Berrian and his bride with a rapturous vision in the moment they approached the city. Flint, along with Francis, had come home to America.

Three years later, in 1829, Flint offered in *George Mason* the kind of parable he avoided in *Francis Berrian*. In *George Mason* the father of a family is lured West by his readings of Chateaubriand and others. Truer to what Flint wrote in his *Geography,* the elder Mason finds only death in the land of Chateaubriand. His son, however, makes his American way by working on one of those steamboats of Dew's industrial vision. He prospers and finally rescues his family from the painful agrarian life to which they had been led by the father's reading of European fantasies. The Masons, young George's new bride and all, quite wealthy now, stay in the West, settling "in a large and populous village,"[31] the growing urban complex that America's wilderness predictably would yield. It was not yet Boston, but as Thomas Dew affirmed, the cities of the West would surely arise to rival their Eastern counterparts.

Without exploring the epistemology of *reality* as opposed to *unreality,* one can safely say that, as the terms are used in every-day discourse, Flint wavered between them in *Francis Berrian,* while committing himself to "reality" in *George Mason* by rejecting Europe's siren call of the West and bringing his hero home to nature's truest form, the city. This same American "reality" is found in the writings of Cooper, who, innovator that he was, helped formulate the cultural idea into a fictional enterprise that others would imitate. In creating his Leatherstocking saga, Cooper gave America one literary model for the theme, although he was less concerned with insisting upon a return to the city specifically than to civilization in general. What sets Cooper apart from his imitators—aside from his superior literary talents—is his brilliantly imaginative invention, a hero—Natty Bumppo—who can stay in Europe's West while his other heroes come home, as Francis Berrian does, to enjoy the fruits of nature in America's civilized place. Cooper no more believed the notion that man in some way belonged in the unchanged wilderness than did Emerson, as the latter expressed in the aphorism on God and frogs. And while the polemics of Cooper in his various fictional enterprises may often warrant derision, he never did anything to deserve the ultimate ridicule of having posterity assume, as it has sometimes actually done, that Natty's world in nature was something other than an alluring and beautiful fantasy seen through Cooper's prism of history. Cooper's marvelous capacity to capture America's ''reality'' and ''unreality'' in the magic of art makes him a major American writer, artistic flaws and all. But no one understood better than Cooper how inextricably tied to property and civilization America was; no one adhered more closely than he did to the valued idea of civilization, whether as the city or otherwise, emerging from nature. For all his sentimentality about Natty, nobody championed the cause of private property more than Cooper did. As Henry Nash Smith so admirably stated, ''The depth and power of Cooper's characterization of Leatherstocking is due to his capacity to respond to [an] anarchic inference from the ideal of forest freedom despite his own commitment to the ideal of an ordered, stratified society based on the secure ownership of land by a leisure class.''[32] To the blessings of civilization, Cooper brought home one hero after another, leaving Natty to die in the world of nature Europe had invented and into which these individuals had entered during episodes of ''unreality'' prior to taking their proper place in the town of Templeton or in other centers of civilization.

Nor are we to take too seriously as a culturally representative idea Cooper's lament for the passing of the wilderness, since even the ''tale'' *his* stories tell validates the incisive observation about nature yielding to civilization given by Robert Montgomery Bird in some notes he made for *Nick of the Woods* (1837):

It is a nobler and more profitable labour to investigate the origin of a people [Americans], whose ancestors fought them [Indians] hand to hand for the possession of the wilderness, and purchasing it with blood and tears, gave it, now *blossoming like the rose* [my italics], to be an inheritance to their children.

It is the fashion of poetry to lament the change. . . .It is right that poetry should do so; for there is something deeply melancholy and humbling in the fate of the Indian. Nevertheless, philosophy has no sigh for the change; for the earth is the dwelling of man, not the brute, and its fair fields are intended for those who will cultivate them and multiply [the conventional anthropology of the day assumed that Indians lacked virility], not for those who harvest it for wild beasts.[33]

By approving of those who "cultivate" the land, Bird does not mean simply farming, since in his *Nick of the Woods* Indians do indeed cultivate the land in an agricultural sense—at least they did so before being slaughtered with Bird's obvious approval. Cooper, desiring the same outcome—the imposition of civilization—mourned as a "poet" what happened in a time that both he and Bird knew to be historical. As a "philosopher" Cooper approved of what the "poet" in him lamented. The gift of nature was the blessing of civilization enjoyed by the heroes of Cooper's America. Recipients of the boon include Oliver Effingham, Duncan Heyward, his grandson Middleton, and Jasper Western. Although Cooper basically departs from the formula in *The Deerslayer* (1841), he picks it up again after his completion of the Leatherstocking series when in *Satanstoe* (1845) Corny Littlepage returns in triumph with Anneke Mordaunt to Lilacsbush, comfortably close to the elegant society of New York City. It was a fitting end—the flower and the city.

9

Cain's City

When James Kirke Paulding observed that "the chief ambition of a western adventurer is to found a great city on speculation," or when John Pendleton Kennedy, in his pastoral idyll *Swallow Barn* (1832) reserved for the city of Richmond the word "sublime,"[1] each was commenting on a geographically definable urban idea. That is, such locations as those evoked by Paulding or Kennedy, or more extravagantly by Dew or Mayo, referred to places that had or would emerge from the American landscape. Regardless of how exotic Kiloam might be, it existed within the realm of physical definition and future possibility. Such urban gardens as Kiloam or the "Ne plus ultra" of Timothy Flint's ambivalent imagination always had some direct relation to the commercial, tangible domain that grew from the wilderness into the city.

No literate person of early nineteenth-century America could remain ignorant of the powerful urban image associated with nature and the developing West. The idea of a journey to nature that yielded the city existed as a cultural commonplace for those who condemned the prospect as well as for those who revered it. Perhaps inevitably, romantic writers, although varying in their personal responses to the secular image of America's city, all found literary occasions for employing the pattern of their culture's mythology of nature and the city. In developing their own private myths of nature as interior vision, they found the typology of their "external world" useful for literary ends. But while the metaphor of the romantic city followed the pattern of an American myth, the romantic city was found in the same "occasional and transient" place as "nature." Moreover, in creating their own "city," romantic writers remained indebted to the theological city long ago defined by St. Augustine. In images drawn from the cities of St. Augustine and William Starbuck Mayo, American Romantics found the literary location for the journey's end.

Although ideas of metaphysical divisions between spiritual and temporal notions are not contingent upon the restrictions of Augustinian theology, in *The City of God* St. Augustine offered Western civilization a crucial metaphor for stating the distinctions. In the early children of Adam, Cain and Abel, St. Augustine saw two archetypes of the basic polarities that for hundreds of years came to mediate ideal Christian theology. The first of these children was Cain, who in Augustinian theology represented the "city of man"; the next was Abel, a type for "the city of God." Just why Cain's offering was so poorly regarded is a theological question more appropriately explored elsewhere. But in having his sacrifice summarily rejected, Cain became the first child of Adam to find that what grew from the earth was insufficient. His offering rejected, he fell on his own resources and built a city, literally in the Bible, but symbolically a place as contemporary to us as the room in Sartre's *No Exit.* Cain walked the world as a creature cut off from any external meaning, and those following him in time, who could find no better way to God than he could, shared the plight described by Emerson in the moments when he felt that if we are without God, we are like the "chill, houseless, fatherless, aimless Cain."[2] When the possible loss of God threatened such a fate, men like Emerson turned to nature, which "is loved," he writes, "by what is best in us. It is loved as the city of God, although, or rather because there is no citizen."[3] This suggests the yielding of the self to the universal, the kind of sacrifice the more memorable "fatherless" individual, Melville's Ishmael, refused to offer and that we associate with transcendentalism.

In loving "as the city of God" this idea of a citizenless "nature," Emerson was reshaping to his own uses an older Augustinian theology. No citizens inhabited his "nature" because man's new allegiance was gravitating toward the internal spiritual self rather than to the external divinity who rejected Cain's offering. Nor did Emerson take this direction without a full awareness of how much a "Cain" he would be if his new myth failed. In moving toward a theology claiming that men contained the very "god-like minds" Cooper would condemn in *The Sea Lions,* Emerson was following a course entirely alien to the citizenship of God's kingdom that Abel enjoyed. This new direction, moreover, implied much more than a rejection of Christian history, although in its perception of man it grew ineluctably from the historical shift in Christianity that we call the Renaissance. It moved away from the ideal embodied in Abel.

Augustinian exegesis represents Abel as symbolic of an ideal Christian type, an individual who subordinates the self into the "city of God," a "place" in one sense remote from man, since its center is the Godhead; but in another sense a "place" that is immanent, since God's radiance shines among those who are of His city. God is the very architecture of the city in which His citizens live. Many years after St. Augustine's definition, however, at the dawn of American history, a subtle shift had occurred in this idea of the city, that key metaphor we associate with the Puritans and which was provided by John Winthrop in his famous sermon on the *Arbella* in 1630. In a way, Winthrop presents a conduct manual. If we do all the right things, he tells his listeners, "the Lord will be our God and delight to dwell upon us, as His own people and will command a blessing upon us in all our ways."[4] It is not hard here to recognize a utopian vision. Although God will surely punish a community that does not heed His word, He will as surely reward the community of His chosen which obeys His commands; those people will prosper in *this* world, as, of course, in the other. And the whole world would be watching, as Winthrop makes clear in his famous simile: ''for we must consider that we shall be as a City upon a Hill; the eyes of all people are upon us'' (p. 199). Without going into all the complexities of free will and predestination that are too familiar to bear repetition here, I believe it is fair to say that the idea stated by Winthrop burdened those voyagers on the *Arbella* with an awesome responsibility for shaping the secular direction of their new society. Since God would form the New World in accordance with their behavior, these religious people were to determine which of two ''cities'' would grow in the land they were settling. They were to choose between dichotomized cultures in *this* world, one promising ''curses upon us till we be consumed out of the good land,'' and the other offering such ''a praise and glory, that men shall say of succeeding plantations: the Lord make it like that of New England'' (pp. 198-99). But this was not quite St. Augustine's ''city of God.'' As one commentator has succinctly stated, ''Augustine is more concerned to describe this vale of tears, and to fortify us for our life in it, than to excogitate ideal types for an ideal environment.''[5] This distinction between St. Augustine and John Winthrop, hairsplitting though it might appear, is central to that momentous change in Western civilization called the Renaissance; and indeed the Puritans, as Perry Miller pointedly observes, were ''spokesmen'' for what the change implied.[6] Winthrop, whose thought was shaped in the turbulence of that period, for all his deep religiosity partook of the process described in another context by Crane Brinton ''as the persistent Christian tension between this world and the next.''[7]

If the process had stopped with the distinction between Winthrop and St. Augustine, the significance might not command our attention. As Perry Miller has shown in the opening chapter of *The New England Mind,* the Puritans owed much to Augustinian theology, so the difference between the two men was perhaps reconcilable. But this process of shifting the world's axis from God to man, showing itself however incipiently in Winthrop's vision, was part of an ongoing phenomenon that in its most signifi-

cant form brought the "city of God" finally to the emanation of
man found in Emerson's theology of nature. This shift in
Western civilization marked an ontology described by Joseph
Campbell as "a spirituality true to this earth and to its life, where
it is in the creatures of this world that the Delectable Mountains
of our Pilgrim's Progress are discovered, and where the radiance
of the City of God is recognized as Man."[8] Or one may call it the
"city of man" to distinguish the romantic "city" from the
secular one at the end of America's journey into nature.[9]

The romantic journey to the city implied the intense self-
reliance that appears not only in the brightest visions of Emerson,
Thoreau, and Whitman, but also in the awesome isolation of
Hester Prynne or Ahab. While such individualism has often been
described as a product of democracy, which it partly was, its most
important antecedents were metaphysical rather than Constitutional. And its impulse was heretical to the oldest ideas of Christianity, as defined by St. Augustine, who so pointedly warned
against the very suppositions that would one day form the nexus
of a new myth. "The devil," he had written, "would not have
trapped man in an obvious and open sin, when he did what God
had forbidden, if man had not already begun to please himself.
That is why he took delight in the assurance 'You shall be as
gods.' Such they might have been more easily, if they had stuck
obediently to their true divine source of origin rather than proud-
ly arrogating the status to themselves."[10] In this we may
recognize Father Mapple's sermon on "delight" and "obedience," while we keep in mind the gam with the *Delight*.[11] We
may also recognize Emerson's or Thoreau's "arrogating" to the
self the "divine source." With exquisite irony an aspect of
religious history had come full circle, since a man such as
Thoreau, who told us he had never quarrelled with God, followed
the way of Emerson's "poet," who is after all St. Augustine's
devil in what he promises, while Melville, who time and again
showed us the dangers of this devil's course, protested God's injustice. But quarrel or no quarrel, justice or injustice, the spiritual

center of the world, rapturous or horrendous, was now far from the old city of God.

The metaphor was alive, however, both in its continuity of spiritual history and in the vitality given to it by America's particular attachment to the city. Although encomiums to the American city rhetorically owed something to the religious city—just as America's garden linguistically owed something to Eden—the American city in the nineteenth century had long been secular in its imaginative connotation. But in the typology of the romantic quest this city became so transformed that American romantic writers often departed from the traditional quest motif of Western civilization where the hero is drawn to a destiny away from the city.[12] While heroes in American romantic quests often left society, their journey, like the national one they knew, frequently led to a "city" emerging from "nature."

Literally, this romantic city might imply the journey *from* nature to an urban place, as in Pierre's movement to New York or Donatello's to Rome. But more important than urban identification is the definition of one's location after the journey into nature, since the quest ends in a city finally belonging neither to St. Augustine nor to William Starbuck Mayo, however much it owes to metaphors associated with them. The fruition of nature in this quest may be the endlessness encountered in *Mardi,* in "Passage to India," or in "El Dorado"; or it may be the return to civilization by Thoreau from Walden Pond, the returns of Coverdale and Hester from their encounters with nature, or the way back for Redburn, Tom, Ishmael, and Israel Potter. It may lead to the madness of *Pym,* or the apotheosis in *Nature.* But what all these have in common is their conformity to the idea that one moves into nature in hope of some kind of gain, and one returns—if at all—to the self, the romantic counterpart to the American city found in nature. Whether resulting in triumph or defeat, no pattern is more constant in American romantic literature.

The problem of identifying the romantic self to which heroes return parallels the difficulty in sorting out America's geographical West from an archetypal one. That is, in its lavish praise of self-reliance, democratic American society endorsed as a political concept an idea that in romantic writing came to transcend the geographical space of America. Categories of thought containing ideas of "individualism" often implied antithetical meanings, for the romantic individual was as remote from the "American" individual as the romantic West was from the geographical one. These differences may be exemplified by the antipodal definitions of two "individualists," Cooper's Natty Bumppo and Melville's Taji.

Natty is an American phenomenon. No matter how relentlessly he pushes westward, he remains tied to a political subdivision of the earth called America. He is an individualist existing in the contradictory world of a commercial, stratified, egalitarian, democratic society. In theory as good as Judge Temple, he may even be superior by virtue of his culture's celebration of the common man; but if Natty were the marrying kind, his society's paradoxical values would never permit him to join with any woman having the judge's social standing. Far from hurting Cooper's myth, conflicts of this kind make Natty the remarkably well-drawn personficiation of logically irreconcilable attitudes existing in the America of Cooper's day. Through Natty, Cooper addresses the problems of freedom and property, and although Cooper has been vastly overrated as a social critic, he did understand that societal conflicts of interest do exist in forms that defy the power of man to remove. It was rather a fine insight for a man so much the product of an age of progress. And since he had to choose sides, he did. Although Cooper apparently believed that America was expanding too fast for its own good,[13] he nevertheless accepted the legitimacy of all the conquests in the West. He would have questioned the sanity of anyone who misunderstood his claim that the Temples were entitled to the land yielded through the victory over that "anarchic" idea Henry Nash Smith described. Readers with an abstract commitment to egalitarianism, if indeed many held such a view, could very well sit in their drawing rooms and enjoy Cooper telling sad stories of the death of Indians and of Natty and of the region of nature they occupied. It was safe. Natty, with almost divine self-sacrifice, had cleared the West for those cities that would one day rise there. Humbly, asking nothing for himself, when his mission had ended, he stood before his God and announced his readiness to leave this world. The legal title to the land was securely in the hands of Judge Temple's inheritors, who were by then prospering in a commercial America. Natty's nature had been God's nature, and God's nature had been America's. In this cooperative enterprise of laying the foundation for America's West, nature—often sublimely beautiful in Cooper's poetic portrayal of it—had yielded great material reward to the Duncan Middletons of America; it had legitimized the crushing of the Indians and the possession of their lands by subsuming the political contest under that rhetorical pose which Robert Montgomery Bird would be too honest, or perceptive, to countenance. Yet few if any were ready to quarrel with Cooper's basic idea of what an individualist was, and Natty Bumppo always ultimately conceded that society, however temporarily unjust, was finally right. America belonged to an ordered, white civilization and not to him nor to his Indian friends. This was Natty Bumppo, an American individualist who in the sacrifice of himself and his Indians prepared the way for the garden of America. Others would build their Kiloams on that land.

Taji, though he moves in an ever-westwardly direction, is remote from Cooper's American individualist. His concern with politics in the long, allegorical visits to almost every conceivable geographical location represents just one of the many modes of failure associated with this individualist's quest for something ineffable. Like Emerson's ''poet,'' like Thoreau at Walden, he insists that the individual must *never* concede to society a role more legitimate than his own. This is, of course, anarchic, and while Thoreau and Emerson never lived out the whole of what their theories implied, Taji shares their kind of individualism. The nature he encounters in his westward journey largely departs

from any American sense of the geographical West, nor does
Melville even depend on America's journey as a central trope in
the way Thoreau does, for example, in "Walking." Melville
creates his own world, the conditions of which require no
dependence upon America. Taji's individualism is not Natty's,
nor do the two enter a similar nature. In the final act of possessing
his own soul and immediately abdicating the kingdom he has
won, Taji does so—in madness or in wisdom—because he *chooses*
such a course. Only in the meaning or meaninglessness of himself
does Taji find a rationale for his behavior. The finest promise of
society is only a Siren's call for him. As with Natty, Taji knows
he has to flee from society, but unlike Leatherstocking, whose
temporal space is the whole of America's unsettled West, Taji's
region is the entire universe rapidly shrinking to embody only the
self. In this creation called *Mardi,* Melville presented the most extreme version of the romantic journey to the self. It went even
beyond the metaphor of a return to civilization, but it did not
lead, as in Whitman's ongoing journey in "Passage to India,"
toward an equation that in some way brought man and God
together.

The story told in *Mardi* was extreme even for Melville, and the
idea of a return to a city is scarcely recognizable in it. As for Natty, his only return is to God, whom he had never really left. But
between the polarities of Taji's ultimate attempt at ordering the
universe to himself and Natty's sacrificial yielding of his world to
America, a range of romantic writing existed that made explicit
use of the city at the end of the journey, though not the city of
those such as Webber, Mayo, or Flint. Drawing from the
American paradigm, such writing brought the journey's end to a
city containing neither the material promise of Mayo nor the
religious certitude of St. Augustine. It was a journey to a city
emerging from religious concerns of the nineteenth century.

One remarkable example of the romantic journey appears in
Longfellow's *Evangeline* (1847). This poem offers the reader a
particularly valuable opportunity to examine the romantic appropriation of America's journey toward the city that blossoms

from nature, since with uncommon clarity and simplicity Longfellow transforms a secular image of nature to romantic myth. As with almost all major nineteenth-century narratives of the West, *Evangeline* is removed from the commercial present and set in the imaginative past. Superficially, the story tells of a woman's absolute fidelity to her man through many years of lamentable separation. After she has pursued him across a continent, Evangeline finds him at the moment of his death, and, united in their old age, the lovers are soon buried side by side. It is a sentimental story, although one not written by a Unitarian white-bearded poet complacently certain of Christian immortality. Through Newton Arvin's insights we see Longfellow's theology as "pervaded by the fragrance of nineteenth-century religious liberalism—undogmatic, eclectic, latitudinarian, and rather vague."[14] Or, a theology filled with the uncertainties of his era that drew him away from the church as his religious center. Consistent with Longfellow's religious doubts, *Evangeline* offers no tale of virtue rewarded by lovers being joined in heaven. In its ironic mode, this poem of human isolation in a doubtful universe narrates the heroine's journey to nature and her dreary return to the city.

Although the setting of Acadie, where the tale begins, is in Canada, it clearly represents an idealized region conforming to the pastoral golden age at times imposed upon America by Europe's old dream for the New World. Society and its physical surroundings are in harmony, although the introduction informs the reader from the beginning that the citizens of this ideal community have been thrust from their Eden and that the forest has regained the land, somewhat as Thomas Cole seemed to fear it might in his "Course of Empire" (1836). Although human action initiates the separation of Evangeline and Gabriel, nature turns temporary separation into extended pathos. A storm at sea sends the lovers in different directions, and Evangeline begins her quest.

It is a westward one, where Longfellow's heroine keeps moving into that region of America's promise, encouraged by the prophecies of Father Felician, who is remarkable in his record of inaccuracy. At one point, weary from the search, Evangeline has a dream of "an opening heaven" illuminating "her soul in sleep with the glory of regions celestial."[15] While the vision reveals itself, a boat approaches.

> Gabriel was it, who, weary with waiting, unhappy and restless,
> Sought in the Western wilds oblivion of self and of sorrow.
> Swiftly they [Gabriel and his party] glided along, close
>   under the lee of the island,
> But by the opposite bank, and behind a screen of palmettos,
> So that they saw not the boat [Evangeline's], where it lay
>   concealed in the willows;
> All undisturbed by the dash of their oars, and unseen,
>   were the sleepers.
> Angel of God was there none to awaken the slumbering maiden.
>   (P. 87)

Although the narration requires for the sake of suspense that Evangeline must sleep, the incident implies more than a mere event to tease the reader's interest. In Gabriel's attempt to seek "oblivion of self" in the West, we recognize the potential for renewal in a fairy-tale world where one might awaken to his goddess and be reborn to her in the fashion of Jonathan Romer. But in Longfellow's version of the story, nature not only fails to yield the heroine, it actually conceals her behind "a screen of palmettos." Nor does any "Angel of God" waken her, as Longfellow works with rather heavy irony on the name of his hero, or as he keeps Father Felician's empty promises of religious hope before us. When Evangeline subsequently, and too late, tells him that Gabriel is near, Father Felician assures her that she and Gabriel will be reunited in the "Eden of Louisiana!" (p. 88). But though Louisiana and the American West prove true to the promise of America's material wealth, Father Felician's assurances remain inevitably wrong. For Evangeline and Gabriel, both of whom seek each other in the promised land of the West, nature yields no prize.

Longfellow relentlessly places this sense of westwardly movement before us, even to the point of sending Gabriel along the
way to Oregon, to the deserted regions in the far West that contemporary Americans believed were not suited for human habitation. Evangeline pursues him, while "the magic Fata
Morgana/Showed them her lakes of light, that retreated and
vanished before them" (p. 92). There is something of the
receding Yillah of *Mardi* in this, of Whittier's "Vanishers."
There is also something demonic, a terror beyond the "demonism"
of Flint's West. We see this particularly in the legend told by the
Shawnee woman of brides lured to the forest in vain quests. Such
stories suggest to Evangeline more than the absence of Eden.

> Filled with the thoughts of love was Evangeline's heart, but
>   a secret,
> Subtile sense crept in of pain and indefinite terror,
> As the cold, poisonous snake creeps into the nest of the
>   swallow.
> It was no earthly fear. (P. 93)

The next day, however, Evangeline returns to her Christian certitude as she urges, " 'Let us go to the Mission, for there good
tidings await us!' " (p. 94). This, just after Jesus and Mary have
been mentioned. But, as Longfellow's perspective becomes more
and more clarified, she misses finding Gabriel again. Haplessly,
she awaits the fulfillment of Father Felician's promise, as once
more Longfellow directs us superficially to bad clerical advice and,
more importantly, to the general uncertainty of religious promise.
Evangeline makes one more trip, only to find the ruined hut of
Gabriel.

Gabriel, as every nineteenth-century Christian knew, appeared
in the Bible as the angel prophecying to Zacharias "glad tidings"
(Luke 1:19) and to Mary the greatest of all Christian prophecies.
Surely, therefore, we have to note carefully that, just before the
virgin Evangeline falls on Gabriel's ruined lodge, Longfellow,
litany-like, had twice repeated, "Gabriel came not" (p. 95).
Longfellow sets no personal precedent in this biblical inversion.

He had manipulated scripture before in, to name only one example, ''The Wreck of the Hesperus,'' written in 1839 at a time when he was still attending church, though what thoughts he held we may wonder from his poetry. In the storm at sea, the skipper urges his daughter not to ''tremble so;/For I can weather the roughest gale/That ever wind did blow.'' But her fears prove to be justified, although the poet compares her bosom to ''hawthorn buds''—which in nineteenth-century floral lexicon meant ''hope''—and although those hawthorn buds open ''in the month of May''—which in Christian tradition and in Catholic dogma is the month of the merciful Virgin Mary. In spite of all this and the assurances of the little girl's father, the ship sinks. But before it goes down, and after her father dies, the child ''clasped her hands and prayed/That savéd she might be;/And she thought of Christ, who stilled the wave,/On the Lake of Galilee.'' The full significance of her futile prayer—for she does drown—becomes apparent only when juxtaposed against the poem's penultimate line, ''Christ save us all from a death like this.'' If this prayer is as efficacious as the little girl's, then heaven will not help us at last. And that is precisely the possibility Longfellow suggests in the vain calls to Gabriel.

The last section of *Evangeline,* nevertheless, initially seems to hold some promise. Evangeline, as American heroes—or in this case, heroines—so often do, comes back to the city. At first, it seems to be the traditionally rewarding place America took its cities to be. The vision of Philadelphia reminds us of the ''magnificent promise'' Francis Berrian saw as he returned to the promised land of Boston.[16] As Evangeline gazes at the city, the ''mists'' that fall ''from her mind'' are compared to the revelation of ''shining rivers and cities and hamlets''; already she has discovered ''Something. . .in the friendly streets of the city,'' nothing less than an association of Philadelphia with ''the old Acadian country'' (p. 95); an association of city with nature.

But Longfellow's city is remote from America's ''garden.'' In the religious rather than secular city Evangeline reformulates her image of Gabriel so that he is now ''transfigured'' (p. 96).

The reality she discovers, however, does not correspond to her vision, since she finds Gabriel alive and not at all "transfigured." Moreover, she finds the only "Consoler"—not Christ, but rather "Death," who, "Laying his hand upon many a heart, had healed it forever" (p. 97). One scarcely need emphasize the irony of "Death," over whom Christ had won His victory, performing the laying on of hands, the healing. It is all there for the reader to see, although Evangeline herself piously thanks God for the particular favor He had bestowed upon her. Bride and groom have come home to a city of plague and pigeon droppings rather than to the City of God, or of Kiloam.

Nor is Longfellow quite through expressing his own "axis of vision." Evangeline and Gabriel, after their brief reunion, are buried together "far away from [the forest's] shadow" (p. 98). New people live in the old region of Acadie, but they are under the same "shadow" of the "forest primeval," the force in the universe from which the ocean and the forest continues to send its gloomy sound whenever the story of Evangeline is told. We have seen something of this "shadow" in Emerson's "Monadnoc" and in Whittier's "Hampton Beach." It implicitly extends to the city where the lovers are "consoled." But this city is not merely Philadelphia; it is the world. That it should be represented as an urban place is due in large measure to an American metaphor. Lovers find only death to console them because the city is no longer assured to be of God, although it remains in *Evangeline* "the vale of tears."

Longfellow's source for *Evangeline* grew from a tale passed on to him by Nathaniel Hawthorne, who subsequently praised the poem that grew from it. The central myth governing *Evangeline*—the quest in nature for redemption through human love—had been examined by Hawthorne ten years before the publication of *Evangeline* in "The Lily's Quest," which appeared in *Twice-Told Tales* (1837). Hawthorne's story, though drawing on the same cultural assumptions as Longfellow's, relies less on American history than *Evangeline* and more on Christian myth. Engaging both, Hawthorne offers a story that exemplifies an inability to find salvation in the city of America or the city of God.

Longfellow had named his lovers Evangeline and Gabriel, giving obvious religious overtones to them and their quest. Hawthorne also carefully chose the names of his lovers: Adam Forrester and Lilias Fay. "Adam Forrester" appropriately describes an individual seeking new happiness in the West, while "Lilias Fay" suggests the impossibility of achieving it. The "Fay" recalls to us the Fata Morgana that had lured Evangeline on. "Lilias," as Hawthorne writes, represents "Lily," which is no accident, since the voguish floral dicitionaries revealed the lily as representing happiness. Adam and Lilias seek the "Temple of Happiness." Or rather, they *sought* it, since once again a romantic narrative of nature takes place in the past. Hawthorne's allegory is simple enough. As others have, the two lovers pursue happiness in this world, but find that the only "lily" is that which grows from the grave. Death, having accompanied them all along, at last makes its point. And Hawthorne makes his. This world promises no new Adam, and temporal happiness remains illusory in a universe where death always stalks us. But the "new Adam" with his "Fay" of happiness has to learn this.

The first temple Hawthorne's Adam wishes to erect "would look towards the West."[17] In his innocence he thinks that the ground on which he walks has never been touched before, but Hawthorne tells us that man has always walked there, that there is no new region in this world. A geographically westward vision holds no promise. Although all the sites planned by the lovers for their "temple" at first seem to be in regions untouched by nature, they all reveal themselves as places where others have been. Fully aware that cities were blooming from America's nature, Hawthorne was saying that no region on earth was fertile ground for a corresponding "temple" of happiness. The journey to nature brings only the death of Lilias and Adam's exclamation of " 'joy!' " that " 'now our happiness is for Eternity!' " (p. 503). Whether this assertion is regarded ironically or not,

Hawthorne has suggested the limitations of any "temple" one might hope to build in the West of America or in the world. St. Augustine might have taken the message for granted, but it was a rather bleak one in the nineteenth century if God did not have His city to offer us. On this Hawthorne was silent in "The Lily's Quest."

Possibly, he was not sure. In the same collection, another story suggests his ambivalence on the point. This is "The Seven Vagabonds," which tells of an apparently aimless pilgrimage, although from the beginning the city had been considered as a possible destination. But at first nature appears so lovely that the ultimate goal of the journey remains subordinate to the beauty of the moment. The more immediate goal is a camp meeting, but very quickly a Methodist minister pronounces that the meeting has ended. Whatever our destiny may be, it is not discovered in Hawthorne's disbanded religious congregation, so the pilgrims continue without purpose, as individuals disperse from the group to go in their own directions. At the end of the story, only the narrator and an Indian remain from the original group. As if each intuitively understands what must now be done, they set out for the "distant city."[18] Whether that "city" would no longer be there, as had been the case with the camp meeting, is not clear, although the white man and the Indian—as they were not asked to do in America—walk the same mysterious path from nature to an unknown city.

While the bleakness of this road in an age of religious uncertainty formed the basis for countless stories throughout Western civilization, the solution that writers were suggesting with increasing frequency was one of salvation in this world through human love. The theme appears in *Evangeline* and in "The Lily's Quest," and is even suggested in "The Seven Vagabonds" when two lovers depart from the pilgrimage to follow their own way. This motif of salvation through human love that Matthew Arnold would suggest in "Dover Beach" (1867) and that Melville would position as a central possibility in *Clarel* (1876) has become so familiar to us that we may easily

forget how new it once was. Not merely the search of men and
women for each other, but the idea that *eros* or *amor* can in some
way fill the void left by the loss of God as traditionally
understood. In Arnold's familiar words,

> The sea of faith
> Was once, too, at the full. . .
> But now I only hear
> Its melancholy, long, withdrawing roar,
> Retreating. . . .
> Ah, love, let us be true
> To one another!

Or as Melville writes in lines that clearly owe something to Arnold, "Ah, Ruth, thine eyes/Abash these base mortalities!"[19]
Although *Evangeline* only tentatively approached this idea,
"The Lily's Quest" faced it more directly. But not until *The
Scarlet Letter* (1850) did the first great examination of the theme
take place in America, as Hawthorne turned to his country's past
and to its metaphors of nature and the city for an exploration of
the idea—one of many themes found in a narrative so rich in its
varieties of meaning.

In the first chapter of *The Scarlet Letter* Hawthorne reminds
his readers that in every "Utopia" some "virgin soil" must be
set aside for a "cemetery" and for a "prison." The echo of
"The Lily's Quest" is immediate, with only the "prison" as
something new in the equation, although the idea of such temporal necessity as our "prison" was implicit in the earlier story.
In *The Scarlet Letter,* Hawthorne more directly approaches the
matter. In front of this "prison" that literally confines Hester at
the beginning, and symbolically along the way, two kinds of
vegetation grow. One contains weeds, the other roses. From the
weeds, in a familiar although inverted metaphorical idea, grows
"the black flower of civilized society, a prison."[20] And,
equivocally presented, on the other side grows "a wild rose-
bush. . .with its delicate gems, which might be imagined to offer
their fragrance and fragile beauty to the prisoner as he went in,

and to the condemned criminal as he came forth to his doom, in token that the deep heart of Nature could pity and be kind to him'' (p. 48). It is tempting at first to pose the blackness of civilization against the beneficence of nature, but before the story ends we find that each is in some way a part of the other, as in America, the country where civilization was the flower of nature. In Hawthorne's story, what grows is "some sweet moral blossom'' (p. 48). Although the meaning of that "moral blossom'' may be debated, it suggests partly that we are pulled toward the prison of society, itself a type for the metaphysical prison that holds us all. This may not be a very "sweet'' flowering, but Hawthorne was quite as "black'' as Melville thought him to be.

The aspect of *The Scarlet Letter* bearing most directly on Hawthorne's rich use of these American metaphors concerns the crucial meeting of Hester and Dimmesdale in the forest—in nature—where each attempts to find some temporal salvation in the other. Hawthorne set this meeting in the wilderness partly because it represented a region that might be less susceptible to the normal restraints of society, but also for its identification with America's nature of infinite promise. In a sense, the scene suggests the "anarchic'' idea of Natty Bumppo, although in her profound individualism Hester finally refuses to accept a societal legitimacy more compelling than her own. She also engages her society's presumption of its capacity to define God's will. Hester is Emerson's self-reliant individual who finally goes to nature for the way out of her plight.

In the forest with Arthur, her prospects momentarily seem bright:

Such was the sympathy of Nature—that wild, heathen Nature of the forest, never subjugated by human law, nor illumined by higher truth—with the bliss of these two spirits! Love, whether newly born, or aroused from a deathlike slumber, must always create a sunshine, filling the heart so full of radiance, that it overflows upon the outward world. Had the

forest still kept its gloom, it would have been bright in Hester's
eyes, and bright in Arthur Dimmesdale's! (P. 203)

That is the promise of nature, although we note here its lack of
"higher truth." Whether or not Hawthorne ironically castigates
this "higher truth" or accedes to it, the story finally shows that
the promise nature made could not be kept. But the reason is not
that nature is bad or deceptive. Rather, in this encounter nature
represents the extension of Hester's will, the world she seeks to
build. Her "axis of vision" sees the possibility of love's fruition.
Hawthorne was to tell us otherwise, although the engimatic ending of the story—the promise that "at some brighter period" (p.
263) another daring and worthy woman might find her
way—may suggest how tempted Hawthorne was by the possibility of this boon from nature—what in *Moby-Dick* is called the
"feminine." But Hawthorne finds a limitation in the myth of
"nature," since the destined prophetess would come "in
Heaven's own time" (p. 263). The individual could not by
herself make it happen.

When Hester throws off her "A" she offers Dimmesdale a
solution in defiance of society; she momentarily becomes the individual triumphantly defeating a social order. All nature seems
on her side, as it often does to the questing hero who has found
the way.[21] For the moment, Arthur seems ready to follow her
path. But Hawthorne poses a matter more complex than whether
a single individual may prevail over society, for between Hester
and Dimmesdale there was nothing less at issue than that
Renaissance clash between the world of man and the world of
God. Hawthorne's lovers act out again a story as old as that
reported to us in the famous tale of Heloise and Abelard, those
earlier lovers whose beliefs so remarkably parallel the theologies
of Hester and Arthur.[22]

I do not wish to enter into a controversy over whether
Hawthorne, in giving his heroine and hero the same "H" and
"A" as Heloise and Abelard and in having them take perfectly
precisely identical positions about their love affair, was in fact us-

ing them as a source. Of much more concern than the possibility
of "influence" is how the older story helps define the fundamental conflict in *The Scarlet Letter* between the temporal world and
a future one. The parallels are fascinating. Heloise and Hester
were exiled from society. Abelard's literal penalty was suffered
symbolically by Arthur. And after a long separation, Heloise, like
Hester after her, sought out the man she loved. In the case of
Heloise, she reproached him for neglecting her, for failing to
understand that whatever may have happened to him, and to
them, her temporal love for him continued. This is what Hester
essentially says to the dying Arthur on the scaffold he has sought
after nature had failed to replace his God. " 'Shall we not meet
again?' " Hester asks. " 'Shall we not spend our immortal life
together? Surely, surely, we have ransomed one another, with all
this woe!' " (p. 256) Dimmesdale responds by cautioning silence
against blasphemy, since he has already withdrawn from
whatever reliance he may have placed upon himself while under
the spell of Hester and her anarchic "nature"; he returns to his
own "reality," his own "axis of vision." He returns to God. In
his dying moment he admonishes Hester for thinking any
thought other than that of her eternal soul. This is exactly what
Abelard told Heloise when he rejected her reproach. And there
the line is drawn in the two stories. Shall we partake of the loves
of this world or the redemption, if any, of the next? With which
do we cast our lot? Whether Hester's choice can be entirely
isolated in that context is questionable, but all readers can be certain where her thoughts are at the moment Arthur dies. As for
him, he surely lives and dies at last for the city of God rather than
for the triumph of man growing from the wilderness of Hester's
"nature." She, in turn, chooses to end her years in the isolated
dwelling by the sea, by the American city of Boston where Arthur Dimmesdale lived and died.

On whose side Hawthorne was in the competing cities that
were defined in the final polarity on the scaffold in Boston, after
Hester and Arthur had returned from their encounter in
"nature," will not be explored here. To ask the question is to

miss the point. Hawthorne can give no answer. Although with some justification, Hawthorne has often been thought of as a moralizer, in *The Scarlet Letter* he seeks to reveal and probe rather than to sermonize. It is enough to understand the alternatives symbolized by Hester and Arthur. We need not choose sides. But we do know that, whether or not Dimmesdale finds heaven, Hester's "nature" cannot impose her dreams upon the world.

In defining *nature* as incapable of achieving such an end, Hawthorne was reasonably consistent. He made a similar point in *The Blithedale Romance* (1852), where the dichotomy between city and nature explicitly emerges. Coverdale journeys to Blithedale and predictably returns. Regardless of how we define what he seeks, like Hollingsworth, Zenobia, and Priscilla, Coverdale finds nothing redemptive in nature. He is left with "nothing, nothing, nothing!"[23] Whatever life means for this individual, it is not to be found in nature. He therefore returns to a "town" in this version of the paradigm. After this he more than once goes to Europe, America's ultimate model of civilization.

And in Europe Hawthorne set his next and final "romance," *The Marble Faun* (1860), where he most directly employs the American motif of nature and the city; he does so through the inversion of relating how the special child of nature, Donatello, goes to the city called Rome and loses his Eden. The attempt to regain it takes him back to nature in search of the prelapsarian world Hawthorne kept assuring us was forever out of our temporal reach. The particular affinity Donatello once had with nature was gone, and in his isolated tower of owls—symbolic of the knowledge and wisdom he had painfully discovered—he recognizes what being disunited from nature implies. It would be absurd to say (and I accuse no critic of believing it) that Donatello's "fall" is remotely tied to an anti-urban theme. The city that corrupts him is this world, the "vale of tears" St. Augustine thought it to be, Emerson's world where man without God lives the experience of Cain, or "Cain's city and citified man," as Melville was to call it years later in *Billy Budd*.[24] Confining us in such a vision is Hester's "prison," or Bartleby's "walls," or the bars enclosing Donatello at the end of *The Marble Faun*.

The symbolism of Donatello in "prison" at the end of Hawthorne's last "romance" was offered to his readers in a delicious retort to those who criticized the ending of his book as obscure. That is, in the original edition of *The Marble Faun*, several mysteries about Hilda and Miriam seem to be left unresolved, while the specific fates of Donatello and Miriam are posed as questions with which the book ends. To the discerning reader, however, nothing needs to be added, since whatever Hawthorne had to say about the ambiguity of sin and human motivation had already been told. Perhaps readers could pose minor questions about some minor details of the story, but it was pointless to ask *where* Donatello and Miriam were, or *what* sin lurked in Miriam's past. The readers who asked these questions were those who needed life explained in the simplicities of Hawthorne's competitors, his irksome "d——d mob of scribbling women."[25] In an exercise of literary arrogance and adroitness rarely if ever matched, Hawthorne responded to those readers who wanted to see life as what we would now call "a well-made novel." The "Postscript" or "Conclusion" (depending on the edition used) that Hawthorne tacked on to his story "explained" precisely nothing, unless one cares to value a handful of unimportant details about Hilda that only raise a few unimportant questions. But as to who Miriam was and as to what sin she had committed, Hawthorne gives his answer in the form of Kenyon's incredulity that someone could actually not know. And as to where Donatello was, Hawthorne has Kenyon merely present in metaphor what the book had already revealed. " 'The Castle of Saint Angelo,' said Kenyon sadly, turning his face towards that sepulchral fortress, 'is no longer a prison; but there are others which have dungeons as deep, and in one of them, I fear, lies our poor Faun.' "[26] From this, the reader may assume, though not with absolute assurance, that Donatello is literally in jail. More certain, and far more important, is the fact that he is "imprisoned" by the boundaries of himself. But " 'why, then, is Miriam at large?' " the narrator asks, as Hawthorne anticipates his reader. The answer is, " 'after all, her crime lay merely in a glance; she did no murder!' " which, if it tells us anything, as it misses the whole point, reveals more about Kenyon, who had made the reply, than about Miriam. The reader who has understood the book prior to Hawthorne's artfully redundant ending knows that Miriam and Donatello are complements of each other, are "types" whose original appeared long ago. Representatives of all humanity, Miriam and Donatello are married to the necessities of spiritual history. As two aspects of one mysterious event, they can have no "conclusion" to their history. Miriam is at large because the world is at large, because we live in the "city" that Cain built, and because in the moments of Hawthorne's deepest truths we see face to face the reality of ourselves as no longer participants of the garden but rather occupants of Cain's city. It is the only place to which one can go from the garden of nature Donatello leaves in coming to what Hawthorne keeps calling "the eternal city" of Rome, as he employs the commonplace phrase to emphasize the bleakness of his vision.

Donatello understands the equation with Cain. We see this in the moment when Kenyon, who scrupulously seeks to avoid touching life, recoils in horror from the very image of Cain he had fashioned himself (p. 272). Donatello cannot prevent Kenyon from rearranging the clay in this parody of the artist as God; nor can Donatello make Kenyon give shape to Cain in the lifeless marble that more and more comes to symbolize both Kenyon and his Hilda. But Donatello can hold the image behind the form of his own face, as the Reverend Hooper hid it behind cloth in "The Minister's Black Veil." Donatello can wear a mask in the "prison" of this world and its awful necessity of "sin." Nor can one really spell out with any precision this mystery of sin and lost innocence that possessed Hawthorne and led him to write "romances" rather than novels as a way of coming closer to his truth through the technique of distorting what we call "reality." And he was arrogant enough to say to his readers that they either comprehended what he meant the first time, or he had nothing else to say. So he ended his "Postscript" or "Conclusion" with the final insult of an awful pun directed at those who had made him give an "explanation"; he had Kenyon reply to the mystery of Donatello's ears! " 'On that point, at all events, there shall be not one word of explanation.' " On that note, *The Marble Faun* ends. Hilda and Kenyon go back to America in their roles of bloodless "marble" (p. 411) lover and "marble woman" (p. 423) with dreams of a "marble Eden" (p. 369), the fool's paradise of an Amasa Delano, while Miriam, the pulsating, human force of the world, remains "at large," and Donatello, having left the garden of illusion—formulated as "nature" —comes to know that he resides in Cain's city.

The only alternative Hawthorne offers to Donatello's journey is the way of Hilda, occupant of the book's other tower, the abode of continuing innocence. In the symmetry of *The Marble Faun,* Hilda, as the other innocent, offers a view of the world by one who generally fails to see evil, and who, as Kenyon does before the statue of Cain, turns away from it. As Hawthorne tells us,

> With respect to whatever was evil, foul, and ugly, in this populous and corrupt city [literally Rome, symbolically the world], she had trodden as if invisible, and not only so, but *blind* [my italics]. She was altogether unconscious of anything wicked that went along the same pathway, but without jostling or impeding her, any more than gross substance hinders the wanderings of a spirit. Thus it is, that, bad as the world is said to have grown, Innocence continues to make a Paradise around itself, and keep it still unfallen. (P. 387)

No wonder that Hawthorne was thought to be a transcendentalist. For Emerson exceeded this promise only by saying that the world might lose its evil. But since the world and man were part of one phenomenon, the distinction between what Emerson promises in *Nature* and what Hilda lives out in *The Marble Faun* narrows perceptibly. Yet a large difference does remain, since Emerson's "poet" *sees,* while Hilda remains "blind." Nor does Hawthorne, in the presentation of Hilda's way, really offer a genuine possibility for this world, since Hilda's innocence approaches perfection, which correspondingly moves her away from humanity. Hawthorne's most "perfect" woman, Georgiana, who appears in his "Birthmark," can only die. In the city where Hilda walks, she can only live as "marble." The alternatives are therefore clearly posed by Hawthorne. In which city is our humanity defined—in Hilda's or in Donatello's? Surely there is little doubt as to which flower grows from nature.

Fourteen years earlier, in *Mosses from an Old Manse* (1846), Hawthorne had clarified the matter in his short story, "The New Adam and Eve," which quite predictably, since it was set in America, took the city as the location for the new garden. In Hawthorne's little story the prison metaphors found in *The Scarlet Letter* or *The Marble Faun* receive more explicit definition. As the only inhabitants of the city, of the world, the new Adam and Eve are appalled when they encounter a prison. They "hurry from the prison. Had they known how the former inhabitants of earth were shut up in artificial error, and cramped and chained by their perversions, they might have compared the whole moral world to a prison-house, and have deemed the removal of the race a general jail-delivery."[27] Even for Hawthorne this view is grim and harsh, but it provides a clue as to how little a living Hilda might find in temporality. For even these newly created children of God, the new Adam and Eve, both discover that once touched by the city of this world the way back to what Adam calls "our home," the place from which they "have strayed"—torn like Thoreau from "Those fair Elysian fields"[28]—proves to be elusive. As Adam says in seeking to return, "something drags us down" (p. 282). It is their humanity, new or old. The "city" this pair—or Hester and Dimmesdale or Donatello and Miriam—lives in was built by Cain. It is the "prison" that holds us. A Hilda or an Amasa Delano can be blind to it.

To "see," however, may offer nothing other than Donatello's prison. This is an idea that Melville explores in *Pierre* (1852), a story that once more leads from nature to the city. In his "Adamic" tale, written a few years before *The Marble Faun,* Melville presents a literal city, recognizable as New York, even though he makes a point of not mentioning it by name. As in Hawthorne's *Marble Faun,* Melville's hero "falls" in the city. But as in Hawthorne's romance, the cause is not urban vice. The city in *Pierre* parallels the familiar urban "blossom" of nature. Ironically, congruent with the American myth, this "city" is "nature"—or Saddle Meadows—revealed in its true and appalling identity. In Melville's vision it is not Kiloam; rather, it is the world stripped of illusions, one of which was Pierre's naive idea of Saddle Meadows as an idyllic place. That Saddle Meadows harbored its serpent from the beginning, as Eden did in this "black" vision, has long been well understood by Melville's critics. Pierre comprehends more slowly, though by degrees he learns, as the deepest horrors of Dante and the previously unfathomed anguish of Hamlet become manifest to him. In retrospect, he sees where his destiny had been determined. Contrary to the views of those social scientists who think Melville spent his time writing anti-urban polemics, it happened long before Pierre reached New York: "When at Saddle Meadows, Pierre had wavered and trembled in those first wretched hours ensuing upon the receipt of Isabel's letter; then humanity had let go the hand of Pierre, and therefore his cry."[29] Pierre flees to the city in an attempt to escape the horrors, while the book's very premise hinges on the idea that in whatever direction Pierre goes disaster will follow. Hamlet had been indecisive and was subsequently destroyed, so Pierre would be decisive; and he is destroyed. His one specific appeal to nature takes the form of a plea to the "Memnon stone" that if his course is ruinous, then the stone should fall and destroy him. As if nature answers, a bird lands on the stone, the stone remains unmoving, and Pierre is ultimately ruined. The particular horrors he encounters are finally neither urban nor rural, since both places symbolize a common blackness. Country and city fail him equally. Lucy, his country goddess, is herself from the city; in her city Pierre takes the "bait. . .set in Paradise" (p. 28) and falls in love with this strange girl, whose last name, Tartan, has the marvelously ironic biblical referent of an Assyrian who assailed the city of Jerusalem.[30] In 1852, the year of *Pierre,* the condition of Melville's world suggested that heaven and hell at times seemed to define each other. New York and Saddle Meadows were both part of the larger city in which Pierre feels his "mark of Cain" (p. 336).

When Pierre and Isabel, along with Delly, move from country to city, the fruits of nature are disclosed. The city is nature's flower in the same way that the "human condition" grows from the flaw symbolized in the biblical Eden. What Melville has to say about Eden, about God, about virtue, and about evil, and about so many other things in the strange novel called *Pierre,* is a subject for more essays than have already been written about a book too readily shrugged off as a failure. But the concern of the moment is not to insist on that aesthetic judgment, nor to argue the case for *Pierre.* Rather, it is to emphasize that a common blackness mediates both country and city. In the country the young man is at first an Amasa Delano; in the city he becomes an Ahab. But both places are metaphors for the changing modes of awareness within Pierre, as well as tropes for the world's underlying disorders. New York is no more wicked than Saddle Meadows, and the prison in which Pierre finally dies is the same prison that would claim Donatello, the "cage" described by Horace Bushnell. Although Hawthorne and Melville did not have identical perceptions of the universe, they did share the notion that for better or for worse, the perceiving individual must come home to what in *The Marble Faun* and *Pierre* are called "prisons," or as Emerson once stated it, "Man imprisoned."[31] They return to the city of the self. In defining this kind of isolation, Melville and Hawthorne happened to use a configuration owing something to America's vision of the city culminating from nature, but to deduce that either tale explores primarily an urban place is to recognize what Melville called "the least part of genius."[32]

In the journeys of Pierre or Donatello, or even in Hawthorne's much anthologized "My Kinsman, Major Molineux," individuals go to a city that defines their fractured world, not their country's urban vision. Although the journey from nature to the city was obviously not used invariably, Melville found the idea important enough to employ it again two years after the appearance of *Pierre.* In *Israel Potter,* published serially in 1854 and as a book in 1855, Melville transforms an urban place called London into "the City of Dis," a form of "hell" owing much less to London than to Dante, from whom Melville took the phrase. Perhaps some of Melville's nineteenth-century readers clucked over the iniquity of London as they read his story in *Putnam's,* just as they no doubt nodded approvingly a year later—1855— when in the same magazine Amasa Delano seemed to triumph over evil. But Melville refers to the world and not merely to London when he flatly states in *Israel Potter*: "Nor marble, nor flesh, nor the sad spirit of man, may in this cindery City of Dis abide white."[33] To clarify that point, blacker than the blackness of Hawthorne, Melville brings his hero home, after the dark comedy of his journey, to the Housatonic mountains of his birth, the region of whatever greenery and joy young Israel might have once known. As he had sent Pierre from the country to the city, so he now returns Israel from the city to the country. Cain, as it were, had come home. But to the surprise only of those who did not comprehend Melville, Israel no more found the promised land in America than in the "City of Dis," where he had been a "prisoner" (p. 6). The land of Israel's childhood was vacant; the old inhabitants had gone "West" (p.225). "Best followed now in this life, by hurrying, like itself, to a close," writes Melville (p. 225). "Few things remain," he says in the penultimate paragraph. In the end, Israel comes home to nature, to the emptiness of his world, and only in the oddest of readings could his location of Dis be regarded as particularly urban.

Even Melville's earlier novels, such as *Typee* (1846) and *Redburn* (1849), which on occasion have been cited as reflecting respectively primitive celebrations and urban anathemas, il-

lustrate how distant the metaphysical horrors were from any form
of social arrangement. In *Redburn*, where the hero reaches Liverpool after the journey across the sea and where he moves from
nature to the city, the sum total of all the definable, gory and
vividly portrayed details of that English city do not for a moment
match the terror embodied in Jackson, whose malign influence
manifests itself at sea rather than in Liverpool, and whose
"mystery of iniquity,"[34] as Melville would call it in *Billy Budd*
(p. 76), was to be deeply explored in much of Melville's work. Indeed, *Redburn* sets a particularly bad example as an anti-urban
novel because of its happy ending—as these things go with
Melville—in the city of New York. As for *Typee*, the island holds
such an indefinable terror that Fayaway's numerous charms notwithstanding, Tom's obsessive concern becomes to escape. When
he succeeds, he lapses into a three-month psychic illness, which
anticipates the three-month illness that would end in the death of
Benito Cereno. Although the terror that Tom seeks to escape
may be in many ways indefinable, one aspect is clearly the threat
to his identity—the same fear of losing himself that Ishmael expresses, the threat from which Whittier retreats in "Hampton
Beach." As with Ishmael and Whittier, Tom returns, in his case
to a ship, although wherever the place happened to be it was likely
to represent in some way the falling back upon the self. At the
end of Tom's journey to nature he reaches a ship; at the end of
Pierre's journey from nature he arrives at a city. But each hero
has in common the attempt to find his elusive place in a
mysterious world. Although containing America's nature-to-city
motif—or some variation of it—the journeys remain directed
toward the city of man.

I do not mean that every time a city is mentioned by Melville,
Hawthorne, Longfellow, or others, that no urban ideas appear. As
people aware of their surroundings, they obviously had thoughts
about urban places. As citizens of their country, as well as of the
Cosmopolitan's universe in *The Confidence-Man*, they had concerns ranging from the elections of political officials to the drain-
ing of swamps. As participants in the daily process of their coun-

try's life, they defined the city at times in accordance with America's idea of it as the blossom of nature. Indeed, in his *Second Series* Emerson formulates the image about as precisely as anyone could:

> If we consider how much we are nature's, we need not be superstitious about towns, as if that terrific or benefic force did not find us there also, and fashion cities. Nature, who made the mason, made the house. We may easily hear too much of rural influences. The cool disengaged air of natural objects makes them enviable to us, chafed and irritable creatures with red faces, and we think we shall be as grand as they if we camp out and eat roots; but let us be men instead of woodchucks and the oak and the elm shall gladly serve us, though we sit in chairs of ivory on carpets of silk.[35]

This nature so familiar to us as the one that will "fashion cities" is not the "occasional and transient" place of Thoreau. It belongs to the "moon," just as chairs really might be of ivory. Every moment was not a metaphysical one, and the literature of the most intensely romantic writers contains celebration and disparagement of both farms and cities. One thinks of Thoreau's ironic confrontation with the bean field in *Walden,* or the skepticism of Margaret Fuller and George Ripley about farm life.[36] And certainly Whittier was far from his pantheistic moments when ridiculing Wordsworth's attempt to "exorcise" railroads "by a sonnet," or in adding that "rocks and trees, rapids, cascades, and other water-works are doubtless all very well; but on the whole, considering our seven months of frost, are not cotton shirts and woollen coats still better?"[37] Nor was Emerson tied to metaphysics when observing that in bitter winter weather, "a hundred miles of prairie. . .are not worth the poorest shed or cellar in the towns."[38] Views such as these, and they are plentiful, find their counterparts in the myriad and familiar stated preferences for the natural world over civilization and its artifacts. At issue, however, is not any quantitative analysis over whether trees or buildings were more likely to be praised, or whether the city was preferred over the country. These were not the important questions faced by romantic artists. The relation of the city to nature in the central matters that were raised treated concerns other than woollen coats or urban cellars. In a world where the "end" purpose of "nature" was "man," as Emerson said it was,[39] buildings might be as remote from cities as the moon of Thoreau's "Walking" could be from nature.

In a letter to his friend Harrison Blake dated August 9, 1850, Thoreau offers us a comment on the city (and on swamps) as valuable as the one he gives in distinguishing the moon from nature: "I see less difference between a city and a swamp than formerly," Thoreau writes. "It is a swamp, however, too dismal and dreary even for me, and I should be glad if there were fewer owls, and frogs, and mosquitoes in it." What "swamp" and what "city" does he mean in saying that he prefers "a more cultivated place, free from miasma and crocodiles?"[40] *Walden,* where swamps are richly praised, had not yet been written when Thoreau wrote these words. Are we to believe that between 1850 and 1854, when *Walden* was published, Thoreau underwent a conversion? No one, it is hoped, can seriously entertain such an idea. Nor is it even likely that, however annoying mosquitoes may have been, Thoreau had any serious quarrel with owls and frogs, or with crocodiles. Yet here is the same man equating the city with the swamp, who in "Walking" would proclaim the much-quoted phrase, "in Wildness is the preservation of the World." Fortunately for proprietors of gift shops, the letter to Blake does not require the abandonment of the slogan. Thoreau loved the "wild," and he wondered about the city.

Thoreau's swamp, his city, his Wildness, were romantic metaphors for modes of consciousness. Although Thoreau had much to say against urban places—as well as much to say for them—his letter to Blake had little to do with that subject. His city was the world, and in equating it with a swamp he revealed one of his moments when that world did not quite conform to the ordered location he wanted it to be, when the polis of the universe might have been mediated by the "swamps" of Donatello's

Rome or Pierre's New York. Thoreau, of course, posited the way
out, the path toward reunion with that nature of which he was no
longer "part and parcel." The great formulation of this experience with nature was defined in *Walden,* where, inevitably
enough, Thoreau told us that a new city could emerge from
man's new relationship with nature.

He describes this in the "Former Inhabitants" chapter of
Walden, where, seizing his culture's configuration of the city
blossoming from the wilderness, he ironically comments on it and
proceeds to offer his own city as a better way. The narrator, we
recall, has wandered from site to site in the Walden region, evoking memories of those who had lived there before but whose
village never grew. Their commercial skills failed to make "the
wilderness to blossom like the rose," as Thoreau puts it in that
familiar American image. But Thoreau's regret is not that the
commercial city failed to emerge. His "former inhabitants" are
like those Hawthorne perceived when using the identical phrase
in his "New Adam and Eve." As Thoreau describes them, these
people are dead, but more important, they never lived—at least
not as Thoreau saw the possibilities of life. Hawthorne's "former
inhabitants" never found a way out of the prison of their city.
Similarly, Thoreau's "former inhabitants" never learned to experience the waters of Walden Pond. So Thoreau hopes, and his
book continually returns to this, that he may start again and build
his own city from the boon of nature, or, more aptly as we know,
from the power of the perceiving self. "Again," he writes,
"perhaps, Nature will try, with me for a first settler, and my
house raised last spring to be the oldest in the hamlet." And
then, after assuring his reader that no "man has ever built on the
spot which I occupy," he invokes what is almost a prayer that the
city he builds will not be the one humanity has known for so long:
"Deliver me from a city built on the site of a more ancient city,
whose materials are ruins, whose gardens cemeteries."[41] We know
that "ancient city" encountered by Emerson's "god in ruins,"
who along with his ancestors and his contemporaries finally encountered spiritual failure in the "gardens." America promised

very little if it built its cities and gardens from such materials. It offered no new direction. In the private enterprise of beginning again, Thoreau looked to the ''rose'' of his own city, the one that would take him not merely beyond America, but beyond whatever was implied in the first city that man had built.

In the ''Wildness'' that would be ''the preservation of the world,'' a mystical self could form from nature the new city, the ''occasional and transient'' place to be made permanent by art or to be experienced in moments of intense illumination, as it happened one day to Thoreau on July 10, 1851:

> How many times I have seen this kind of sunset—the most gorgeous sight in nature! From the hill behind Minott's [a friend] I see the birds flying against this red sky, the sun having set; one looks like a bat. Now between two stupendous mountains of the low stratum under the evening red, clothed in slightly rosaceous amber light, through a magnificent gorge, far, far away, as perchance may occur in pictures of the Spanish coast viewed from the Mediterranean, I see a city, the eternal city of the west, the phantom city, in whose streets no traveller has trod, over whose pavements the horses of the sun have already hurried, some Salamanca of the imagination. But it lasts only for a moment, for now the changing light has wrought such changes in it that I see the resemblance no longer.[42]

In that moment Thoreau sees the world rightly ordered, the universe unfolding to the same perfection as Dante had long ago seen in *his* beatific vision of the rose after having escaped the darkness that Pierre had seen in him. But the theology of Dante's journey could no longer lead either Melville or Thoreau to the ''phantom city,'' and the psychology that would advise us how to categorize such experiences was only being born. So in that time of history, which Thoreau thought to be the best of times, the view from Minott's hill might remain uncluttered by the dogmas of science or theology, and ''the eternal city'' could be as wondrous as one's own power to ''see'' into the distance of the ''west.'' Or as terrible.

Walden offers the brighter vision. But the promise could only be redeemed by an interior force that might free man from his prison, the same force that would hold him if he failed to turn it to the way of redemption. As Thoreau observes with a premise basic to his vision, confronting "nature" revealed that "one could no longer accuse institutions and society, but must front the true source of evil."[43] Now surely, in this vindication of social institutions from the stigma of having caused evil, Thoreau did not mean to place the onus on trees, or rocks, or mosquitoes, or any manifestation of the physical world external to him. This source of evil was neither urban nor rural, nor "Wildness" manifested as uncultivated wilderness. Nature, in this vision, was "part and parcel" of man. The source of evil, as well as of good, of demonism or of divinity, was the individual. Whatever evil existed in the world had its original source in that idea of biblical, psychological or mythic history—however one wishes to explain it—of the supreme flaw man inflicted upon himself, as Thoreau saw it, when he fell away from his divine source. Since man had shattered his own world, he could put it together again, as in *Walden* where the hero journeys to nature and perhaps discovers how he might awaken to the divine self that existed before Cain built his city. It all had very little to do with owls and frogs, this emulation of an American paradigm where the city emerges from nature.

Nor was the outcome of the romantic journey always as certain. Thoreau's "true source of evil" oscillated between embracing the faith of *Walden* and moving toward the doubts revealed in the letter to Blake or in the often-quoted passage describing his frightening assent of "Titanic" Mt. Ktaadn, the place where, in Thoreau's very own words, in an analogy rarely—if ever—commented upon, "nature" defines a "stepmother" world, as it did to Ahab. But in the wonderful art of *Walden,* in the penetrating eye of its enlightened hero, the kinds of disorders found in the Mt. Ktaadn of *The Maine Woods* are obliterated by the poet's triumphant vision.[44] Yet in this nature beyond the moon, the logical and always implicit corollary to Emerson's dream of prevailing over the "sordor and filths of nature" was that failure to do so would make nature even more monstrous. As it happened when the whale and Ahab each made the other more demonic, even though Melville held more closely to the idea that behind it all was an external and manipulative force. For the metaphysical "axis of vision" whereby Melville differed primarily from Emerson and Thoreau was not in any strict adherence to optimism or pessimism, but in a different idea of the extent to which man could break from the "prison" that held Ahab to the whale, that united the "divine" Thoreau with the "beasts" in an alliance he sought to break. But all three shared the belief that no physical journey, either to the nearest woods or to the whale fishery, would lead them to Melville's "final harbor" as a place of religious discovery. Redemption would not be found in the old God that Melville intensely wanted back, nor in a theology created from the world of physical things. If found, it would be in the mystery of the self, the interior worlds of discovery postulated in the art of Emerson or Thoreau.

As a very young man, Emerson in 1823 learned this; he discovered how remote any physical journey to nature was, how little it helped one find the nature he would later define as an emanation of the self. I refer to the time when he took his revered aunt's advice and looked for inspiration in the forest: "When I took my book therefore to the woods—I found Nature not half poetical, not half visionary enough. . . .In short I found that I had only transported into the new place my entire personal identity, & was grievously disappointed."[45] Unlike Melville's Tom in *Typee,* who so wanted to retain his identity, Emerson was seeking a way to change himself and his world. In the years to follow his experience in the forest—the event occurring in 1823—Emerson would build his own world, improve upon nature, and offer the new way to redemption—or, more modestly, the means to encounter those personal tragedies of which life had given him more than his share. Through the private alembic of poetic illumination, he created such a world. At times it almost appeared to offer the promise of his vision.

It seemed to in 1831 when, after the death of his beloved Ellen, he spent a fortnight "wandering" in "the Green Mountains and Lake Champlain" searching for his bride, who was "nowhere and yet everywhere" to be found.[46] His surroundings appeared to be suffused with her. However, the world Emerson built was tenuously constructed. Three years later, in 1834, Ellen remained very much in his troubled thoughts. And after walking in the "companionable" woods with his "Reason" and his "Understanding," Emerson expresses the doubt that no poetry of nature could quite remove:

> I have my glees as well as my glooms alone. Confirm my faith (and when I write the word, Faith looks indignant), pledge me the word of the Highest that I shall have my dead and my absent again, and I could be content and cheerful for a thousand years.

The "Highest," however, was part of what Emerson had lost. "[W]ere I assured of meeting Ellen tomorrow," he continues, "would it be less than a world, a personal world. Death has no bitterness in the light of that thought."[47] Closer to a Hester Prynne than a Reverend Dimmesdale, Emerson conceived the continuity of love, although the heaven of the lovers' joining could exist for him only precariously in the mystery of the mind, in the location of the single individual shaping the world to a better order.

A few years later, in 1842, in trying to comprehend the death of his son Waldo, his thoughts, like Ishmael's at the end of *Moby-Dick,* gravitated toward the hell of his own "Ixion."[48] It was not that Emerson had revised his definition of nature, since its conditions remained what they were in 1836. The promise in *Nature* had been that the world was heaven or hell in accordance with one's interior vision, and Emerson sought no hypocritical turn toward a "good man." Nor did he expect that the stars would give what he had naively sought in 1823. Whatever the implications, and Emerson was always prepared to accept them, he knew that temporal disorders were not to be dissipated by a trip to the woods, no matter how beautiful one might find such a place to be. Thus, it was not merely to ridicule the minor vogue of temporarily living in isolated huts that turned Emerson, as early as 1825, against praising any "wolfish misanthropy that retreats to thickets from cheerful towns, and scrapes the ground for roots and acorns, either out of a grovelling soul, or a hunger for glory that has mistaken grimace for philosophy. *It is not the solitude of place,"* he continues, *"but the solitude of soul which is so inestimable to us"* (my italics).[49] These "thickets" and "cheerful towns" do something other than dichotomize nature and the urban places of America. Emerson's attack is clearly not against a rural environment; not simply a defense of civilization. It is rather an affirmation of the interior world as the place for the romantic quest. However far one went into "nature," by whatever "causeway" one crossed the "moon," the passage covered ground quite different from the geographical place of America and inwardly took one much farther west than Whitman's India. For Melville this required the passionate insistence on his own identity; for Emerson it meant the same thing, except that the identity would be created anew. But whether the journey took one to madness or to redemption—and to approach the edge of one was to risk the precipice of the other—the movement into nature led toward what Emerson called in 1841 the "hermit's lodge" of the self, which was to be "the Holy City and the Fair of the whole world."[50] And whatever the outcome of this journey to the "Holy City," one traveled an intensely private route. Even "Columbus," Emerson tells us, "discovered no isle or key so lonely as himself."[51]

As for the literal city, where one attended concerts, conducted business, or simply mingled with the crowd, the responses to it were as varied as the individuals and their moods of the moment. In a poem, one might state a preference for the city over nature, as Whitman did in "Give me the Splendid Silent Sun"; or, as in the case of Longfellow's "Mezzo Cammin," one might equate it with life. Or, as was sometimes the case, one might choose to condemn it. But the deep and imaginative questions that the world asked of our greatest writers led them elsewhere, took them to an exploration of such questions as Melville posed within the mind of Pierre:

> Is it possible, after all, that spite of [sic] bricks and shaven faces, this world we live in is brimmed with wonders, and I and all mankind, beneath our garbs of common-placeness, conceal enigmas that the stars themselves, and perhaps the highest seraphim can not resolve? (Pp. 138-39)

Whether found or not, such "wonders" belonged neither to nature as merely a physical place nor to the city, whether of Rome, New York, or Kiloam. Nor in a special way did they even belong to the stars, as Emerson pointedly observed a decade earlier, in 1841, when he wrote that "the moment I *am*, I despise city and the seashore, yes, earth and the galaxy also."[52]

From the intensity of such mysterious experiences, metaphors of nature or of cities could emanate. But although American society at large knew that their cities would blossom from nature, the romantic writers never had similar assurances. As they searched for some New Jerusalem in their "nature," the counter-threat of Cain's city too frequently intruded. Whether as Ahab or as Emerson, the individual embarking on the daring quest, on Whitman's "Passage to more than India," took an interior journey somewhat bolder than the national one that did not happen to emphasize the recurring spiritual questions of Western civilization. "*Wherefore unsatisfied soul?*" asks Whitman in "Passage to India." "*Whither O mocking life?*" Writers who asked similar questions could only be sure that the answers transcended any nature or any city to be found in the geographical location of America.

Notes

Chapter 1: Introduction: Journeys to Nature

1. Ralph Waldo Emerson, *The Complete Works of Ralph Waldo Emerson,* intro. Edward Waldo Emerson, 12 vols. (Boston and New York: Centenary edition, 1903), 2:9-10. Subsequently cited as *Works.*

2. AN Kaul, *The American Vision* (New Haven, Conn.: Yale University Press, 1963); Richard Poirier, *A World Elsewhere* (New York: Oxford University Press, 1966).

3. Leo Marx, *The Machine in the Garden* (New York: Oxford University Press, 1964), p. 71.

4. Henry David Thoreau, *The Writings of Henry David Thoreau,* 20 vols. (Boston and New York: Walden edition, 1906; reprint, New York: AMS Press, 1968), 5:214. Subsequently cited as *Writings.*

5. I am using *myth* as Emile Durkheim does in another context by referring to "mythology" as "the system of beliefs common to [a] group. The traditions whose memory it [mythology] perpetuates express the way in which society represents man and the world. . . ." In using the word *myth* I do not make a judgment as to whether "the system of beliefs" is true or false. For my use of Durkheim, see *The Elementary Forms of the Religious Life,* trans. Joseph Ward Swain (1912; New York: Free Press, 1965), pp. 419-20.

Since this definition of *myth* might seem to apply equally to a definition of history, I want to make explicit the implicit distinction between the two. History presupposes a true ordering of events independent of any "system of beliefs." It proceeds from the assumption that truth is absolute and chronologically recoverable. Thus, when Thoreau finds inadequate "any history of America" he questions the very idea that history can exist in such terms. Truth is found in immediate poetic experience rather than in recorded events. The association of his society with myth is mine and not his.

6. Arthur O. Lovejoy, "On the Discrimination of Romanticisms," *PMLA 39* (June, 1924): 229-53. For the basic attack on Professor Lovejoy's position, see René Wellek, "The Concept of 'Romanticism' in Literary History." *Comparative Literature* 1 (Winter 1949): 1-23; and (Spring 1949): 147-72.

7. Northrup Frye, *A Study of English Romanticism,* (New York: Random House, 1968), pp. 37-38. Subsequently cited parenthetically in the text.

8. R. W. B. Lewis, in his seminal study of the American Adamic theme, *The American Adam* (Chicago: University of Chicago Press, 1955), appears to accept the idea that America's literary "Adam" was in important instances not fallen. For clarifying discus-

sions of how fallen "Adam" was in American literature, see Roy Harvey Pearce, *The Continuity of American Poetry* (Princeton, N.J.: Princeton University Press, 1961) and Frederic I. Carpenter, " 'The American Myth': Paradise (to be) Regained," *PMLA* 74 (December 1959): 599-606. I examine the whole subject at length in chapter 6 of this study.

9. M. H. Abrams, *Natural Supernaturalism* (New York: W. W. Norton, 1971), p. 13.

10. Herman Melville, "Hawthorne and His Mosses," in *The Shock of Recognition*, ed. Edmund Wilson (New York: Farrar, Straus and Cudahy, 1943), pp. 195-96.

11. Ibid., p. 196.

12. All quotations of Whitman's poetry are from *Leaves of Grass*, eds. Harold W. Blodgett and Sculley Bradley (New York: New York University Press, 1965)—for "Passage to India," see pp. 411-21. Citations of Melville's *Mardi* are from the Newberry edition, eds. Harrison Hayford, Hershel Parker, and G. Thomas Tanselle (Evanston and Chicago: Northwestern University Press, 1970), pp. 654, 556.

13. Emerson, *Nature, Works*, 1: 73-74.

14. Thoreau, *Writings*, 5: 167.

15. Thoreau, *A Week on the Concord and Merrimack Rivers, Writings*, 1: 69.

16. Melville, *Mardi*, p. 654.

Chapter 2: Nature in the Land of Milk and Honey

1. Perry Miller, "The Location of American Religious Freedom,' " *Nature's Nation* (Cambridge, Mass.: Harvard University Press, 1967), pp. 158-59.

2. *Godey's Lady's Book* 10 (January 1835): 48.

3. Daniel Drake, *Discourse on the History, Character, and Prospects of the West*, intro. Perry Miller (1834; Gainesville, Fla.: Scholars' Facsimiles & Reprints, 1955), p. 2.

4. George Ripley, *The Harbinger* 1 (October 1845): 267.

5. Richardson Wright, *The Story of Gardening: from the Hanging Gardens of Babylon to the Hanging Gardens of New York* (New York: Dover Publications, 1963), p. 368.

6. The almost endless connotations of *nature* have been discussed by Arthur O. Lovejoy and George Boas, *Primitivism and Related Ideas in Antiquity* (New York: Octagon Books, 1965). For an extraodinarily useful study of nature in Western civilization, see Clarence J. Glacken, *Traces on the Rhodian Shore* (Berkeley and Los Angeles, Calif.: University of California Press, 1967).

7. Although I will discuss Flint at several points in this study, for a fuller discussion of him see my introduction to *A Condensed Geography and History of the Western States or the Mississippi Valley* (1828; Gainesville, Fla.: Scholars' Facsimiles & Reprints, 1970), as well as the broader discussion by George R. Brooks in his edition of *Recollections of the Last Ten Years in the Valley of the Mississippi* (1826; Carbondale, Ill.: Southern Illinois University Press, 1968). Both books by Flint are enormously useful for insights into

American society at that time. Even Flint's misconceptions, and they are numerous, tell us much about his day. In my view, no writer offers a more representative picture of how Americans regarded the western regions.

8. Timothy Flint, *Geography,* 1: 10.

9. Ibid., p. 62. Or compare J. Hector St. John Crèvecoeur's earlier variation of this dualism in his reference ''to pestilential infections which lay nature waste'' (*Letters from an American Farmer,* note by W. P. Trent; intro. Ludwig Lewisohn [New York: Fox, Duffield, and Company, 1904], p. 239).

10. Thomas Farnham, *Travels in the Great Western Prairies, the Anahuac and Rocky Mountains, and in the Oregon Territory* (1841; London, 1843), in Reuben Gold Thwaites, ed., *Early Western Travels* (New York: AMS Press, 1966), 28: 192.

11. Edmund Flagg, *The Far West* (New York, 1838), in Reuben Gold Thwaites, ed. *Early Western Travels* (New York: AMS Press, 1966), 27: 21.

12. Ibid., p. 118.

13. Amos A. Parker, *Trip to the West and Texas* (Concord, N.H.: William White, 1836), p. 34.

14. John K. Townsend, *Narrative of a Journey Across the Rocky Mountains to the Columbia River* (Philadelphia, 1839), in Reuben Gold Thwaites, ed., *Early Western Travels* (New York: AMS Press, 1966), 21: 124-27.

15. C. W. Dana, *The Garden of the World, or The Great West* (Boston: Wentworth, 1856), pp. 13-15.

16. Ibid., p. 137.

17. Ibid., p. 20.

18. Ibid., p. 55.

19. Frances Trollope, *Domestic Manners of the Americans,* ed. Donald Smalley (New York: A. A. Knopf, 1949), p. 34.

20. N. P. Willis, *American Scenery* (London: G. Virtue, 1840), 1: 1.

21. Ibid., p. 2.

22. Ibid., 2: 26. Leo Marx's *The Machine in the Garden* (New York: Oxford University Press, 1964) is the most important study to date on the relationship of American landscape to society and art. Abundant evidence supports his thesis on technology and pastoral ideals. It is important to realize, as I am sure Leo Marx does, that ideal form was not a pressing concern for most people, especially when they were conquering the wilderness, or even visiting it. The ideal so effectively defined in *The Machine in the Garden* is best understood as one poetical ideal—at times even an empty rhetorical one employed by politicians—rather than a broad, national concern.

23. M. H. Abrams, *The Mirror and the Lamp* (New York: Oxford University Press, 1953), p. 122.

24. Arthur Hobson Quinn and Edward H. O'Neill, eds., *The Complete Poems and Stories of Edgar Allan Poe,* (New York: A. A. Knopf, 1946), 1:392. Subsequently cited as *Poems and Stories.*

25. George Ogden, *Letters from the West* (New Bedford, 1823) in Reuben Gold Thwaites, ed., *Early Western Travels* (New York: AMS Press, 1966), 19: 40.

26. Ibid., p. 25.

27. Basil Hall's important works on America were *Forty Etchings from Sketches Made with the Camera Lucida, in North America in 1827 and 1828,* (1829: London: Simpkin

and Marshall, 1830) and *Travels in North America in the Years 1827 and 1828* (Edinburgh: Cadell and Co., 1829).

28. Francis J. Grund, *The Americans in Their Moral, Social, and Political Relations* (London: Longman, 1837), 1: 165-66.

29. Drake, *Discourse on the History, Character, and Prospects of the West,* p. 55.

30. Ogden, *Letters from the West,* p. 33.

31. Robert Baird, *View of the Valley of the Mississippi* (1832; Philadelphia: H. S. Tanner, 1834), p. iii.

32. Ibid., pp. 104-5.

33. Harriet Martineau, *Society in America* (London: Saunders and Otley, 1837), 1: 212.

34. Richard Hofstadter, *The American Political Tradition and the Men Who Made It* (New York: A. A. Knopf, 1948), pp. 55-56.

35. Martineau, *Society in America,* 1: 213.

36. Max Lerner, introduction to Adam Smith, *An Inquiry into the Nature and Causes of the Wealth of Nations,* ed. Edwin Cannan (New York: The Modern Library, 1937), p. ix.

37. Timothy Dwight, *Travels; in New-England and New-York* (New Haven, Conn.; Privately printed, 1821-22), 3: 34.

38. Washington Irving, *Astoria* (1836; New York: John B. Alden, 1884), p. 269.

Chapter 3: The Garden of America

1. Herman Melville, *Mardi,* ed. Harrison Hayford, Hershel Parker, and G. Thomas Tanselle. (Evanston and Chicago: Newberry edition, Northwestern University Press, 1970), p. 384.

2. Catherine Sedgwick, *Linwoods* (New York: Harper, 1835), 2:189.

3. Fanny Kemble (Frances Anne Butler), *Journal* (London: J. Murray, 1835), 2:256.

4. Gustave De Beaumont, *Marie, or Slavery in the United States,* trans. Barbara Chapman, intro. Alvis L. Tinnin (Stanford, Calif.: Stanford University Press, 1958), p. 136.

5. Michael Chevalier, *Society, Manners, and Politics in the United States: Letters on North America;* ed. John William Ward and trans. after the T.G. Bradford edition (1839; reprint, Gloucester, Mass.: Peter Smith, 1967), pp. 295-96.

6. Frances (Fanny) Wright, *Views of Society and Manners in America,* ed. Paul R. Baker (1821; Cambridge, Mass.: Harvard University Press, 1963), p. 104; Harriet Martineau, *Retrospect of Western Travel* (London: Saunders and Otley, 1838), 2: 39; Charles Fenno Hoffman, *A Winter in the Far West* (London: Harper and Brothers, 1835), 2: 308.

7. Alexis de Tocqueville, *Democracy in America,* trans. Henry Reeve (1835; New York: Schocken Books, 1961), 2: 89.

8. Alexander Philip Maximilian, *Travels in the Interior of North America,* trans. H. Evans Lloyd (London, 1843), in Reuben Gold Thwaites, ed., *Early Western Travels* (New York: AMS Press, 1966), 22:25.

9. Theodore Dwight. *The Northern Traveller* (New York: Goodrich and Wiley, 1834), p. 34. This is revised from a more descriptive segment in earlier editions. The book was first published in 1825. Such use of *romantic*, of course, differs from my own use of the word as described in Chapter 1.

10. Timothy Flint, *Recollections of the Last Ten Years in the Valley of the Mississippi,* ed. George R. Brooks (1826; Carbondale, Ill.: Southern Illinois University Press, 1968), p. 15.

11. Dwight, *The Northern Traveller,* p. 363.

12. P. Stansbury, *A Pedestrian Tour of Two Thousand Three Hundred Miles, in North America* (New York: J. D. Myers and W. Smith, 1822), p. 45.

13. Catherine Sedgwick, *Hope Leslie* (New York: White, Gallaher, and White, 1827), 1:137.

14. Annabel Newton, *Wordsworth in Early American Criticism* (Chicago: The University of Chicago Press, 1928), p. 6.

15. Charles Dickens, *American Notes,* ed. Andrew Lang, *The Works of Charles Dickens* (1842; London: Chapman and Hall, 1897), 28:181.

16. Flint, *Recollections,* p. 41.

17. C. W. Dana, *The Garden of the World, or The Great West* (Boston: Wentworth, 1856), p. 16.

18. Timothy Dwight, *Travels; in New-England and New-York* (New Haven, Conn.: Privately printed, 1821-22), 4:35.

19. Flint, *Recollections,* p. 11.

20. Henry Schoolcraft, *Travels in the Central Portions of the Mississippi Valley* (New York: Collins and Hannay, 1825), p. 121.

21. Timothy Flint, *A Condensed Geography and History of the Western States or the Mississippi Valley* (1828; Gainesville, Fla.: Scholars' Facsimiles & Reprints, 1970), 1:206.

22. DeBeaumont, *Marie,* p. 116.

23. Robert Baird, *View of the Valley of the Mississippi* (1832; Philadelphia: H. S. Tanner, 1834), pp. 91-92. For a much wider examination of American attitudes toward Indians, see Roy Harvey Pearce, *The Savages of America* (Baltimore, Md.: The Johns Hopkins Press, 1953).

24. Achille Murat, *America and the Americans,* ed. and trans. Henry J. Bradfield (New York: William H. Graham, 1849), p. 41. Bradfield's translation is apparently from material written by Murat about 1832. This date is suggested on p. 260.

25. Ibid., p. 212.

26. Washington Irving, *A Tour of the Prairies* (1835; New York: James B. Millar & Co., 1884), p. 27.

27. J. Watson Webb, ed. *Altowan,* by William Stewart (New York: Harper, 1846), 1:iii-iv.

28. Catherine Sedgwick, "Our Burial Place," *Tales and Sketches* (1835; New York, Harper, 1868), p. 396.

29. Edgar Allan Poe, *Julius Rodman, The Complete Works of Edgar Allan Poe,* ed. James A. Harrison (New York: Thomas Y. Crowell & Co., 1902), 4:41-42.

30. Meriwether Lewis, *History of the Expedition under the Command of Lewis and Clark,* ed. Elliott Coues (New York: F. P. Harper, 1893), 2:368. (Text based on 1814 edition).

31. Timothy Flint, ed., *Inland Trade with New Mexico*, in Reuben Gold Thwaites, ed., *Early Western Travels* (New York: AMS Press, 1966), 18:341-42. Originally published in *Western Monthly Review* (April and May 1829).

32. Ralph Walso Emerson, "Nature," *Essays Second Series*, in *The Complete Works of Ralph Waldo Emerson*, intro. Edward Waldo Emerson (Boston and New York: Centenary edition, 1903), 3:177. Subsequently cited as *Works*.

33. Edmundo O'Gorman, *The Invention of America* (Bloomington, Ind.: Indiana University Press, 1961). Although I will not attempt to summarize Professor O'Gorman's position, his study should be of interest to all those interested in America as an idea.

34. Thomas Farnham, *Travels in the Great Western Prairies, the Anahuac and Rocky Mountains, and in the Oregon Territory* (1841; London, 1843), in Reuben Gold Thwaites, ed., *Early Western Travels* (New York: AMS Press, 1966), 28:143.

35. Hoffman, *A Winter in the Far West*, 1:182.

36. Chevalier, *Society, Manners, and Politics in the United States*, pp. 266-67.

37. Edmund Flagg, *The Far West*, (New York, 1838), in Reuben Gold Thwaites, ed., *Early Western Travels* (New York: AMS Press, 1966), 27:94.

38. Charles Brockden Brown, *Edgar Huntly* (1801; Philadelphia: David McKay, 1887), p. 164.

39. Stansbury, *A Pedestrian Tour*, p. 66.

40. For example, see Theodore Dwight, *Sketches of Scenery and Manners in the United States* (New York: A. T. Goodrich, 1829), p. 68; or Charles Lyell, *A Second Visit to the United States of North America* (New York: Harper and Brothers, 1849), 1:61.

41. Dwight, *Travels*, 3:91.

42. Inness's picture is reproduced in Leo Marx, *The Machine in the Garden* (New York: Oxford University Press, 1964), p. 220.

43. J. K. Paulding, *Westward Ho!* (New York: J. and J. Harper, 1832), 2:10.

44. Reproduced in David Grimsted, ed., *Notions of the Americans: 1820-1860* (New York: George Braziller, 1970), p. 262.

45. Lydia Sigourney, *Scenes in My Native Land* (Boston: James Monroe, 1845), pp. 168-69.

46. *The Western Farmer* 1 (July 1840) : 311.

47. Perhaps Nathaniel Hawthorne, *Complete Short Stories* (Garden City, N.Y.: Hanover House, 1959), p. 585. This story originally appeared in "The Token," 1831. For comments on its ascription to Hawthorne, see George E. Woodberry, *Nathaniel Hawthorne* (Boston and New York: Houghton, Mifflin and Company, 1902), pp. 38-39. For the argument rejecting Hawthorne's authorship, see William Charvat, Roy Harvey Pearce, and Claude M. Simpson, eds., *The Snow Image* (Columbus, Ohio: Ohio State University Press, Centenary edition, 1974), pp. 406-7.

48. Emerson, "The Young American," *Works*, 1:367-68.

49. N. P. Willis, *American Scenery*, 2: 55. Anne Royall, who complained of poor private gardens—and a lack of public ones—in Washington, had observed more than a decade earlier that "a very handsome public garden is laid out near the capitol, but suffered to remain in a state of nature" (*Sketches of History, Life, and Manners, in the United States* [New Haven, Conn.: Privately printed, 1826,] pp. 154-55).

50. Hoffman, *A Winter in the Far West*, 1: 80.

51. Hoffman, *A Winter in the Far West*, 1: 153.

52. DeBeaumont, *Marie*, p. 135.

53. John Pendleton Kennedy, *Swallow Barn* (1832; New York: Putnam's, 1872; edition revised by Kennedy), p. 145.

54. Dickens, *American Notes,* p. 203.

55. Baird, *View of the Valley of the Mississippi,* p. 28.

56. Ibid., pp. 39-40.

57. Ibid., p. 32.

58. Henry David Thoreau; *The Maine Woods, The Writings of Henry David Thoreau,* 20 vols. (Boston and New York: Walden edition 1906; reprint, New York: AMS Press, 1968), 3:78.

59. Emerson, "Fate," *Works,* 6:8.

Chapter 4: Mammon's Cave

1. Francis J. Grund, *The Americans in Their Moral, Social, and Political Relations* (London: Longman, 1837), 1:173.

2. Supra. See chap. 2.

3. James Fenimore Cooper, *The Prairie,* illus. F.O.C. Darley (1827; New York: W. A. Townsend and Company, 1859), p. 104. Publication dates in this collection of Cooper's writings are 1859-61.

4. Mark Twain, "Fenimore Cooper's Literary Offenses," *The Portable Mark Twain,* ed. Bernard DeVoto (New York: Viking Press, 1946), p. 541.

5. Edwin Fussell in his *Frontier: American Literature and the American West* (Princeton, N.J.: Princeton University Press, 1965) argues that for Hawthorne, and indeed for other major writers, the contemporary West played an important literary role. Those interested in the subject of the West on American imagination will want to examine his arguments.

6. Nathaniel Hawthorne, "The Hall of Fantasy," *Mosses From an Old Manse,* eds., William Charvat, Roy Harvey Pearce, and Claude M. Simpson (Columbus, Ohio: Ohio State University Press, Centenary edition, 1974), p. 178. Subsequently cited as *Works.*

7. Hawthorne, *Works,* 1965, *The House of the Seven Gables* (1851), p. 18.

8. Patrick F. Quinn, "Poe's Imaginary Voyage," *Hudson Review* 4 (Winter 1952): 563-64.

9. For Melville's use of Flint, see John D. Seelye, "Timothy Flint's 'Wicked River' and *The Confidence-Man,*" PMLA 78 (March 1963):75-79. H. Bruce Franklin has argued that Melville used Dickens's *Martin Chuzzlewit* (1844), and this is certainly possible. See Franklin's edition of *The Confidence-Man* (Indianapolis and New York: Bobbs-Merrill Company, Inc., 1967), pp. 71, 179. Since so much was written about this region, it is impossible to determine all the sources Melville may have used.

10. Herman Melville, *The Confidence-Man,* ed. Elizabeth S. Foster (New York: Hendricks House, 1954), p. 146.

11. Henry Nash Smith, *Virgin Land* (Cambridge, Mass.: Harvard University Press, 1950), p. 4.

12. James Hall, *Letters from the West* (London: Henry Colburn, 1828), p. 14.

13. Timothy Flint, *A Condensed Geography and History of the Western States or the*

Notes 235

Mississippi Valley (1828; Gainesville, Fla.: Scholars' Facsimiles & Reprints, 1970),
1:141.
14. P.J. De Smet, *Letters and Sketches: With a Narrative of a Year's Residence among the Indian Tribes of the Rocky Mountains* (Philadelphia, 1843), in Reuben Gold Thwaites, ed., *Early Western Travels* (New York: AMS Press, 1966), 27:333.
15. James O. Pattie, *The Personal Narrative of James O. Pattie*, ed. Timothy Flint (Cincinnati, Ohio, 1831), in Thwaites, ed. *Early Western Travels,* 18:44.
16. Review cited in Jay Ledya, ed., *The Melville Log* (New York: Gordian Press, 1969), 2:570.
17. Ibid., pp. 572-73.
18. Ibid., p. 565.
19. For Melville and Mather, see Daniel G. Hoffman, *Form and Fable in American Fiction* (New York: Oxford University Press, 1961), p. 290.

Chapter 5: Causeways over the Moon

1. Edgar Allan Poe, "Eldorado," in *The Complete Poems and Stories of Edgar Allan Poe,* eds. Arthur Hobson Quinn and Edward H. O'Neill (New York: A. A. Knopf, 1946), 1:83.
2. Henry David Thoreau, "Walking," *The Writings of Henry David Thoreau* (Boston and New York: Walden edition, 1906), 5:224. Subsequently cited as *Writings.*
3. Ibid., p. 231.
4. Ibid., p. 211.
5. Ibid., p. 242.
6. Ralph Waldo Emerson, "Nature," *Essays Second Series,* in *The Complete Works of Ralph Waldo Emerson,* intro. Edward Waldo Emerson (Boston and New York: Centenary edition, 1903), 3:192. Subsequently cited as *Works.*
7. *Writings,* 5:242.
8. Perhaps Dickens gave the best capsule statement on the public's response to transcendentalism: "On inquiring what this appellation [transcendentalism] might be supposed to signify, I was given to understand that whatever was unintelligible would be certainly transcendental" (Charles Dickens, *American Notes,* ed. Andrew Lang, *The Works of Charles Dickens* (1842; London: Chapman and Hall, 1897), 28:66.
9. Thoreau, *Writings,* 5:218. This point has been made effectively by Lawrence Willson, "The Transcendentalist View of the West," *Western Humanities Review* 14 (Spring 1960) :183-91.
10: Thoreau, *Journal,* 7, *Writings,* 13:496.
11. Thoreau, *Writings,* 6:210.
12. Ibid., 5:219.
13. Ibid., p. 228.
14. Thoreau, *The Maine Woods, Writings,* 3:78-79. Compare also the separation of the self from the body described in Thoreau's *Journal,* 1, *Writings,* 7:321: "I must confess there is nothing so strange to me as my own body. I love any other piece of nature, almost, better."

15. Thoreau, *Writings*, 5:222.

16. Ibid., p. 206.

17. Francis Grund, *The Americans in Their Moral, Social, and Political Relations* (London: Longman, 1837), 2:1-2.

18. Herman Melville, "The Berg," *Collected Poems of Herman Melville*, ed. Howard P. Vincent (Chicago: Hendricks House, 1947), p. 204. For *Satanstoe*, see James Fenimore Cooper, illus. F. O. C. Darley (New York: W. A. Townsend and Company, 1859-61), p. 275.

19. James Fenimore Cooper, *The Last of the Mohicans*, illus. F. O. C. Darley (New York: W. A. Townsend and Company, 1859-61), p. 55.

20. James Fenimore Cooper, *The Prairie*, illus. F. O. C. Darley (1827; W. A. Townsend and Company, 1859-61), p. 449.

21. James Fenimore Cooper, *The Pioneers*, illus. F. O. C. Darley (New York: W. A. Townsend and Company, 1859-61), p. 121. Cooper's use of "natural right" corresponds to the idea which I have discussed of nature affirming private truth.

22. Robert E. Spiller et al., eds., *Literary History of the United States*, rev. ed. (New York: Macmillian, 1959), p. 304.

23. Parke Godwin, ed., *Prose Writings of William Cullen Bryant* (1884; reissued Russell and Russell, New York, 1964), 1:222.

24. Thoreau, *The Maine Woods*, *Writings*, 3:3-4.

25. Ralph Waldo Emerson, *Journals of Ralph Waldo Emerson*, eds. Edward Waldo Emerson and Waldo Emerson Forbes (Boston and New York: Houghton Mifflin Company, 1909-14), 7:293-94. Subsequently cited as *Journals*.

26. Thoreau, *A Week on the Concord and Merrimack Rivers*, *Writings*, 1:202.

27. Ibid., p. 408.

28. Thoreau, "Cliffs and Springs," *Collected Poems of Henry Thoreau*, ed. Carl Bode (Baltimore, Md.: The Johns Hopkins Press, 1965), p. 92. Subsequently cited at *Poems*.

29. Thoreau, *The Maine Woods*, *Writings*, 3:30.

30. See Richard Hofstadter, *Social Darwinism in American Thought: 1860-1915* (Philadelphia: University of Pennsylvania Press, 1944), p. 30 ff.

31. Francis Parkman, *The Oregon Trail*, intro. Henry Sinclair Drago (New York: Dodd, Mead and Company, 1964), p. 233.

32. Timothy Flint, *A Condensed Geography and History of the Western States or the Mississippi Valley* (1828; Gainesville, Fla.: Scholars' Facsimiles & Reprints, 1970), 1:167;Emerson, *Journals*, 5:64.

33. Thoreau, *Journal*, 1, *Writings*, 7:92.

34. Emerson, *Journals*, 1:224-25.

35. Ibid., 3:282.

36. James Fenimore Cooper, *Oak Openings*, illus. F. O. C. Darley (New York: W. A. Townsend and Company, 1859-61), pp. 9-10.

37. Thoreau, *Walden*, *Writings*, 2:101.

38. Thoreau, *Journal*, 4, *Writings*, 10:459.

39. Thoreau, *Journal*, 1, *Writings*, 7:272.

40. Thoreau, *Journal*, 4, *Writings*, 10:459.

41. Emerson, *Journals*, 2:120.

42. Walt Whitman, "This Compost," *Leaves of Grass,* eds. Harold W. Blodgett and Sculley Bradley (New York: New York University Press, 1965), pp. 369-70.

43. William Cullen Bryant, "Midsummer," *Poetical Works of William Cullen Bryant* (New York: D. Appleton and Co., 1906), p. 107. The poem deals specifically with the destructiveness of the sun, but the implications are broader. The sun, symbolizing death, exerts its power over the life-sustaining force of the earth.

44. Emerson, "The Chartist's Complaint," *Works,* 9:232. The possibility exists that Emerson offers a sarcastic comment on the Chartists, but I do not think he does. Emerson's attitude toward them was what we might expect. He was repelled by mob activity, but was sympathetic to the people who were victims of injustice. Furthermore, in praising Carlyle, Emerson was to write that "he. . .stood for the people, for the Chartist, for the pauper. . . ." (*Works* 10:497). If one still insists on reading the poem as a mocking commentary on the Chartists, the message remains almost the same: men may be fools for cursing the sun, but the world is unjust, nevertheless. Read either way, the poem presents the image of men resorting to acts of futile anger in nature's unjust world.

45. Thoreau, *The Maine Woods, Writings,* 3:79.

46. Thoreau, "Epitaph on the World," *Poems,* p. 154.

47. Thoreau, "I am a Parcel of Vain Strivings Tied," *Poems,* p. 81.

48. Johann Wolfgang von Goethe, *The Sufferings of Young Werther* trans. Harry Steinhauer (1774; New York: W. W. Norton, 1970), pp. 6-7; Percy Bysshe Shelley, "The Triumph of Life," lines 47-48.

49. See chap. 7, note 14.

50. Mary Shelley, *Frankenstein,* intro. Robert E. Dowse and D. J. Palmer (New York and London: Everyman, 1963), p. 134.

51. Emerson, *Journals,* 8:247.

52. Ibid., 4:327.

53. Herman Melville, *Moby-Dick,* eds. Luther S. Mansfield and Howard P. Vincent (New York: Hendricks House, 1952), p. 225.

54. Emerson, *Journals,* 7:277.

Chapter 6: Adam Once More

1. Ralph Waldo Emerson, "Nature," *Essays Second Series, The Complete Works of Ralph Waldo Emerson,* intro. Edward Waldo Emerson (Boston and New York: Centenary edition, 1903), 3:178. Subsequently cited as *Works.*

2. The quotation, from "Experience," is cited as an epigraph to Chapter 1 of Roy Harvey Pearce's *Continuity of American Poetry* (Princeton, N.J.: Princeton University Press, 1961). It appears in Emerson, *Works,* 3:75.

3. Henry David Thoreau, *Walden, The Writings of Henry David Thoreau,* 20 vols. (Boston and New York: Walden edition, 1906; reprint, New York: AMS Press, 1968), 2:243. Subsequently cited as *Writings.*

4. Thoreau, *Journal,* 9, *Writings,* 15:121.

5. Emerson, "The Poet," *Works*, 9:315.

6. Nathaniel Hawthorne, *Mosses From an Old Manse*, eds. William Charvat, Roy Harvey Pearce, and Claude M. Simpson (Columbus, Ohio: Ohio State University Press, Centenary edition, 1974), p. 185.

7. Lines 2847-2848 in any standard edition of *The Canterbury Tales.* I have obviously modernized the language.

8. Hawthorne, *Mosses From an Old Manse*, pp. 403-4.

9. John Greenleaf Whittier, "The World's End," *The Writings of John Greenleaf Whittier in Seven Volumes* (Boston and New York: The Riverside Press, 1889), 5:420-21.

10. Ralph Waldo Emerson, *Journals of Ralph Waldo Emerson*, eds. Edward Waldo Emerson and Waldo Emerson Forbes (Boston and New York: Houghton Mifflin Company, 1909-14), 8:69. Subsequently cited as *Journals.* Emerson, apparently taking seriously his injunction against a "foolish consistency," some years later—in 1857—specifically rejected such a linear model. See *Journals*, 9:114. This should not be construed as a change in perception from one generation to the next, a movement from "pessimism" to "optimism," but rather should be understood as part of the problem inherent in welding a coherent philosophy out of metaphors with shifting meanings. It also reflects the simple fact that people feel differently on different days.

11. Thoreau, *Journal*, 3, *Writings*, 9:378.

12. Thoreau, *Journal*, 1, *Writings*, 7:321.

13. John Greenleaf Whittier, "The Vanishers," *The Complete Poetical Works of Whittier* (Cambridge, Mass.: Cambridge edition, 1884), p. 157.

14. Emerson, *Poems, Works*, 9:17.

15. Those wishing to examine the matter might begin with Erich Neumann's *Art and the Creative Unconscious* (1959) or with his more famous study, *The Great Mother* (1955). Both works, translated by Ralph Manheim, appear in Princeton University Press' Bollingen Series (1972).

16. Emerson, *Journals*, 1:119-20. Emerson's editors refer to this passage as "florid oratory then in vogue," which may help to explain the quality of Emerson's prose here. But it will not do as an explanation for his sense of the terrors he describes.

17. Emerson, *Journals*, 6:435.

18. Emerson, *Nature, Works*, 1:73-74.

19. Emerson, *Journals*, 4:248.

20. Emerson, *Nature, Works*, 1:48.

21. Ibid., pp. 58-59.

22. Emerson, *Journals*, 4:248-49.

23. Emerson, *Journals*, 9:132.

24. Horace Bushnell, *Nature and the Supernatural* (New York: Charles Scribner's, 1860), p. 68. As with others, I am indebted to R. W. B. Lewis for bringing this important work to the attention of modern scholars.

25. Ibid., p. 410.

26. Ralph Waldo Emerson, "Holiness," in *The Early Lectures of Ralph Waldo Emerson*, eds. Stephen E. Whicher, Robert E. Spiller and Wallace E. Williams (Cambridge, Mass.: Harvard University Press, 1964), 2:342.

27. Emerson, *Journals*, 3:454.

28. Herman Melville, *Mardi,* eds. Harrison Hayford, Hershel Parker and G. Thomas Tanselle (1849;Evanston and Chicago: Newberry edition, Northwestern University Press, 1970), p. 30.

29. Thoreau, *The Maine Woods, Writings,* 3:190.

30. Emerson, *Journals,* 4:258. Roy Harvey Pearce, in *The Continuity of American Poetry* (Princeton, N.J.: Princeton University Press, 1961), p. 149, calls attention to a similar perception by Poe.

31. The poem appeared in Emerson's *Poems,* probably before the public in 1846, although imprinted 1847. For the dating of the poem see *Works,* 9:424 and Ralph L. Rusk, *The Life of Ralph Waldo Emerson* (New York: Columbia University Press, 1957), p. 312.

32. *Poems, Works,* 9:61. Subsequent entries are cited parenthetically in the text.

33. See, for example, Frances S. Osgood, ed. *The Poetry of Flowers,* (New York: J. C. Riker, 1846), pp. 261, 263.

34. Cited in Herman Melville, *The Melville Log,* ed. Jay Leyda (New York: Gordian Press, 1969), 1:292.

35. Herman Melville, *Pierre,* eds. Harrison Hayford, Hershel Parker, and G. Thomas Tanselle (1852; Evanston and Chicago: Newberry edition, Northwestern University Press, 1971), p. 342. Citations in the text are from this edition.

36. Herman Melville, *Moby-Dick,* eds. Luther S. Mansfield and Howard P. Vincent (1851; New York: Hendricks House, 1952), p. 428.

37. Emerson, *Nature,* in *Works,* 1:73-74.

38. Melville, *Pierre,* p. 284. Melville's brilliant insight will be recognized by those well-versed in cross-cultural initiation and rite of passage myths. There is a plentitude of studies to examine, from Frazer's *Golden Bough* to Joseph Campbell's *The Masks of God* (see Bibliography).

39. Melville, *Pierre,* ed. Henry A. Murray (New York: Hendricks House, 1949), p. 499.

Chapter 7: The Oceans of America

1. Henry David Thoreau, *The Writings of Henry David Thoreau,* 20 vols. (Boston and New York: Walden edition, 1906; reprint, New York: AMS Press, 1968) 1:323. Subsequently cited as *Writings.*

2. Thomas Philbrick, *James Fenimore Cooper and the Development of American Sea Fiction* (Cambridge, Mass.: Harvard University Press, 1961), p. ix.

3. Ibid., p. 209 ff.

4. James Fenimore Cooper, *The Sea Lions,* illus. F. O. C. Darley (New York: W. A. Townsend and Company, 1859-61), p. 6.

5. Ibid.

6. Herman Melville, "Cooper's New Novel," *The Literary World,* No. 117 (April 28, 1849) :370. The entire review appears on p. 370.

7. Joseph C. Hart, *Miriam Coffin, or The Whale-Fisherman* (New York: G. and C. and H. Carville, 1834), 2:6.

8. J. N. Reynolds, *Mocha Dick,* intro. L. L. Balcom (New York: C. Scribner's Sons, 1932), pp. 84-85, 90.

9. Captain Adam Seaborn, *Symzonia,* intro. J. O. Bailey (Gainesville, Fla.: Scholars' Facsimiles and Reprints, 1965). *Symzonia* has often been ascribed to John Cleves Symmes, writing under the pseudonym of Captain Adam Seaborn with the intention of advancing the hollow earth theory. However, the novel itself points out erroneous aspects of the theory (for example, pp. 34-35, 82-83). Symmes may only have been debating with himself, although it seems more likely that he did not write the book. In his introduction to *Symzonia* J. O. Bailey faces the authorship problem, pointing out that the Library of Congress catalogued the book as a burlesque on the theories of Symmes (which it seems in part to be). Professor Bailey also notes that the copy he used from the library of the University of North Carolina had the name of Symmes pencilled in after that of Seaborn, and that the library of North Carolina originally ascribed the book to Symmes. One must, of course, be reluctant to ascribe authorship on the basis only of library cataloguing, and since the two libraries are in any event at odds with each other, different evidence must be employed. Since I know of no substantial external evidence, the internal evidence seems to carry the most weight. In my opinion it points away from Symmes. Even the diagram of the earth in *Symzonia* is at odds with certain geographical assumptions held by Symmes in his remarkable and much-discussed theory of ''holes in the poles.'' While I agree to a point with Professor Bailey that the book is not a burlesque—although I do see aspects of this in it—I disagree that *Symzonia's* intention is to prove the theories of Symmes. Ascribing authorship of such a minor book would not ordinarily warrant this attention, but since Poe seemed so interested in the theories of Symmes, and since *Pym* certainly does appear to have some relation to the theories of Symmes, the matters of authorship and how the book was received may be worth pursuing. For another discussion of this question, one rejecting the Symmes theory of authorship, see Henri Petter, *The Early American Novel* (Columbus, Ohio: Ohio State University Press, 1971), pp. 163-64.

10. Stephen Whicher, *Freedom and Fate* (Philadelphia: University of Pennsylvania Press, 1953), p. 25.

11. Herman Melville, *White-Jacket,* eds. Harrison Hayford, Hershel Parker, and G. Thomas Tanselle (Evanston and Chicago: Newberry edition, Northwestern University Press, 1970), pp. 398-99.

12. Ted N. Weissbuch and Bruce Stillians, ''Ishmael the Ironist: The Anti-Salvation Theme in *Moby-Dick,*'' *Emerson Society Quarterly,* No. 31 (1963) :71-75.

13. Herman Melville, *Moby-Dick,* eds. Luther S. Mansfield and Howard P. Vincent (1851; New York: Hendricks House, 1952), p. 1. Citations in the text are from this edition.

14. Harrison Hayford and Hershel Parker have suggested in the Norton Critical Edition of *Moby-Dick,* (New York, 1967), pp. 493-94, that the speaker is Ahab rather than Ishmael. A careful reading of the ''Gilder'' chapter certainly seems to support them, even though their ''conservative'' principles keep them from making the emendation in the text. If the speaker is Ishmael, as has been traditionally assumed, the bleak prose of one who has already completed the journey reinforces the idea that he has found no salvation. If the speaker is Ahab, the particular passage would define a similar attitude in

Ishmael to the extent that he comes to identify himself with Ahab's perceptions, as I believe he has done by this time in *Moby-Dick*. It is unambiguously Ishmael, and not Ahab, who reminds us in the same chapter that "when beholding the tranquil beauty and brilliancy of the ocean's skin, one forgets the tiger heart that pants beneath it; and would not willingly remember, that this velvet paw but conceals a remorseless fang." By the day of the last chase, toward the end of the final chapter of *Moby-Dick*, it is Ishmael who sees in the whale "eternal malice." Ahab, the Promethean side of Ishmael's consciousness, makes no judgment darker or more monomaniacal than this.

15. Edmund Wilson, ed. "Hawthorne and his Mosses," in *The Shock of Recognition* (New York: Farrar, Straus and Cudahy, 1943), p. 195. See chap. 1.

16. Henry David Thoreau, *Collected Poems of Henry Thoreau*, ed. Carl Bode (Baltimore, Md.: Johns Hopkins Press, 1965), p. 46.

17. Thoreau, *Writings*, 1:237.

18. John Greenleaf Whittier, *The Complete Poetical Works of Whittier* (Cambridge, Mass.: Riverside Press, 1884), pp. 142-43. Subsequently cited as *Poems*.

19. Walt Whitman, *Leaves of Grass*, eds. Harold W. Blodgett and Sculley Bradley (New York: New York University Press, 1965), p. 255.

20. Melville, *Moby-Dick*, p. 255.

21. Gay Wilson Allen, *The New Walt Whitman Handbook* (New York: New York University Press, 1975), p. 41.

22. Edgar Allan Poe, *The Complete Poems and Stories of Edgar Allan Poe*, eds. Arthur Hobson Quinn and Edward H. O'Neill (New York: A. A. Knopf, 1946), 2:738. Subsequently cited as *Poems and Stories*. Melville, *Moby-Dick*, p. 412.

23. Ralph Waldo Emerson, *Journals of Ralph Waldo Emerson*, eds. Edward Waldo Emerson and Waldo Emerson Forbes (Boston: Houghton Mifflin, 1904-14), 7:245; Washington Irving, "The Voyage," in *The Sketch Book* (1819-20; New York: John Wurtle Lovell, 1881), pp. 13-14; Richard Henry Dana, *Two Years Before the Mast* (1840; Boston and New York: Riverside Press, 1911), p. 8.

24. Whittier, *Poems*, p. 56.

25. Thoreau, *Cape Cod, Writings*, 4:187; Emerson, "Fate," in *The Complete Works of Ralph Waldo Emerson*, intro. Edward Waldo Emerson (Boston and New York: Centenary edition, 1903-4), 6:8; Hawthorne, "The Ambitious Guest," *Twice-told Tales*, eds. William Charvat, Roy Harvey Pearce, and Claude M. Simpson, (Columbus, Ohio: Ohio State University Press, Centenary edition, 1974), p. 332.

26. Dana, *Two Years Before the Mast*, p. 402.

27. Thoreau, *Cape Cod, Writings*, 4: 125.

28. Melville, *Moby-Dick*, p. 274.

29. Thoreau, *Cape Cod, Writings*, 4:188.

30. Thoreau, *Writings*, 5:224.

31. For Melville's use of Marryat see Bernard Rosenthal, "Melville, Marryat, and the Evil-Eyed Villain," *Nineteenth-Century Fiction* 25 (September 1970) :221-24; and "Elegy for Jack Chase," *Studies in Romanticism* 10 (Spring 1971): 213-29.

32. For comparisons of these motifs of whiteness in *Pym* and *Moby-Dick*, see Patrick F. Quinn, "Poe's Imaginary Voyage," *Hudson Review* 4 (Winter 1952) :562-85.

33. Edward H. Davidson, *Poe: A Critical Study* (Cambridge, Mass.: Harvard University Press, 1957), p. 182.

34. Poe, *Poems and Stories*, 2:725.

35. See Poe's letter to William E. Burton, June 1, 1840 in *The Letters of Edgar Allan Poe*, ed. John Ward Ostrom (New York: Gordian Press, Inc., 1966), 1:130. Poe's judgment of *Pym* in this letter must be qualified by two factors. First, he was pleading a financial matter with Burton and may have deprecated his own story as a ploy to show his sense of fairness, since Burton had judged the tale harshly. Secondly, Professor Ostrom, facing the difficult task of deciphering Poe's handwriting, editorially cautions us that the phrase in which the word *silly* seems to appear is not entirely clear in the manuscript.

Chapter 8: The Urban Garden

1. Henry David Thoreau, *Cape Cod, The Writings of Henry David Thoreau*, 20 vols. (Boston and New York: Walden edition, 1906; reprint, New York: AMS Press), 4:188.

2. See Poe's laudatory review of an address by Dew to the students of William and Mary, *The Southern Literary Messenger* 2 (October 1836):721-22. Poe's authorship of this review has been established by William Doyle Hull in his unpublished doctoral dissertation, *A Canon of the Critical Works of Edgar Allan Poe with a Study of Poe as Editor and Reviewer* (University of Virginia, 1941), pp. 158-61.

3. James Fenimore Cooper, *The Monikins*, illus. F. O. C. Darley (New York: W. A. Townsend, 1859-61), p. 406.

4. C. C. Hazewell, "Agrarianism," *Atlantic Monthly* 3 (April 1859): 393-403. This essay, as well as its authorship by Hazewell, came to my attention in Louis H. Douglas' excellent collection, *Agrarianism in American History* (Lexington, Mass.: D. C. Heath and Co., 1969), p. 24.

5. Hazewell, "Agrarianism," p. 394.

6. Thomas Dew, "An Address on the Influence of the Federative Republican System of Government upon Literature and the Development of Character," *The Southern Literary Messenger* 2 (March 1836):266.

7. Cooper, *The Monikins*, p. 405.

8. Walt Whitman, "Ages and Ages Returning at Intervals," *Leaves of Grass*, eds. Harold W. Blodgett and Sculley Bradley (New York: New York University Press, 1965), p. 107.

9. J.K. Paulding, *Westward Ho!* 2 vols. (New York: J. and J. Harper, 1832), 1:87-88.

10. Robert Montgomery Bird, *Peter Pilgrim* (Philadelphia: Lee and Blanchard, 1838), 1:20.

11. Michael Chevalier, *Society, Manners, and Politics in the United States*, ed. John William Ward (1839; Gloucester, Mass.: Peter Smith, 1967), p. 31. I use the dating of the first American edition.

12. Thomas Farnham, *Travels in the Great Western Prairies, the Anahuac and Rocky Mountains, and in the Oregon Territory* (London, 1841) in Reuben Gold Thwaites, ed. *Early Western Travels* (New York: AMS Press, 1966), 28:119-20.

13. Nathaniel Chipman, *The Legal Mind in America*, ed. Perry Miller (New York: Doubleday, 1962), p. 26.

14. Elisha Ayers, *A Journey of Travel* (Preston, Conn.: Privately printed, 1847) p. 7.

15. James Fenimore Cooper, *The Crater,* ed. Thomas Philbrick (1847; Cambridge, Mass.: Harvard University Press, 1962), p. 139.

16. For example, see Thomas Nuttall, *Journal of Travels into the Arkansa Territory, During the Year 1819* (Philadelphia, 1821), in Reuben Gold Thwaites, ed., *Early Western Travels* (New York: AMS Press, 1966), 13:85.

17. Alexis de Tocqueville, *Democracy in America,* trans. Henry Reeve (1835; New York: Schocken, 1961), 2:153, 155.

18. Catherine Sedgwick, *Hope Leslie,* (New York: White, Gallaher, and White, 1827), 1:v.

19. Perry Miller, "The Location of American Religious Freedom," *Nature's Nation* (Cambridge, Mass.: Harvard University Press, 1967). See particularly pp. 150-53.

20. William Starbuck Mayo, *Kaloolah* (New York and London: G. P. Putnam's Sons, 1849), p. 40.

21. D. H. Lawrence, *Studies in Classic American Literature* (1923), in Edmund Wilson, ed. *The Shock of Recognition* (New York: Farrar, Straus and Cudahy, 1943), p. 909.

22. Timothy Flint, *Recollections of the Last Ten Years in the Valley of the Mississippi,* ed. George R. Brooks (1826; Carbondale, Ill.: Southern Illinois University Press, 1968), p. 137.

23. Paulding, *Westward Ho!* 1:94.

24. Henry Nash Smith, *Virgin Land* (Cambridge, Mass.: Harvard University Press, 1950), pp. 71-74.

25. Ibid., p. 72.

26. Ralph Waldo Emerson, *Journals of Ralph Waldo Emerson,* eds. Edward Waldo Emerson, and Waldo Emerson Forbes (Boston and New York: Houghton Mifflin Co., 1904-14), 9:153.

27. Charles Webber, *Old Hicks the Guide; or, Adventures in the Camanche Country in Search of a Gold Mine* (New York: Harper and Brothers, 1848), p. 318.

28. Lawrence, *Studies in Classic American Literature, The Shock of Recognition,* p. 951: "Fenimore, lying in his Louis Quatorze hotel in Paris, passionately musing about Natty Bumppo and the pathless forest, and mixing his imagination with the Cupids and Butterflies on the painted ceiling, while Mrs. Cooper was struggling with her latest gown in the next room, and the *déjeuner* was with the Countess at eleven. . . ."

29. Timothy Flint, *Francis Berrian, or The Mexican Patriot* (Philadelphia: Key and Biddle, 1834), 1:106.

30. Timothy Flint, *A Condensed Geography and History of the Western States or the Mississippi Valley* (1828; Gainesville, Fla.; Scholars' Facsimiles & Reprints, 1970), 1:206. See also chap. 3. Although perceiving Europe's view of the West as deceptive, Flint's own ambivalence toward the region reflects the lingering force of Europe's image. For Flint's discussion of the West's intangible appeal for immigrants, see *Recollections,* p. 175. Flint argues here that this appeal of the West is instrumental in bringing foreign immigrants there, even when they believe that their primary motive is economic. He also reveals the extent to which he himself sees a poetry in the West unrelated to economic concerns. This appeal for Flint finds expression in *Francis Berrian.*

31. Timothy Flint, *George Mason, The Young Backwoodsman; or 'Don't Give up the Ship,' A Story of the Mississippi* (Boston: Hilliard, Gray, Little, and Wilkins, 1829), p. 144.

32. James Fenimore Cooper, *The Prairie,* intro. Henry Nash Smith (New York: Holt, Rinehart and Winston, 1966), p. xviii.

33. Robert Montgomery Bird, *Nick of the Woods,* ed. Cecil B. Williams (New York: American Book Co., 1939), pp. xxx-xxxi.

Chapter 9: Cain's City

1. J.K. Paulding, *Westward Ho!* (New York: J. and J. Harper, 1832), 1:125, John Pendleton Kennedy, *Swallow Barn* (1832; New York: Putnam's, 1872), p. 18.

2. Ralph Waldo Emerson, "Holiness," *The Early Lectures of Ralph Waldo Emerson,* eds. Stephen E. Whicher, Robert E. Spiller, and Wallace E. Williams (Cambridge, Mass.: Harvard University Press, 1959-72), 2:342.

3. Ralph Waldo Emerson, "Nature," *Essays Second Series, The Complete Works of Ralph Waldo Emerson,* intro. Edward Waldo Emerson (Boston and New York: Houghton Mifflin, 1903-4), 3:178. Subsequently cited as *Works.*

4. John Winthrop, "A Model of Christian Charity," *The Puritans,* eds. Perry Miller and Thomas H. Johnson (New York: Harper and Row, 1963), p. 198. The text is originally taken by the editors from *Winthrop Papers,* 2 (Boston: Massachusetts Historical Society, 1931). My subsequent citations of Winthrop are also from Miller and Johnson, although I have modernized spelling and capitalization where appropriate.

5. Marthinus Versfeld, *A Guide to the City of God* (London and New York: Sheed and Ward, 1958), p. 6.

6. Perry Miller, *The New England Mind: The Seventeenth Century* (New York: Macmillan Co., 1939), p. ix.

7. Crane Brinton, *Ideas and Men* (New York: Prentice-Hall, Inc., 1950), p. 298.

8. Joseph Campbell, *The Masks of God* (New York: The Viking Press, 1968), 4: 35-36.

9. I obviously make no claim to having coined the phrase, the city of man, which dates back at least to St. Augustine. To the best of my knowledge, the most important recent use of it in literary criticism is found in Michael H. Cowan's *City of the West: Emerson, America, and Urban Metaphor* (New Haven, Conn. and London: Yale University Press, 1967). Although Professor Cowan uses this idea of the "city of man" for rather different purposes than I do and reaches different conclusions, his study is in my judgment required reading for those interested in the idea of the city as an imaginative concept. A similarly important book—one that also breaks away from the rigid literalness that dominates many studies of the city—is David R. Weimer's *The City as Metaphor* (New York: Random House, 1966).

10. Aurelius Augustinus, *City of God,* abrdg. and trans., J.W.C. Wand (London: Oxford University Press, 1963), p. 234. I have used this translation from an abridged edition because of its particular clarity in expressing points important to my discussion. For a comparison, I cite the same passage from John Healey's translation (London: Everyman edition, 1945), 2:44: the "devil could not have seduced man-kind to such a palpable transgression of God's express charge, had not evil will and self-love got place in them before, for he delighted in that which was said: 'Ye shall be as gods': which they might sooner

have been by obedience and coherence with their Creator than by proud opinion that they were their own beginners.''

11. See chap. 7.

12. See chap. 1.

13. James Fenimore Cooper, *The Crater,* ed. Thomas Philbrick (1847; Cambridge, Mass.: Harvard University Press, 1962), p. 380.

14. Newton Arvin, *Longfellow: His Life and Work* (Boston: Little, Brown & Co., 1963), p. 10.

15. Henry Wadsworth Longfellow, *The Complete Poetical Works of Henry Wadsworth Longfellow,* ed. Horace E. Scudder (Boston and New York: Cambridge edition, 1893), p. 87.

16. Timothy Flint, *Francis Berrian or The Mexican Patriot* (1826; Philadelphia: Key and Biddle, 1834), 2:245.

17. Nathaniel Hawthorne, *Twice-told Tales,* eds. William Charvat, Roy Harvey Pearce, and Claude M. Simpson (Columbus, Ohio: Ohio State University Press, Centenary edition, 1974), p. 443. Subsequently cited as *Works.*

18. Ibid., p. 369.

19. Herman Melville, *Clarel,* ed. Walter E. Bezanson (New York: Hendricks House, Inc., 1960), p. 374.

20. Hawthorne, *Works,* 1962, *The Scarlet Letter,* p. 48.

21. Joseph Campbell in *The Hero with a Thousand Faces* (Princeton, N.J.: Princeton University Press, 1949) defines the traditional relationship between the questing hero and ''Mother Nature'' in a way that seems to be particularly applicable to Hester: ''One has only to know and trust, and the ageless guardians will appear. Having responded to his own call, and continuing to follow courageously as the consequences unfold, the hero finds all the forces of the unconscious at his side. Mother Nature herself supports the mighty task'' (p. 72). The apparent betrayal of Hester by nature may suggest Hawthorne's own divided feelings on Hester's solution.

22. For the interpretation given to the Heloise and Abelard story, I am indebted to Joseph Campbell, *The Masks of God* (New York: Viking, 1968), 4:53 ff. See also Leslie Fiedler, *Love and Death in the American Novel* (rev. ed., New York: Delta, 1966), p. 229.

23. Hawthorne, *Works,* 1964, *The Blithedale Romance,* p. 245.

24. Herman Melville, *Billy Budd,* eds. Harrison Hayford and Merton M. Sealts, Jr. (Chicago: University of Chicago Press, 1962), p. 53.

25. Nathaniel Hawthorne, *Letters of Hawthorne to William D. Ticknor, 1851-1864* (Newark, N.J.: The Carteret Book Club, 1910), 1:75. The letter is dated January 19, 1855.

26. This passage appears on the last page of most editions of *The Marble Faun,* although the editors of the Centenary edition have removed it—erroneously, in my opinion. The editorial explanation is given in this edition (*Works,* 1968, p. cxxvi). My own subsequent citations of the ''Postscript,'' as it is called in this edition, or the ''Conclusion'' as in other editions, is from the Centenary text.

Since the burden of any editor is sufficiently great, I take no pleasure in disagreeing with a textual decision. I simply state that the reason for excluding the passage in the Centenary edition is one of critical judgment, a belief that its inclusion makes the book too bleak and that one of the two original editions did not carry the passage. I believe that even the reading preferred by the editors—Kenyon's simple assertion that Donatello is in prison—implicitly carries the same meaning found in the more extensive passage that I have used. My disagreement with the editors over the bleakness of *The Marble Faun* should not be construed as any negative reflection upon the massive and thorough scholarship that went into creating the text.

27. Hawthorne, *Works*, 1974, *Mosses from an Old Manse* (1846), p. 255.

28. Henry David Thoreau, *Collected Poems of Henry Thoreau*, ed. Carl Bode (Baltimore, Md.: Johns Hopkins Press, 1965), p. 81. Also see chap. 5.

29. Herman Melville, *Pierre*, eds. Harrison Hayford, Hershel Parker, and G. Thomas Tanselle (Evanston, Ill: Northwestern University Press, 1971), p. 296.

30. 2 Kings 18:17; see also Isaiah 20:1.

31. Emerson, "Nature," in *Essays Second Series, Works*, 3:196.

32. Herman Melville, "Hawthorne and his Mosses," in Edmund Wilson, ed., *The Shock of Recognition*, (New York: Farrar, Straus and Cudahy, 1943), p. 193.

33. Herman Melville, *Israel Potter*, (1855; New York: Russell and Russell, 1963), p. 212. Although Melville used an earlier story in the creation of *Israel Potter*, as he did in "Benito Cereno," the particular meaning he gave it was his own. The passage cited here is his, as is the whole metaphysical, symbolic, and comic thrust of the story.

Readers wanting to compare Melville's story with his source may wish to examine Israel R. Potter, *Life and Remarkable Adventures of Israel R. Potter* (1824), which is available in an edition introduced by Leonard Kriegel (New York: Corinth Books, 1962). More recently, a full-length study of *Israel Potter* has been written by Arnold Rampersad, *Melville's Israel Potter* (Bowling Green, Ky.: Bowling Green University Popular Press, 1969).

34. 2 Thessalonians 2:7.

35. Emerson, "Nature," in *Essays Second Series, Works*, 3:182-83.

36. For Margaret Fuller, see Perry Miller, ed., *Margaret Fuller: American Romantic*, (New York: Anchor Books, 1963), pp. 219-21; for Ripley, see *The Harbinger* I (August 9, 1845), 142-43.

37. John Greenleaf Whittier, "Patucket Falls," *The Writings of John Greenleaf Whittier in Seven Volumes* (Boston: Riverside Press, 1889), 5:364-65.

38. Ralph Waldo Emerson, *Journals of Ralph Waldo Emerson*, eds. Edward Waldo Emerson and Waldo Emerson Forbes (Boston and New York: Houghton Mifflin Company, 1904-14), 9:7. Subsequently cited as *Journals*.

39. Emerson, "The Conservative," *Works*, 1:317.

40. Henry David Thoreau, *The Writings of Henry David Thoreau* (Boston and New York: Walden edition, 1906), 6:187. Subsequently cited as *Writings*.

41. Thoreau, *Walden*, in *Writings*, 2:291.

42. Thoreau, *Journal*, 2, *Writings*, 8:296.

43. Thoreau, *The Maine Woods, Writings*, 3: 18.

44. Compare Thoreau's two statements:

Occasionally, when the windy columns broke in to me, I caught sight of a dark, damp crag to the right or left; the mist driving ceaselessly between it and me. It reminded me of the creations of the old epic and dramatic poets, of Atlas, Vulcan, the Cyclops, and Prometheus. Such was Caucasus and the rock where Prometheus was bound. Aeschylus had no doubt visited such scenery as this. It was vast, Titanic, and such as man never inhabits. Some part of the beholder, even some vital part, seems to escape through the loose grating of his ribs as he ascends. He is more lone than you can imagine. There is less of substantial thought and fair understanding in him than in the plains where men inhabit. His reason is dispersed and shadowy, more thin and subtile, like the air. Vast, Titanic, inhuman Nature has got him at disadvantage, caught him alone, and pilfers him of some of his divine faculty. She does not smile on him as in the plains. She seems to say sternly, Why came ye here before your time. . . .Why seek me where I have not called thee, and then complain because you find me but a stepmother? (*Writings,* 3:70-71)

Now *Walden:*

We can never have enough of nature. We must be refreshed by the sight of inexhaustible vigor, vast and titanic features, the sea-coast with its wrecks, the wilderness with its living and its decaying trees, the thundercloud, and the rain which lasts three weeks and produces freshets. We need to witness our own limits transgressed, and some life pasturing freely where we never wander. We are cheered when we observe the vulture feeding on the carrion which disgusts and disheartens us, and deriving health and strength from the repast. (*Writings,* 2:350)

45. Ralph Waldo Emerson, *The Letters of Ralph Waldo Emerson,* ed. Ralph L. Rusk (New York: Columbia University Press, 1939), 1:133.

46. Emerson, *Journals,* 2:384-85.

47. Ibid., 3:392.

48. Emerson, *Letters,* 3:9.

49. Emerson, *Journals,* 2:51.

50. Ibid., 5:531.

51. Emerson, "Society and Solitude," *Works,* 7:7.

52. Emerson, *Journals,* 6:6.

Selected Bibliography

A Bibliographical Note

The subject of nature and America has generated an enormous body of scholarship, even if much of it only touches peripherally on the subject. The attention has been warranted, since the history of America particularly has lent itself to an examination of the topic, although the history of this scholarship would in itself offer subjects for more than one valuable study. To have taken the reader through all these works would have drawn too much attention away from my own perspective and would have risked reshaping my book into a study I did not wish to pursue. I hasten to add that neither the inclusion nor the exclusion of a given secondary source necessarily implies agreement or disagreement with its premises or its arguments. With this in mind, I note a few uncited works that may help exemplify the wide range of perceptions about nature in the age of American Romanticism: Ekirch A. Arthur, *Man and Nature in America* (New York: Columbia University Press, 1963); W.H. Auden, *The Enchafèd Flood: or The Romantic Iconography of the Sea* (New York: Vintage, 1950); Wilson O. Clough, *The Necessary Earth* (Austin, Texas: University of Texas Press, 1964); Carlton F. Culmsee, *Malign Nature and the Frontier,* Utah State Monograph Series, Vol. 7, no. 2 (Logan, Utah: Utah State University, 1959); Norman Foerster, *Nature in American Literature* (New York: Macmillan Co., 1923); Lucy Lockwood Hazard, *The Frontier in American Literature* (New York: Thomas Y. Crowell, 1927); Philip Marshall Hicks, *The Development of the Natural History Essay in American Literature* (Ph.D. dissertation, University of Pennsylvania, 1924); Hans Huth, *Nature and the American* (Berkeley, Calif.: University of California Press, 1957); Roderick Nash, *Wilderness and the American Mind* (New Haven, Conn.: Yale University Press, 1967); Tony Tanner, *The Reign of Wonder* (Cambridge: Cambridge University Press, 1965); and John Kirtland Wright, *Human Nature in Geography* (Cambridge, Mass.: Harvard University Press, 1966).

The reader examining these studies, along with those I cite, will have a reasonably adequate sampling of the subject, although certainly not a comprehensive listing. The very useful bibliography found in Edward Halsey Foster's *Civilized Wilderness* (New York: Free Press, 1975) carries valuable titles I have not mentioned. This bibliography, along with Roderick Nash's *Wilderness and the American Mind,* will lead the reader to an abundant selection of thoughtfully chosen primary and secondary sources.

Some of my most valuable primary sources of information have been nineteenth-century periodicals, only a few of which I have specifically cited. Some uncited ones of particular value to me include *The Horticulturist* (September 1846); *The Literary Union* (June 1849); *The Pioneer* (January 1843); *The Western Farmer* (July 1840); and *The Western Journal* (January and April 1848). Other selected primary sources that I have found extremely useful but have not cited include Robert Beverly, *The History and Present State of Viriginia* (1705); W. Bullock, *Sketch of a Journey through the Western States of North America* (1827); William Cobbett, *The American Gardener* (1819) and *A Year's Residence in the United States of America* (1818); Robert H. Collyer, *Lights and Shadows of American Life* (ca. 1843); David Crockett, *An Account of Colonel Crockett's Tour to the North and Down East* (1835); Edmund Dana, *Geographical Sketches on the Western Country* (1819); J. J. Flatters, *The Paradise Lost, of Milton, Translated into Fifty Four Designs by J. J. Flatters, Sculptor* (1843); Margaret Fuller, *Summer on the Lakes* (1844); Chandler Robbins Gilman, *Life on the Lakes* (1836); Josiah Gregg, *Commerce of the Prairies* (1844); James Hall, *Sketches of History, Life, and Manners, in the West* (1835); Charles Fenno Hoffman, *Wild Scenes in the Forest and Prairie* (1839); Charles Joseph Latrobe, *The Rambler in North America* (1835); James Russell Lowell, *The Complete Poetical Works of James Russell Lowell,* ed. Horace E. Scudder (Cambridge, Mass.: Cambridge edition, 1952); Louis Legrand Noble, *The Life and Works of Thomas Cole,* ed. Elliott S. Vesell (1853; Cambridge, Mass.: Harvard University Press, 1964); Joel Parker *Journal of Travels over the Rocky Mountains* (1847); J. K. Paulding, *John Bull in America* (1825); Anne Royall, *The Black Book; or A Continuation of Travels in the United States* (1828-29); Philip Schaff, *America* (1855); Henry Schoolcraft, *Narrative of an Expedition through the Upper Mississippi to Itasca Lake* (1834); Benjamin Silliman, *Remarks, Made on a Short Tour, between Hartford and Quebec in the Autumn of 1819* (1820); Alexander Wilson, *The Foresters: A Poem, Description of a Pedestrian Tour to the Falls of Niagara in the Autumn of 1804* (1818); and John B. Wyeth, *Oregon* (1833).

The list that follows includes works specifically cited by title in the text of the book. Where my text has mentioned works not specifically cited in a note, I have in a very few cases silently added an appropriate source.

Primary Sources

Arnold, Matthew. *Poetical Works of Matthew Arnold.* Edited by C.B. Tinker and H. F. Lowry. London: Oxford University Press, 1950.

Augustinus, Aurelius. *City of God.* Translated by John Healey. 2 vols. London: Everyman, 1945.

———.*City of God.* Translated and abridged by J. W. C. Wand. London: Oxford University Press, 1963.

Ayers, Elisha. *A Journey of Travel.* Preston, Conn.: Privately printed, 1847.

Baird, Robert. *View of the Valley of the Mississippi* (1832). Philadelphia: H. S. Tanner, 1834.

Bird, Robert Montgomery. *Nick of the Woods* (1837). Edited by Cecil B. Williams. New York: American Books, 1939.

———.*Peter Pilgrim.* 2 vols. Philadelphia: Lee and Blanchard, 1838.

The Broadway Journal. September 1845.

Brown, Charles Brockden. *Arthur Mervyn* (1799-1800). Philadelphia: David McKay, 1887.

———.*Edgar Huntly* (1801). Philadelphia: David McKay, 1887.

Bryant, William Cullen. *Poetical Works of William Cullen Bryant.* New York: D. Appleton, 1906.

——— *Prose Writings of William Cullen Bryant.* Edited by Parke Godwin. 2 vols. 1884. Reprint. New York: Russell and Russell, 1964.

Bushnell, Horace. *Nature and the Supernatural* (1858). New York: Scribner's, 1860.

Chevalier, Michael. *Society, Manners, and Politics in the United States: Letters on North America* (1839). Edited by John William Ward and translated after the T.G. Bradford edition. 1961. Reprint. Gloucester, Mass.: Peter Smith, 1967.

Coleridge, Samuel Taylor. *The Complete Poetical Works of Samuel*

Taylor Coleridge. Edited by Ernest Hartley Coleridge. 2 vols. Oxford: Clarendon Press, 1912.

Cooper, James Fenimore. *The Crater* (1847). Edited by Thomas Philbrick. Cambridge, Mass.: Harvard University Press, 1962.

————.*The Novels of James Fenimore Cooper*. Illustrated by F. O. C. Darley. 32 vols. New York: W. A. Townsend and Co. 1859-61.

————.*The Prairie* (1827). Introduction by Henry Nash Smith. New York: Holt, Rinehart and Winston, 1966.

Crèvecoeur, J. Hector St. John. *Letters from an American Farmer* (1782). Note by W. P. Trent; introduction by Ludwig Lewisohn. New York: Fox, Duffield, 1904.

Dana, C. W. *The Garden of the World, or The Great West*. Boston: Wentworth, 1856.

Dana, Richard Henry. *Two Years before the Mast* (1840). Boston: Riverside Press, 1911.

De Beaumont, Gustave. *Marie, or Slavery in the United States* (1835). Translated by Barbara Chapman; introduction by Alois L. Tinnin. Stanford, Calif.: Stanford University Press, 1958.

De Smet, P. J. *Letters and Sketches: With a Narrative of a Year's Residence among the Indian Tribes of the Rocky Mountains* (1843). In Reuben Gold Thwaites, ed. *Early Western Travels* (1904-7). Vol. 27. Reprint. New York: AMS Press, 1966.

Dew, Thomas. "An Address on the Influence of the Federative Republican System of Government upon Literature and the Development of Character." *The Southern Literary Messenger* 2 (1836): 261-82.

The Dial. 1840-44.

Dickens, Charles. *The Works of Charles Dickens*. Edited by Andrew Lang. 38 vols. London: Chapman and Hall, 1897.

Dickens, Charles, and Collins, Wilkie. *The Wreck of the Golden Mary* (1856). Introduction by Herbert van Thal; illustrations by John Dugan. London: Arthur Barker, 1955.

Drake, Daniel. *Discourse on the History, Character, and Prospects of the West* (1834). Reprint. Introduction by Perry Miller, Gainesville, Fla.: Scholars' Facsimiles and Reprints, 1955.

Dwight, Theodore. *The Northern Traveller* (1825). New York: Goodrich and Wiley, 1834.

————.*Sketches of Scenery and Manners in the United States.* New York: A. T. Goodrich, 1829.

Dwight, Timothy. *Travels; in New-England and New-York.* 4 vols. New Haven, Conn.: Privately printed, 1821-22.

Emerson, Ralph Waldo. *The Complete Works of Ralph Waldo Emerson.* Introduction by Edward Waldo Emerson. 12 vols. Boston and New York: Centenary edition, 1903-4.

————.*The Early Lectures of Ralph Waldo Emerson.* Edited by Stephen E. Whicher, Robert E. Spiller, and Wallace E. Williams. 3 vols. Cambridge, Mass.: Harvard University Press, 1959-72.

————.*Journals of Ralph Waldo Emerson.* Edited by Edward Waldo Emerson and Waldo Emerson Forbes. 10 vols. Boston and New York: Houghton Mifflin Co., 1904-14.

————.*The Letters of Ralph Waldo Emerson.* Edited by Ralph L. Rusk. 6 vols. New York: Columbia University Press, 1939.

Farnham, Thomas. *Travels in the Great Western Prairies, the Anahuac and Rocky Mountains, and in the Oregon Territory* (1841). In Reuben Gold Thwaites, ed. *Early Western Travels* (1904-7). Vol. 28. Reprint. New York: AMS Press, 1966.

Flagg, Edmund. *The Far West* (1838). In Reuben Gold Thwaites, ed., *Early Western Travels* (1904-7). Vols. 26-27. Reprint. New York: AMS Press, 1966.

Flint, Timothy. *A Condensed Geography and History of the Western States or the Mississippi Valley* (1828). Reprint. Introduction by Bernard Rosenthal. 2 vols. Gainesville, Fla.: Scholar's Facsimiles and Reprints, 1970.

————.*Francis Berrian, or The Mexican Patriot* (1826). 2 vols. Philadelphia: Key and Biddle, 1834.

————.*George Mason, The Young Backwoodsman; or 'Don't Give up the Ship,' A Story of the Mississippi.* Boston: Hilliard, Gray, Little, and Wilkins, 1829.

————.*Recollections of the Last Ten Years in the Valley of the Mississippi* (1826). Edited by George R. Brooks. Carbondale, Ill.: Southern Illinois University Press, 1968.

Godey's Lady's Book. January 1835.

Goethe, Johann Wolfgang von. *The Sufferings of Young Werther* (1774). Translated by Harry Steinhauer. New York: W. W. Norton, 1970.

Gordon, R. K., ed. and trans. *Anglo-Saxon Poetry.* New York: Everyman, 1970.

Grant, Anne MacVicar. *Memoirs of an American Lady* (1808). New York: G. Dearborn, 1836.

Grund, Francis J. *The Americans in Their Moral, Social, and Political Relations.* 2 vols. London: Longman, Rees, Orme, Brown, Green, and Longman, 1837.

Hall, Basil. *Forty Etchings from Sketches Made with the Camera Lucida, in North America in 1827 and 1828* (1829). London: Simpkin and Marshall, 1830.

———.*Travels in North America in the Years 1827 and 1828.* Edinburgh: Cadell and Co., 1829.

Hall, James. *Letters from the West.* London: Henry Colburn, 1828.

The Harbinger. August and October 1845.

Hart, Joseph C. *Miriam Coffin, or the Whale-Fisherman.* 2 vols. New York: G. and C. and H. Carville, 1834.

Hawthorne, Nathaniel. *The Centenary Edition of the Works of Nathaniel Hawthorne.* Edited by William Charvat, Roy Harvey Pearce, and Claude M. Simpson. 13 vols. Columbus, Ohio: Ohio State University Press, 1962-77.

———.*Letters of Hawthorne to William D. Ticknor, 1851-1864.* Foreword by C. E. Frazer Clark, Jr. 2 vols. Newark, N.J.: Carteret Book Club, 1910.

———.*Complete Short Stories.* New York: Hanover House, 1959.

Hazewell, C. C. "Agrarianism." *The Atlantic Monthly* 3 (1859): 393-403.

Hoffman, Charles Fenno. *A Winter in the Far West.* 2 vols. London: Harper and Brothers, 1835.

Ingraham, Joseph Holt. *The Lady of the Gulf: A Romance of the City and the Seas.* New York: Burgess and Garrett, ca. 1845.

Irving, Washington. *Astoria* (1836). New York: John B. Alden, 1884.

———.*The Sketch Book* (1819-20). New York: John Wurtle Lovell, 1881.

———.*A Tour of the Prairies* (1835). New York: James B. Millar and Co., 1884.

Irving, Washington; Bryant, William Cullen; Cooper, James Fenimore;

et al. *Home Book of the Picturesque.* New York: G. P. Putnam, 1852.

Kemble, Fanny. *Journal.* 2 vols. London: J. Murray, 1835.

Kennedy, John Pendleton. *Swallow Barn* (1832). New York: Putnam's, 1872.

Ladies' Companion. October 1842.

Lewis, Meriwether. *History of the Expedition under the Command of Lewis and Clark* (1814). Edited by Elliott Coues. 4 vols. New York: F. P. Harper, 1893.

Longfellow, Henry Wadsworth. *The Complete Poetical Works of Henry Wadsworth Longfellow.* Edited by Horace E. Scudder. Boston: Riverside Press, 1893.

Lyell, Charles. *A Second Visit to the United States of North America.* 2 vols. New York: Harper and Brothers, 1849.

Marryat, Frederick. *The Novels of Captain Marryat.* Edited by R. Brimley Johnson. 22 vols. London: J. M. Dent and Co., 1896.

——.*The Pirate, and the Three Cutters* (1836). London: Bohn, 1861.

Marsh, George. *Man and Nature* (1864). Edited by David Lowenthal. Cambridge, Mass.: Harvard University Press, 1965.

Martineau, Harriet. *Retrospect of Western Travel.* 2 vols. London: Saunders and Otley, 1838.

——.*Society in America.* 2 vols. New York: Saunders and Otley, 1837.

Mather, Cotton. *Magnolia Christi Americana.* London: T. Parkhurst, 1702.

Maximilian, Alexander Philip. *Travels in the Interior of North America* (1843). Translated by H. Evans Lloyd. In Reuben Gold Thwaites, ed. *Early Western Travels* (1904-7). Vol. 22. Reprint. New York: AMS Press, 1966.

Mayo, William Starbuck, *Kaloolah.* New York: Putnam's, 1849.

Melville, Herman, *Billy Budd.* Edited by Harrison Hayford and Merton M. Sealts, Jr. Chicago: University of Chicago Press, 1962.

——.*Clarel* (1876). Edited by Walter E. Bezanson. New York: Hendricks House, 1960.

——.*Collected Poems of Herman Melville.* Edited by Howard P. Vincent. Chicago, Ill.: Hendricks House, 1947.

————.*The Confidence-Man* (1857). Edited by Elizabeth S. Foster. New York: Hendricks House, 1954.

————.*The Confidence-Man* (1857). Edited by H. Bruce Franklin. Indianapolis, Ind.: Bobbs-Merrill, 1967.

————."Cooper's New Novel." *The Literary World* 4 (1849): 370.

————.*Israel Potter* (1855). Reprint. New York: Russell and Russell, 1963.

————.*The Melville Log.* Edited by Jay Leyda. New York: Gordian Press, 1969.

————.*Moby-Dick* (1851). Edited by Harrison Hayford and Hershel Parker. New York: Norton Critical Edition, 1967.

————.*Moby-Dick* (1851). Edited by Luther S. Mansfield and Howard P. Vincent. New York: Hendricks House, 1952.

————.*Pierre* (1852). Edited by Henry A. Murray. New York: Hendricks House, 1949.

————.*The Writings of Herman Melville.* Edited by Harrison Hayford, Hershel Parker, and G. Thomas Tanselle. Evanston and Chicago: Newberry Edition, Northwestern University Press, 1970- .

Miller, Perry, ed. *The Legal Mind in America.* New York: Doubleday, 1962.

————.ed. *Margaret Fuller: American Romantic.* New York: Anchor Books, 1963.

Miller, Perry, and Johnson, Thomas H., ed. *The Puritans.* 2 vols. New York: Harper and Row, 1963.

Murat, Achille. *America and the Americans* (ca. 1832). Edited and translated by Henry J. Bradfield. New York: William H. Graham, 1849.

Nuttall, Thomas. *Journal of Travels into the Arkansa Territory, during the Year 1819* (1821). In Reuben Gold Thwaites, ed. *Early Western Travels* (1904-7). Vol. 21. Reprint. New York: AMS Press, 1966.

Ogden, George. *Letters from the West* (1823). In Reuben Gold Thwaites, ed. *Early Western Travels* (1904-7). Vol. 19. Reprint. New York: AMS Press, 1966.

Osgood, Frances S., ed. *The Poetry of Flowers* (1840). New York: J. C. Riker, 1846.

Paine, Thomas. *The Writings of Thomas Paine.* Edited by Moncure Daniel Conway. 4 vols. New York: G. P. Putnam's Sons, 1894.

Parker, Amos A. *Trip to the West and Texas* (1835). Concord, N.H.: William White, 1836.

Parkman, Francis. *The Oregon Trail* (1849). Introduction by Henry Sinclair Drago. New York: Dodd, Mead, 1964.

Pattie, James O. *The Personal Narrative of James O. Pattie* (1831). Edited by Timothy Flint. In Reuben Gold Thwaites, ed. *Early Western Travels* (1904-7). Vol. 18. Reprint. New York: AMS Press, 1966.

Paulding, J.K. *Westward Ho!*. 2 vols. New York: J. and J. Harper, 1832.

Poe, Edgar Allan. *The Complete Poems and Stories of Edgar Allan Poe.* Edited by Arthur Hobson Quinn and Edward H. O'Neill. 2 vols. New York: A. A. Knopf, 1946.

———.*The Complete Works of Edgar Allan Poe.* Edited by James A. Harrison. 17 vols. New York: Thomas Y. Crowell, 1902.

———.*The Letters of Edgar Allan Poe.* Edited by John Ward Ostrom. New York: Gordian, 1966.

Potter, Israel Ralph. *Life and Remarkable Adventures of Israel R. Potter* (1824). Edited by Leonard Kriegel. New York: Corinth Books, 1962.

Reynolds, J. N. *Mocha Dick* (1839). Introduction by L. L. Balcom. New York: Scribner's, 1932.

Royall, Anne. *Sketches of History, Life, and Manners, in the United States.* New Haven, Conn.: Privately printed, 1826.

Schoolcraft, Henry. *Travels in the Central Portions of the Mississippi Valley.* New York: Collins and Hannay, 1825.

Scott, Walter. *Waverly Novels.* 48 vols. Westminster: A. Constable, 1895-96.

Seaborn, Captain Adam [pseud.]. *Symzonia* (1820). Reprint. Introduction by J. O. Bailey. Gainesville, Fla.: Scholars' Facsimiles and Reprints, 1965.

Sedgwick, Catherine. *Hope Leslie.* 2 vols. New York: White, Gallaher, and White, 1827.

———.*The Linwoods.* 2 vols. New York: Harper, 1835.

———.*Tales and Sketches* (1835). New York: Harper, 1868.

Shelley, Mary. *Frankenstein* (1818). Introduction by Robert E. Dowse and D. J. Palmer. New York: Everyman, 1963.

Shelley, Percy Bysshe. *The Complete Poetical Works of Percy Bysshe*

Shelley. Edited by Thomas Hutchinson. New York: Oxford University Press, 1933.

Sigourney, Lydia. *Scenes in My Native Land.* Boston: James Monroe, 1845.

Smith, Adam. *An Inquiry into the Nature and Causes of the Wealth of Nations* (1776). Edited by Edwin Cannan. New York: Modern Library, 1937.

The Southern Literary Messenger. October 1836.

Stansbury, Philip A. *A Pedestrian Tour of Two Thousand Three Hundred Miles, in North America.* New York: J. D. Myers and W. Smith, 1822.

Stewart, William. *Altowan.* Edited by J. Watson Webb. 2 vols. New York: Harper, 1846.

Stowe, Harriet Beecher. *Uncle Tom's Cabin* (1852). Edited by Kenneth S. Lynn. Cambridge, Mass.: Harvard University Press, 1962.

Thoreau, Henry David. *Collected Poems of Henry Thoreau.* Edited by Carl Bode. Baltimore, Md.: Johns Hopkins Press, 1965.

———.*The Writings of Henry David Thoreau.* 20 vols. Boston and New York: Walden Edition, 1906. Reprint. New York: AMS Press, 1968.

Tocqueville, Alexis de. *Democracy in America* (1835). Translated by Henry Reeve. 2 vols. New York: Schocken, 1961.

Townsend, John K. *Narrative of a Journey across the Rocky Mountains to the Columbia River* (1839). In Reuben Gold Thwaites, ed. *Early Western Travels* (1904-7). Vol. 21. Reprint. New York: AMS Press, 1966.

Trollope, Frances. *Domestic Manners of the Americans* (1832). Edited by Donald Smalley. New York: A.A. Knopf, 1949.

Twain, Mark. *The Portable Mark Twain.* Edited by Bernard DeVoto. New York: Viking, 1946.

[Tyas, Robert]. *The Sentiment of Flowers.* London, 1836.

U. S. Telegraph (Washington, D.C.). 6 April 1836.

Webber, Charles. *Old Hicks the Guide; or, Adventures in the Camanche Country in Search of a Gold Mine.* New York: Harper and Brothers, 1848.

The Western Farmer. July 1840.

Whitman, Walt. *Leaves of Grass*. Edited by Harold W. Blodgett and Sculley Bradley. New York: New York University Press, 1965.

Whittier, John Greenleaf. *The Complete Poetical Works of Whittier*. Cambridge, Mass.: Riverside Press, 1884.

———.*The Writings of John Greenleaf Whittier in Seven Volumes*. Boston: Riverside Press, 1889.

Willard, Dr. *Inland Trade with New Mexico* (1829). Edited by Timothy Flint. In *Early Western Travels*. Edited by Reuben Gold Thwaites (1904-7). Vol. 18. Reprint. New York: AMS Press, 1966.

Willis, N. P. *American Scenery*. 2 vols. in 1. London: G. Virtue, 1840.

Wilson, Edmund, ed. *The Shock of Recognition*. New York: Farrar, Straus and Cudahy, 1943.

Wordsworth, William. *The Poetical Works of William Wordsworth*. Edited by E. de Selincourt and Helen Darbishire. 5 vols. Oxford: Clarendon Press, 1940-49.

Wright, Frances. *Views of Society* and *Manners in America* (1821). Edited by Paul R. Baker. Cambridge, Mass.: Harvard University Press, 1963.

Secondary Sources

Abrams, M. H. *The Mirror and the Lamp*. New York: Oxford University Press, 1953.

———.*Natural Supernaturalism*. New York: W. W. Norton, 1971.

Allen, Gay Wilson. *The New Walt Whitman Handbook*. New York University Press, 1975.

Arvin, Newton. *Longfellow: His Life and Work*. Boston: Little, Brown, 1963.

Brinton, Crane, *Ideas and Men*. New York: Prentice-Hall, 1950.

Campbell, Joseph. *The Hero with a Thousand Faces*. Princeton, N.J.: Princeton University Press, 1949.

———.*The Masks of God*. 4 vols. New York: Viking, 1968.

Carpenter, Frederic I. " 'The American Myth': Paradise (to be) Regained." *PMLA* 74 (1959): 599-606.

Cowan, Michael H. *City of the West: Emerson, America, and Urban Metaphor.* New Haven, Conn.: Yale University Press, 1967.

Davidson, Edward H. *Poe: A Critical Study.* Cambridge, Mass.: Harvard University Press, 1957.

Douglas, Louis H. *Agrarianism in American History.* Lexington, Mass.: D. C. Heath, 1969.

Durkheim, Emile. *The Elementary Forms of the Religious Life* (1912). Translated by Joseph Ward Swain (1915). New York: Free Press, 1965.

Fiedler, Leslie. *Love and Death in the American Novel.* Revised edition. New York: Delta, 1966.

Frazer, George. *The Golden Bough.* Abridged ed. New York: Macmillan Co., 1922.

Frye, Northrup. *A Study of English Romanticism.* New York: Random House, 1968.

Fussell, Edwin. *Frontier: American Literature and the American West.* Princeton, N.J.: Princeton University Press, 1965.

Glacken, Clarence J. *Traces on the Rhodian Shore.* Berkeley, Calif.: University of California Press, 1967.

Grimsted, David. ed. *Notions of the Americans: 1820-1860.* New York: Braziller, 1970.

Hoffman, Daniel G. *Form and Fable in American Fiction.* New York: Oxford University Press, 1961.

Hofstadter, Richard. *The American Political Tradition and the Men Who Made It.* New York: A. A. Knopf, 1948.

———.*Social Darwinism in American Thought: 1860-1915.* Philadelphia: University of Pennsylvania Press, 1944.

Hull, William Doyle. "A Canon of the Critical Works of Edgar Allan Poe." Ph.D. dissertation, University of Virginia, 1941.

Kaul, A N. *The American Vision.* New Haven, Conn.: Yale University Press, 1963.

Lewis R. W. B. *The American Adam.* Chicago: University of Chicago Press, 1955.

Lovejoy, Arthur O. "On the Discrimination of Romanticisms." *PMLA* 39 (1924): 229-53.

Lovejoy, Arthur O. and Boas, George. *Primitivism and Related Ideas in Antiquity* (1935). New York: Octagon Books, 1965.

Marx, Leo. *The Machine in the Garden*. New York: Oxford University Press, 1964.

Miller, Perry. *Nature's Nation*. Cambridge, Mass.: Harvard University Press, 1967.

———.*The New England Mind: The Seventeenth Century*. New York: Macmillan Co., 1939.

Neumann, Erich. *Art and the Creative Unconscious*. Translated by Ralph Manheim (1959). Princeton, N.J.: Princeton University Press, 1972.

———.*The Great Mother*. Translated by Ralph Manheim (1955). Princeton, N.J.: Princeton University Press, 1972.

Newton, Annabel. *Wordsworth in Early American Criticism*. Chicago: University of Chicago Press, 1928.

O'Gorman, Edmundo. *The Invention of America*. Bloomington, Ind.: Indiana University Press, 1961.

Pearce, Roy Harvey. *The Continuity of American Poetry*. Princeton, N.J.: Princeton University Press, 1961.

———.*The Savages of America*. Baltimore, Md.: Johns Hopkins Press, 1953.

Petter, Henri. *The Early American Novel*. Columbus, Ohio: Ohio State University Press, 1971.

Philbrick, Thomas. *James Fenimore Cooper and the Development of American Sea Fiction*. Cambridge, Mass.: Harvard University Press, 1961.

Poirier, Richard. *A World Elsewhere*. New York: Oxford University Press, 1966.

Quinn, Patrick F. "Poe's Imaginary Voyage." *Hudson Review* 4 (1952): 562-85.

Rampersad, Arnold. *Melville's Israel Potter*. Bowling Green, Ohio: Bowling Green University Popular Press, 1969.

Rosenthal, Bernard. "Elegy for Jack Chase." *Studies in Romanticism* 10 (1971): 213-29.

———."Melville, Marryat, and the Evil-Eyed Villain." *Nineteenth-Century Fiction* 25 (1970): 221-24.

Rusk, Ralph L. *The Life of Ralph Waldo Emerson*. New York: Columbia University Press, 1957.

Seelye, John D. "Timothy Flint's 'Wicked River' and *The Confidence-Man*." *PMLA* 78 (1963): 75-79.

Smith, Henry Nash. *Virgin Land.* Cambridge, Mass.: Harvard University Press, 1950.

Spiller, Robert E., et al., eds. *Literary History of the United States.* Rev. ed. New York: Macmillan Co., 1959.

Versfeld, Marthinus. *A Guide to the City of God.* London: Sheed and Ward, 1958.

Weimer, David R. *The City as Metaphor.* New York: Random House, 1966.

Weissbuch, Ted N., and Stillians Bruce. "Ishmael the Ironist: The Anti-Salvation Theme in *Moby-Dick.*" *Emerson Society Quarterly,* no. 31 (1963): 71-75.

Wellek, René. "The Concept of 'Romanticism' in Literary History." *Comparative Literature* 1 (1949): 1-23 and 147-72.

Whicher, Stephen. *Freedom and Fate.* Philadelphia: University of Pennsylvania Press, 1953.

Willson, Lawrence. "The Transcendentalist View of the West." *Western Humanities Review* 14 (1960): 183-91.

Woodberry, George E. *Nathaniel Hawthorne.* New York: Houghton Mifflin, 1902.

Wright, Richardson. *The Story of Gardening: From the Hanging Gardens of Babylon to the Hanging Gardens of New York.* New York: Dover, 1963.

White, Hayden. *Tropics of Discourse: Essays in Cultural Criticism.* Baltimore: Johns Hopkins University Press, 1978.

Williams, Raymond. *Marxism and Literature.* Oxford and New York: Oxford University Press, 1977.

Williams, William Carlos. *In the American Grain.* New York: New Directions, 1956.

Wolff, Janet. *The Social Production of Art.* New York: St. Martin's Press, 1981.

Wordsworth, William. *The Prelude.* New York: Penguin, 1995.

Worster, Donald. *Nature's Economy: A History of Ecological Ideas.* Cambridge: Cambridge University Press, 1994.

Worster, Donald, ed. *The Ends of the Earth: Perspectives on Modern Environmental History.* Cambridge: Cambridge University Press, 1988.

Zwinger, Ann. *Run, River, Run: A Naturalist's Journey Down One of the Great Rivers of the American West.* New York: Harper & Row, 1975.

Index